Exalting Christ

Essays in Honor of Fred A. Malone

Exalting Christ

Essays in Honor of Fred A. Malone

Edited by
Steve Martin
and
Mitch Axsom

Founders Press
Cape Coral, Florida

Published by
Founders Press

P.O. Box 150931 • Cape Coral, FL 33915
Phone (239) 772-1400 • Fax: (239) 772-1140
Electronic Mail: founders@founders.org
Website: http://www.founders.org

Printed in the United States of America

13 ISBN: 978–1–943539–09–3

Contents

Foreword

Ingratitude is one of the great sins of our time and one the Scripture singles out as a serious step down a slippery slope (Romans 1:18-19). When the creature does not give thanks and honor the Creator, reality is turned upside down and personal and cultural destruction are not far behind (Romans 1:18-32). Coupled with sinful ingratitude is a failure to give honor to whom honor is due. We honor God first and foremost and then the gifts He gives to men, especially to His Church.

The book you hold in your hand seeks to honor God and His gift to the Church, Fred Malone—Christian, husband, father, pastor, citizen, theologian, and man of God. A team of eager participants jumped at the chance to honor God's servant—and were thankful that they were asked to participate. When the editors approached each of these people, they did not hesitate to jump on board and help show various facets of the jewel that God has made of Fred Malone. As Fred has labored over his life to exalt Christ in all things, the participants help us see more of the glory of God in their contributions.

Daughter Joanna wrote for herself and her two brothers, John and Josh, in showing how Fred exalted Christ is his home. Theologians Jim Renihan , Mike McKelvey and Tom Nettles, pastor-theologians Richard Barcellos, Raymond Perron, Tom Ascol, Earl Blackburn, Conrad Mbewe, Walter Chantry and Tom Hicks, pastor-historians Joe Nesom and Jerry Slate, missionary Allen Beardmore, and pastors Stephen Murphy and Mitch Axsom join ARBCA Coordinator Steve Martin in using their gifts in showing forth the glories of Christ in connection with the life and ministry of Fred Malone. God has used Fred for much good and God alone gets the glory for all this.

Soli Deo Gloria

Steve Martin and Mitch Axsom
April, 2018

Contributors

Tom Ascol met Fred during their PhD studies at Southwestern Baptist Theological Seminary where Tom studied Systematic Theology. They are both founding board members of Founders Ministries and have shared each other's pulpits many times. Tom has been the Senior Pastor of Grace Baptist Church in Cape Coral, Florida since 1986.

Mitch Axsom has had the privilege of serving with Fred Malone in the eldership of the First Baptist Church of Clinton, Louisiana since 2005 and his family has been under his faithful, loving, pastoral care since 1993. Mitch has an MA of Religion from RTS Seminary.

Richard Barcellos, PhD Historical Theology, is pastor of Grace Reformed Baptist Church, Palmdale, CA. He has known Dr. Malone for about 20 years and has worked with him on various writing and ministerial education projects. He is glad to serve with him as part of the core faculty for the IRBS Theological Seminary.

Allen Beardmore first sat under Pastor Malone's pulpit ministry in August 2004, while attending graduate school at Louisiana State University. Subsequently, Pastor Malone's biblical counsel and Christ-centered preaching provided an excellent foundation for Allen's early years of marriage and child-rearing. Prior to being sent to Perth, Australia as a missionary by First Baptist Church, Allen served for two years as Associate Pastor of FBC alongside of Pastor Malone.

Earl Blackburn is Senior Pastor of Heritage Baptist Church, Shreveport, LA. He has served with Dr. Malone in the gospel ministry, on various administrative councils and committees, for over a quarter of a century. Earl esteems and treasures his trusted friendship; a friendship and intimacy borne of things shared—a love of the law and gospel of Jesus Christ the Lord.

Walt Chantry, now retired from the ministry, was pastor for 39 years at Grace Baptist Church in Carlisle, PA. Having taken counsel together with Pastor Fred Malone on many issues over many years, he has come to value greatly Fred's biblical insights and to love his devotion to our Lord and Savior, Jesus Christ.

Tom Hicks is the Senior Pastor at First Baptist Church of Clinton, Louisiana. He has a PhD in Church History from The Southern Baptist Theological Seminary. He studied under Fred Malone for four summer internships during seminary and now serves with him as a fellow pastor at First Baptist.

Joanna Jones is the daughter of Fred Malone. She has a MS in Counseling and Development from Texas Woman's University. Joanna is married to Todd Jones and resides in Fort Worth, Texas, with their daughter, Grace.

Steve Martin serves as the Coordinator of ARBCA (Association of Reformed Baptist Churches of America) and the Dean of Students of the IRBS Theological Seminary in Texas. A native of the Midwest, he attended Trinity Evangelical Divinity School in Chicago. He has been married for 45 years to Cindy and they have two children and six grandchildren. He has contributed to *Dear Timothy* (Founders Press) and *Biblical Shepherding of God's Sheep* (Day One Publications). He lives in the Dallas/Ft. Worth area.

Conrad Mbewe is pastor of Kabwata Baptist Church and chancellor of the African Christian University in Lusaka, Zambia. Though living in Africa, he owes a lot to Dr. Fred Malone as a role model in faithful pastoral ministry and not least for his priceless Foreword in his book *Foundations for the Flock*.

Michael G. McKelvey is Associate Professor of Old Testament at Reformed Theological Seminary in Jackson, Mississippi. He has a PhD in Old Testament from the University of Aberdeen. He was mentored by Dr. Malone over several years as an intern, and Dr. Malone continues to be an encouragement and counselor to him.

Stephen Murphy has served for 30 years as pastor of Dundalk Baptist Church in Ireland. He has an MA in Theology from the University of Chester. He is a frequent visitor to the ARBCA GA, and has preached for Dr. Malone in Clinton. He and his wife Marie have hosted Dr. Malone and Debbie in Ireland, where Dr. Malone has ministered as a visiting preacher.

Joe Nesom has served as pastor of First Baptist Church, Jackson, LA, for 35 years. He taught at New Orleans Baptist Theological Seminary (1976-1981), received his PhD from Smith Baptist University, a school in southern California that later was absorbed in the Conservative Resurgence. He has two daughters and six grandchildren.

Tom Nettles is a Senior Professor at The Southern Baptist Theological Seminary in Louisville, Kentucky. He and Dr. Malone have been friends since around 1980. They have served together on the Founders Ministries board since its inception in 1982.

Raymond Perron is an ARBCA missionary in the Province of Quebec, Canada. He came to know Dr. Malone in 1991 as he was pastoring in Texas and as his church has been among the first to provide him with a support. It didn't take long before Fred and he became good friends. Pastor Fred came many times to visit the churches in Canada to teach courses on different subjects like Hermeneutics and Covenant Theology. Raymond says that Fred had a great impact on his own ministry as well as on their Quebec association. He has the greatest esteem for him because of his deep love for our Lord and his strong desire to see the advancement of God's Kingdom.

Jim Renihan, PhD is President of IRBS Theological Seminary. Dr. Malone has served with him as a Trustee of the Institute of Reformed Baptist Studies, and is a core Faculty member of IRBS Theological Seminary. He considers Dr. Malone to be a good friend and a great encouragement.

Jerry Slate serves as pastor of Berean Baptist Church in Hiram, GA. He has had the privilege of knowing, admiring, and serving alongside Fred Malone in the Association of Reformed Baptists of America (ARBCA) since 2009.

Part One

Exalting Christ in the Home

1

Exalting Christ by Honoring Him in the Home

The Christ-Exalting Father

Joanna Jones

Introduction

My name is Joanna, and I am Fred Malone's daughter. This is not a blessing that I take lightly. Especially now that I am grown and have learned the ways of the world, I realize what an incredible and undeserved gift I have been given by my Heavenly Father. I continue to learn from my dad what it means to be a Christ-centered parent. He is such an encouragement as my husband and I strive to raise our daughter in the same manner.

As I was growing up, I often…usually because of sin…did not understand how God was using my dad to help shape my life. I am ashamed to admit that there were times of rebellion deep in my heart that probably would surprise many people because I kept many of my thoughts and feelings hidden. However, as I look back, I realize that God was working in my heart and using my dad to model the love of my Heavenly Father. There were many times that Dad would sit in my room with me and listen to my heart, sharing wisdom and pointing me to Christ. Those are the memories that I cherish and that I strive to re-create with my own child. In this chapter, I would like to share the characteristics that my dad modeled as a Christ-centered father.

The Christ-Exalting Father Loves God

"We love, because He first loved us" (1 John 4:19, NASB).

When I think of my dad, I have a mental image of him sitting in his study or on the porch, pouring over Scripture. His worn and well-used Bible is in his hands. A cat is curled up on his lap. A cup of coffee is nearby. There are piles of reference books and notes all around, but he is reading his Bible. He loves God's Word.

My dad's relationship with God is a visible and real testimony to his family. When he speaks of his faith, he always points me to Christ. The fact that God would send his only Son to die a horrible death on the cross for us…sinners…should evoke in us a deep desire to love and serve Him in every way. The wonder of the cross is foremost in every spiritual conversation. The gospel never loses its power, and it never gets old or repetitive. It is the foundation that governs every area of our lives. It inspires us to love Him, to read His Word, and to model that love to others.

Any time my dad is faced with a decision, he searches for God's will in his life. I am particularly reminded of his decision to leave his ministry in Fort Worth, Texas and receive the call to serve in Clinton, Louisiana. Instead of relying on human wisdom or personal desires, he poured over Scripture and prayed for many, many weeks. This was a testimony to me of how he sought the Lord's will. What I learned is that we should have a deep desire to honor God in every decision…great or small.

Dad communicated to me that as a believer, we have a unique perception of the world. We choose to live our lives through the lens of the Gospel. We rely on the Holy Spirit to change our hearts and help us filter the problems of the world through Christ's sacrifice. Do our choices honor God or own selfish desires? Is what I am doing a testimony of what God has done for me? Am I modeling God's love for me?

Practically, what I witnessed from my father was open acknowledgement of God's love for him. He communicated a deep desire to serve Him. He spent time in Bible study. He constantly talked about the message of the Gospel. He spent time in prayer, both alone and with his family. He made choices based on God's laws and a desire to honor them.

When Dad's father died, my dad spoke at his funeral. My granddaddy was a simple man with a simple faith. He loved God and strove to live a Godly life. I saved a copy of the words my dad shared at his funeral, and I rejoice that this is the message my dad wishes to share with the world:

> "Believe that Jesus Christ is alive and is God the Son. Repent of sin and trust in Him alone to save you, not your good deeds. Live a godly life

according to the Ten Commandments and be a light with your life in a dark world. Be faithful to a Bible reading and teaching church; read your Bible daily and pray; love your family; teach your children; enjoy your friends; work hard and earn a good name; serve others unselfishly with every chance you get and make a difference. And die with hope in Christ so that your children, your grandchildren, and your friends can be comforted at your grave."

The Christ-Exalting Father Loves His Wife

> "Enjoy life with the woman whom you love all the days of your fleeting life which He has given you under the sun; for this is your reward in life and in your toil in which you have labored under the sun" (Ecclesiastes 9:9, NASB).

There was never any doubt that my dad is in love with his wife. Their story is sweet and simple. They were high school sweethearts who met in band, dated, and married young. By the Lord's grace, they have just celebrated their 50th anniversary.

My dad has often reminded me that it truly is God's grace that they have remained together. The early years of their marriage were rough. But God chose to save them both at the age of twenty-one and they have strived to honor God in their relationship since that time. For that I am eternally grateful.

Words cannot express the sense of security that is given to a child when parents love and honor each other. In today's world, this is something that I do not take for granted. In my chosen career as a teacher and school counselor, I have witnessed families ripped apart by divorce and the severe consequences it bestowed upon their children. As a child, I never had the fear that this would happen in our family. I felt secure in their love for each other and their commitment to marriage and family.

Growing up, my dad modeled a deep love for my mom. One way he did this was physical expression. He often said he loved her…both directly to her and to us. Even though he said it often, we knew he meant it every time. He would tell stories of when they first met. He took joy in her physical beauty and often said she grew more beautiful as she aged. He was physically affectionate with her in front of his children. Hugs were common, often for no reason other than she was standing there.

I often think of the time that I received a new stereo for Christmas. Our whole family loves music, and up until that time we had an old turntable that shakily played records. Imagine my joy to see a beautiful new stereo under the Christmas tree! I was so proud to move it into my bedroom and listen to the radio or tapes play clear, lovely sounds. One day, I came home from school and opened my bedroom door to find my parents slow-dancing in an embrace to the strains of music from my stereo. At the time, the teenager in me thought, "Ewwww…", but that moment is etched in my memory as an example of the love my dad showed for my mom.

Another way Dad showed love for my mom is in his protection and care for her. Mom and Dad had a shared desire for her to work full-time in the home, especially while my brothers and I were young. Dad showed his love by working hard at various jobs in addition to his ministry in order for her to do this. It was a beautiful way for him to show honor to the role she loved as mother and caregiver. And it was of infinite value to us, their children.

He also showed his love by taking care of her in sickness. My mom had various health issues as I was growing up and survived cancer in recent years. He makes sure that she receives the best medical care that is available. He often helps by easing her load of household duties. He is quick to tell her to rest while he cooks dinner or sweeps the floor. I remember one particular time when I was around six years old and I got sick in the middle of the night. Mom was in bed with back problems and Dad was quick to get up and take care of me. He lovingly cleaned me up with the same nurturing manner that my mom always showed.

Dad protected Mom from over-extending herself with duties to the church, friends, and family. He sometimes encouraged her to say "no" to things in order to protect her health and well-being. This didn't (and doesn't) always sit well with Mom, but she knows that his motive is love for her.

Dad always speaks highly of Mom in and out of the home. He is proud of her and constantly recognizes what she does for our family. He does not take her for granted. He praises her efforts and successes to his children and all others.

Dad loves to spend time with my mom. They often go on dates together. He has told me that there is no person on earth that he would rather spend time with than his wife. I love to hear both of them talk about their trips to Gulf Shores or other places where they can just be together. He shows us what it means to "…rejoice in the wife of your youth" (Proverbs 5:18, NASB).

Perhaps the most important way he shows love for her is in their spiritual relationship. He knows that Christ is the most important model for a loving marriage. If Christ can sacrifice Himself for our eternal life, we can sacrifice ourselves for our spouse. If Christ can love us unconditionally, we can love our spouse unconditionally. If Dad or Mom sin against each other, they confess their sin, ask for forgiveness, and work to change. It is the foundation of their marriage, and it is powerful. I witnessed it many times, and it was a wonderful testimony to me. It is the message that he shares with me now as an adult in a marriage relationship. And it is a message that I now strive to share with my husband and daughter.

The Christ-Exalting Father Loves His Children

> "Behold, children are a gift of the Lord,
> The fruit of the womb is a reward.
> Like arrows in the hand of a warrior,
> So are the children of one's youth.
> How blessed is the man whose quiver is full of them;
> They will not be ashamed when they speak with their enemies in the gate."
> (Psalm 127:3–5, NASB)

My dad has shared with me that he and my mom had a deep desire to raise a large family. They wanted at least seven children. Despite physical obstacles, God saw fit to give them three children. We knew we were wanted, and we knew we were loved. In my sin, I sometimes doubted my dad's methods of raising me, but his constant love was a reflection of God's love for me. I believe that children form ideas of God's character by the character of their earthly father. My dad's character is patient, loving, kind, forgiving, self-sacrificing, and honorable. What a gift it is that Dad models the attributes of God in his relationship with me! Even though I did not fully understand as a child, this earthly relationship set the foundation for a spiritual relationship with Christ.

Dad showed his love by spending time with his children. For me, that meant sitting and having long talks together. He would often enjoy relaxing and listening to me play the piano. He took me on simple dates to get ice cream. He took my brothers and me to the park. And this is where the sacrifice was real...he played board games with us. For anyone that knows my father, he hates board games. I mean hates them. But at our insistence, he willingly and happily played Clue or even (gasp!) Monopoly. And it makes me tear up to watch my dad play Candy Land or Chutes and Ladders with my daughter now.

For my brothers, showing love meant spending time outside with sports. T-ball, baseball, football, and golf were times that they bonded together. He was at every game and many practices. He taught them about sportsmanship and winning/losing with grace. He took them fishing and taught them to appreciate and love being outdoors in God's creation. He used their experiences in sports activities to teach them spiritual lessons.

My dad planned fun activities for the family. Growing up, we did not have the money for frequent vacations, but dad worked hard to provide experiences that I will never forget. We travelled to Williamsburg, Virginia and Washington, D.C. to enjoy time together while learning about history. When we travelled to visit family in Alabama, he took us to special places from his childhood to teach us about our heritage. In my college and adult years, he has taken us to Gulf Shores, Alabama to enjoy the beauty of the ocean. As a teenager, I remember one particular time that he took our family to Six Flags Over Texas. My brother Josh and I were older, and we had been to Six Flags on several occasions with friends, school, and church. That day gave me a mental image of my dad that I will never forget…golf shirt, short shorts, camera around his neck, socks pulled up to his knees, and holding a map of the park in his hands. Josh and I were so embarrassed and kept asking him to put the map away because we knew our way around. He looked like the ultimate tourist instead of the cool dudes we thought we were! But what a blessing it is to remember this day that my dad chose to spend with his family, doing something that he knew we would enjoy.

Music activities were another way that my dad showed his love for us as children. As a musician himself, he encouraged me to play the piano and clarinet. My brother Josh was a fine French horn player. My brother Jon enjoyed playing the saxophone in band and is now a wonderful guitar player. Dad was at every band concert and half-time show and piano recital that we ever performed. When I was in fifth grade and wanted to quit piano lessons, he encouraged me to continue to use the gifts that God gave me in music. Through his encouragement (and demand), I continued lessons and grew to be thankful that he did not allow me to quit when I was discouraged. It is a huge part of my life and service to my church today, and playing the piano gives me immeasurable joy.

Dad is always affectionate with us. He hugs us, tells us he loves us, and shows us his love through his actions. He does the same with his grandchildren. His love is constant in times of joy, sorrow, discipline, success, and everyday life.

The Christ-Exalting Father Shows Love for Others

> "A new commandment I give to you, that you love one another, even as I have loved you, that you also love one another. By this all men

> will know that you are My disciples, if you have love for one another" (John 13:34–35, NASB).

The best example of my dad showing love for others is through his ministry. He has a deep desire to communicate the love of Christ to all people. Soon after he first became a Christian at the age of twenty-one, he felt the call to minister to others. He was a young man who was gifted in the areas of math and science, and until that time felt compelled to pursue a career in those fields, perhaps as a doctor. God had other plans and gave him the desire to attend seminary and begin pastoral ministry.

He has shown himself to be a true pastor in every sense of the word. He pours over Scripture and does his best to prepare messages that point to Christ. He visits the sick and the elderly, ministering to them through Bible reading and prayer. He provides counsel to the members of his church and others in the community. He mentors young pastors and guides them in the principles of a Christ-centered ministry. He teaches classes and seminars to students. He holds parenting lessons for the young couples in his church. He writes articles and books about God's grace. He meets with young children and new believers about what it means to trust Christ and follow Him. He helps prepare young couples for marriage by teaching them about Christ and the church. He is a calm and wise presence to help people in times of crisis. And, perhaps most importantly, he prays for people. As his daughter, he has told me that he prays for me daily, and I believe it. What a comfort it is to me to know that he lifts my name daily to the throne of God!

Dad respects others. I saw this especially in the way he treated his father and mother. He loved and honored his parents during their lives. Although we lived far away, he made every effort to visit them as much as possible. Even when he disagreed with them about certain issues, he showed grace and patience. He forgave them and asked forgiveness if he sinned against them. He takes care of his older sister and ministers to her on a faithful basis.

Dad is not quick to argue with others. He lives firmly by the Gospel, and witnesses to others through his actions. Instead of a critical nature, he shows love and patience. I believe that God uses this in his ministry to help win souls to Christ. Sometimes we laugh about the fact that strangers will open up to my dad and tell him their life story while standing in line at the grocery store. There is just something about him that invites people to be comfortable and vulnerable. God uses this gift for His glory.

The Christ-Exalting Father Trains His Children

> "Train up a child in the way he should go, even when he is old he will not depart from it" (Proverbs 22:6, NASB).

When I was seven years old, I stole something from a store. My dad worked in a Christian book store and we would often go pick him up after working a shift. One day, I wandered into the children's section and spied a beautiful yellow pencil eraser. It was shaped like an animal and it was soooo cute. I was delighted. I was so delighted that I put it in my pocket! I knew what I was doing was wrong. I knew that I was breaking God's commandment not to steal. I knew my parents would be horrified if they ever found out. We left the store and piled into our old blue station wagon. Then something happened. An incredible feeling of guilt descended on me and I began to feel physically ill. All the way home, I could feel the beautiful yellow eraser burning a hole in my pocket. When we arrived at the house, I could stand it no longer. I confessed to my dad and showed him the eraser I had stolen. I saw shock and sadness in his eyes, which was infinitesimally worse than the discipline that followed. But the discipline was a relief because the burden of guilt was heavier. Part of the discipline process was going back to the store and confessing what I had done to the manager, Mr. Jack. Dad took me back to the store and led me to Mr. Jack. I did all the talking and apologizing. Thankfully, he forgave me and even gave me my first job nine years later in his bookstore! I will forever be grateful for that experience.

My mom and dad were both committed to raising their children in the training and discipline of the Lord. It was a learning process for them. I have often heard Dad say that he wishes he could go back and do it all over again using what he knows now. Even though I know he made mistakes, I am forever grateful for the way he raised me.

There is so much more to training children than just discipline. From the earliest of ages, Dad taught me about God. Almost every conversation had a spiritual element. Bible study was a part of our everyday life. He both modeled it and did it with us. We memorized the Catechism and practiced it every day. I will admit that at the time, I disliked it. However, the simple answers to these Catechism questions have stuck with me during adulthood and I have come to love and appreciate their guidance. I remember that Dad would set goals for us in our reading and memorization. When we completed a goal, he took us on a "date" for ice cream. A Peanut Buster Parfait from Dairy Queen was a great motivator! The end result was that my brothers and I had a strong foundation in the Word of God and what it meant to be a Christian.

Perhaps the most lasting impression that my dad gave me in my childhood was the way he conducted discipline. The first thing he did was talk with us about what we had done. We identified the commandment we had broken and who we had sinned against. The second thing he did was teach us what we should have done differently. Sometimes we role-played how we should have acted. I appreciate that he did not just punish us, but he taught us to act in a godly way. Thirdly, he spanked us. Corporal punishment was never a reaction or done in anger. It was a calm, consistent part of the whole discipline event. Fourth, we prayed. We asked God to forgive us for our sin and help us to obey Him. Lastly, we apologized and made peace with the person we sinned against. This discipline procedure was consistent. All five elements were present each time there was discipline. This was beneficial to me in so many ways. I always knew what to expect. There were no surprises. Discipline was not an angry reaction of a parent who was at their wit's end. It was a calm event of which the main purpose was to teach, not just punish.

Another way my dad trained us was through godly counsel. Both in my childhood and adulthood, he was always willing and eager to listen to our heart. Some of my most precious memories are of Dad propped up on his elbows on my bed talking with me about life. He listened and gently guided me in finding answers to problems. We have had many conversations in the kitchen, sitting on a barstool and just enjoying being together. As an adult, Dad has written letters to me full of wisdom that I will treasure always. Every time of sharing was part of the whole picture of training up a child.

Now that I am a parent myself, I am encouraged to use these same principles of training in the way I raise my daughter. I am so thankful that I experienced this training and I am not starting from scratch. Not only was Dad training up a child, but he was training up a parent.

The Christ-Exalting Father is a Spiritual Leader

> "You shall love the Lord your God with all your heart and with all your soul and with all your might. These words, which I am commanding you today, shall be on your heart. You shall teach them diligently to your sons and shall talk of them when you sit in your house and when you walk by the way and when you lie down and when you rise up. You shall bind them as a sign on your hand and they shall be as frontals on your forehead. You shall write them on the doorposts of your house and on your gates" (Deuteronomy 6: 5–9, NASB).

Almost every time we sat down for a meal as a family, we ended with a devotional. Dad would read through a passage of the Bible, sometimes following up with a brief comment or questions to us about what it meant. Often he would read that day's excerpt from Spurgeon's *Morning and Evening*. We would pray together as a family. If time permitted, we would grab a hymnal that we kept in the dining room and sing the doxology or another hymn of the faith. I still love to hear my dad's clear tenor voice. I would often sing alto along with my mom. These simple times of family devotions are etched in my memory with fondness.

There were many times that Dad would start conversations with my brothers and me like, "Tell me about your devotions. What are you reading?" He asked in such a way that I knew he was truly interested and it made me want to read more. It sent the message that he loved us and cared about our spiritual growth.

We knew that Dad was our spiritual leader. He was the authority in our household in all matters, and it was a source of comfort. The decisions he made for our family were prayerfully considered through the lens of Scripture. Even as a small child, I sensed this and knew that I was safe and secure. As a matter of fact, my feeling of security led to a fear of what might happen if the Lord took my parents from me before I was an adult. I remember one night I woke up in a panic from a nightmare that my parents had been killed in a car wreck. Mom and Dad were still awake, and I went into the kitchen crying and told Dad about my dream. Instead of assuring me that a tragedy would never happen, he took the opportunity to tell me to put my trust in Christ. As believers, we do not need to worry about the unknown. He is enough. I do not know if Dad even remembers that conversation—we have not spoken about it since—but it is a lesson that I remember well. Do not place your trust and happiness in people. Rather, place it in Christ.

Dad led me to Christ at the age of nine. I had a deep desire to be baptized and join the church. Up until that time, I'm not sure if I was a Christian. I believed what I had been taught and I strove to live a Christian life. But, I didn't really understand and feel the sacrifice that Jesus made for me on the cross. When I told Dad that I wanted to be baptized, he spent many hours with me examining my heart and answering questions that I had. I realized that, while I could not pinpoint an exact time that I was saved, my faith had matured and I was ready to be baptized. He arranged for me to speak with the elders of the church, and I shared my testimony with them. It was with great joy that he baptized me, his daughter, a few weeks later. What a special time that was! Thirty years later, I cried with joy as I watched my dad baptize my daughter after a similar experience. I am truly grateful for the heritage of faith that has been passed down through my family.

The Christ-Exalting Father Models a Strong Work Ethic

> "Whether, then, you eat or drink or whatever you do, do all to the glory of God" (1 Corinthians 10:31).

Dad demanded a lot from us as children. However, he did not demand perfection. What he wanted was a sincere effort to do our best. We were to take our jobs seriously…whether it was schoolwork or sports or mowing the grass. He showed us this in his own life.

When I was younger, Dad often worked two or three jobs to support his family, in addition to his ministry. He performed manual labor loading and unloading boxes; he was a security guard; he worked in a bookstore; and he was a substitute teacher. Nothing was beneath him and he taught me the value of hard work. He learned this work ethic from his own daddy, and he passed it down to his children.

Dad believes that doing your best shows honor to our Lord. He would often explain that we were given gifts, and it pleased God when we used our gifts for His glory. He encouraged my brothers and me to do the best we could in school. As a result, all three of us excelled in our studies and enjoyed our academic experience. We all achieved advanced degrees and successful careers. He was proud of our successes, but he made a point to praise the actual work that we put into our studies.

I mentioned earlier that piano lessons were an important part of my life. I often had piano recitals and performances. Stage fright has often been an issue for me, and there was more than one time that I bombed a performance. Dad was always there with a hug, telling me he was proud of the hard work I had put into the music. He praised the process, not the result.

Dad continues to model a strong work ethic. He takes his calling to the ministry seriously and grieves that he does not have more time to do the things that he wants to do in his job. He works hard to prepare sermons, writings, and speaking engagements at the expense of personal down-time.

I am thankful that I have an earthly father who models the value of hard work. Through this hard work, we show thankfulness for the gifts that God has given us and bring honor to His name.

The Christ-Exalting Father Remains Humble

> "For by grace you have been saved through faith; and that not of yourselves, it is the gift of God; not as a result of works, so that no one may boast" (Ephesians 2:8–9, NASB).

The words I have written about my dad are true. But it is also true that he is a sinful man who is in need of a Savior. There were times that he sinned against us and others. Until he reaches ultimate glory in heaven, he will continue to sin. He understands this truth, and it grieves him deeply. I know my dad well enough to predict that when he reads the words in this book, he will be filled with shame about all the times he failed as a husband, father, and pastor. But I also know that he will rejoice in the great demonstration of God's grace in his life that enables others to write these words about him.

That's what it is…God's grace. God took a sinful young husband who was unhappy in his marriage and who even denied the existence of God and showed great mercy on his soul. God revealed to him the cross and the forgiveness of sins that we can obtain through Christ's sacrifice. God saved his marriage and brought his wife to faith in Christ as well. These are things that Dad joyfully shares with others. He doesn't forget what he was, and is, and what he will be one day in glory.

These beautiful facts keep him humble. He is quick to admit his shortcomings and quick to share God's mercy and grace. I hear it in every sermon that he preaches. I hear it in every spiritual conversation that we have. He desires no glory or recognition for himself, but points only to Christ. This is his legacy and the message that he has spent his entire Christian life sharing: Saved by grace alone, through faith alone, in Christ alone.

Part Two

Exalting Christ in the Pulpit

2

Exalting Christ by Preaching Him from All the Scriptures

Tom Hicks

I had never heard Christ preached so consistently, until I experienced Fred Malone's preaching. He faithfully proclaims the Lord Jesus from every passage of Scripture so that lost men can be saved and saints can be edified. Fred's goal in preaching is never simply to fill his hearer's minds with truth or to change their behavior, but to lead them to Christ in worship so that the Triune God is glorified in the face of Jesus. A good deal of what is contained in this chapter, I learned first from Fred and saw him practice it faithfully in his ministry. His teaching and ministry proved to me that Christians can only grow and persevere in a balanced and healthy way when they always keep Christ before them. Therefore, it is with great joy that I contribute this chapter on preaching Christ from all the Scriptures to his Festchrift. Thank you, brother Fred, for determining to know nothing but Christ and Him crucified, not only in your preaching, but in all your pastoral ministry and life. Thank you too for teaching me to "Remember Jesus Christ, risen from the dead, the offspring of David as preached in my gospel" (2 Timothy 2:8). I pray that the numbers of Christ-centered pastors, preachers, and Christians increase for the health of the church and to the glory of our great Triune God.

The thesis of my chapter is that Christian preachers must preach Jesus Christ at the center of all their sermons. My plan is to summarize (1) the biblical hermeneutics of Christ-centered preaching, (2) the biblical mandate of Christ-centered preaching, and (3) the Trinity and Christ-centered preaching. In this way, the chapter will move from theology, to specific passages, to practical application, and to the goal of it all.

The Hermeneutics of Christ-Centered Preaching

Biblical "hermeneutics" is the art and science of biblical interpretation. It is the theory of how we ought to read and understand the Bible so that we can know God. Make no mistake, the goal of faithful interpretation is the knowledge of God for eternal life. Louis Berkhof says, "Hermeneutics is the science that teaches us the laws, principles and methods of interpretation. It precedes exegesis logically as theory does to application."[1] A sound hermeneutic ensures that we're "reading out" the intended meaning of the Bible (exegesis) rather than "reading into" the Bible our own thoughts and preferences (eisegesis). It begins with the presuppositional conviction that the Bible is the very Word of God, that each word of the Bible is inspired by God (1 Corinthians 2:13; 2 Peter 1:20–21; 2 Timothy 3:16–17) and that the Bible is without error in the autographs (Numbers 23:9; Psalm 12:6; Proverbs 30:5).[2] Hermeneutics is an aspect of theology, which means we should derive our theory of biblical interpretation, or hermeneutics, from the Bible itself. The Second London Baptist Confession 1.9 says, "The infallible rule of interpretation of Scripture is the Scripture itself." The Bible teaches us how to read the Bible.

1. Grammatical, Historical, Theological Hermeneutics

All evangelicals believe we should interpret the Bible according to the grammatical-historical hermeneutic. Not all agree, though, that there is a "theological" level of interpretation. But consider first what evangelicals readily agree upon: the grammatical-historical hermeneutic. Grammatical interpretation simply means that we need to take the words, sentences, context, literary devices, and genre of biblical texts into account when we study the Bible. When we account for grammar, we simply recognize that the Bible is written as literature in normal human language; therefore, our interpretation should follow the normal rules of language. Jesus taught us to interpret the Bible grammatically in Matthew 22:41–45, where He explained Psalm 110:1 to the Pharisees, paying careful attention to the grammatical relationship among the words in the Psalm.

[1] Louis Berkhof, *Principles of Biblical Interpretation* (Grand Rapids, MI: Baker, 1950; reprint, 1994), 11. For a good but short outline of the principles of biblical hermeneutics, see Sam Storms, *Kingdom Come: The Amillennial Alternative* (Ross-Shire, Scotland, UK: 2013), 15–42.

[2] See The Chicago Statement on Biblical Inerrancy for a good summary of the doctrine.

> Now while the Pharisees were gathered together, Jesus asked them a question, saying, 'What do you think about the Christ? Whose son is he?' They said to him, 'The son of David.' He said to them, 'How is it then that David, in the Spirit, calls him Lord, saying, 'The Lord said to my Lord, sit at my right hand, until I put your enemies under your feet'? [Psalm 110:1] If then David calls him Lord, how is he his son?

Jesus invited the Pharisees to carefully interpret the grammar of Psalm 110:1. The grammar shows that David called Christ his "Lord" and therefore, the Christ could not merely be David's human son. Instead, Christ is far more than David's human son.

In this same passage, Christ considered history in His interpretation. Interpreters need to take the historical context into account when they study the Bible. Jesus accounted for history by acknowledging the historical David. Jesus understood that David was the author of the Psalm. Christ also considered the passage in relationship to David's human sons. Therefore, Jesus interpreted Scripture according to the grammatical-historical hermeneutic.

Evangelicals differ, however, over the question of the "theological" aspect of biblical hermeneutics. Dispensationalist interpreters, for example, insist that grammatical-historical hermeneutics alone yield the correct meaning of the biblical text. Charles Ryrie asserts that grammatical-historical interpretation "might also be called normal interpretation" and "plain interpretation."[3] He flatly denies the need for "theological interpretation" saying that the one who uses it "is not a consistent literalist."[4]

Over and against Dispensationalism, historic Reformed theology has always taught that in addition to "grammatical-historical" interpretation, "theological interpretation" is absolutely necessary to arrive to at the true meaning of the biblical text. Reformed interpreters have argued that there is a theological center of the Bible because the Bible has only one Divine Author who reveals Himself in its pages. Louis Berkhof explains, "Scripture contains a great deal that does not find its explanation in history, nor in the secondary authors, but only in God as the *Auctor pirmarius*."[5] In other words, while the Bible has numerous human authors, the *primary Author* of the Bible is God Himself, and we will only be able to understand certain truths of Scripture when we account for God's primary authorship of the Bible. That is to say, the whole Bible is the Word *of God*, which means that we should expect there to be one unifying center of Scripture,

[3] Charles C. Ryrie, *Dispensationalism* (Chicago, IL: Moody, 1966; revised and expanded, 2007), 91.

[4] Ibid., 95.

[5] Berkhof, *Principles of Biblical Interpretation*, 133.

which reveals or discloses God, the Divine Author, to men. Paul referred to this theological unity of the Bible, when he spoke of the "whole counsel of God" (Acts 20:27). The Second London Baptist Confession 1.5 speaks of the Bible's theological center when it refers to "the consent of all the parts, the scope of the whole." This is what older interpreters called the *Scopus Scriptura* or the "scope" of Scripture, which takes a broad look at the unified whole of the Bible and finds that it discloses one message about God redeeming sinners in Christ. Jesus Christ is the perfect revelation of God to men.

Many places of Scripture show that the theological scope of Scripture is centered on Christ. Luke 24:27 says that when Christ was with His disciples on the road to Emmaus, "beginning with Moses and all the Prophets, He interpreted to them in all the Scriptures the things concerning Himself."[6] 1 Peter 1:10–12 says:

> Concerning this salvation, the prophets who prophesied about the grace that was to be yours searched and inquired carefully, inquiring what person or time the Spirit of Christ in them was indicating when he predicted the sufferings of Christ and the subsequent glories. It was revealed to them that they were serving not themselves but you, in the things that have now been announced to you through those who preached the good news to you by the Holy Spirit sent from heaven, things into which angels long to look.

The Old Testament prophets spoke of Christ's sufferings and resurrection because the "Spirit of Christ" was in them. They were moved to write and prophesy of Christ by Christ Himself.

Other passages teach the same thing. Colossians 2:3 says that in Christ "are hidden all the treasures of wisdom and knowledge." No treasures of wisdom and knowledge are found outside of Jesus. 2 Corinthians 1:20 says, "For all the promises of God find their Yes in Him." No promises of Scripture find their "yes" outside of Jesus. The Apostle John tells us that Jesus is the "Word" of God (John 1:1) and that "He has made Him known" (John 1:18). The words "made Him known" could be translated "explained Him."

[6] Notice the emphasis on the totality of Scripture in this verse. Jesus began with "Moses and *all* the Prophets." He used "*all* the Scriptures" in His teaching. The trip to Emmaus was hours long; so, Christ would have had a great deal of time to touch upon many Old Testament connections to Himself. Christ doubtlessly left out many of the Old Testament types, shadows, and allusions to Himself, since this walk would not have been long enough to explain everything in the Scriptures concerning Himself. Christ used all the Scriptures on this long walk to Emmaus to explain many of the things concerning Himself to His disciples.

Jesus explains God. Jesus reveals God. Jesus is the final Word on God. All of Scripture points to Jesus as the revelation of God Himself. Therefore, preachers of Scripture need to center on Jesus because Scripture itself centers on Jesus as the highest revelation of God to men. If preachers fail to center on Christ, then they fail to preach the Christian God. And they fail to lead their hearers into worship.

2. New Testament Priority

One important governing rule of "theological interpretation" is the principle of "New Testament priority." At the beginning of the Middle Ages, Augustine of Hippo (354–430) expressed New Testament priority with the phrase, "The New is in the Old concealed; the Old is in the New revealed." In those words, Augustine meant that the Old Testament contains shadowy types and figures that are only clearly revealed in the New Testament. He meant that the New Testament explains the Old Testament. The Protestant Reformers never attempted to modify Augustine's hermeneutic. Instead, they held firmly to it, and sought to apply it consistently in all of their biblical exegesis, looking to the New Testament to govern their interpretation of the Old. An early confessional Baptist, Nehemiah Coxe, agreed with this Reformed interpretive principle and wrote: "…the best interpreter of the Old Testament is the Holy Spirit speaking to us in the new."[7]

The interpretive principle of New Testament priority is derived from an examination of the Scriptures. As we read the Bible, we notice that earlier texts never explicitly interpret later texts. Earlier texts provide the interpretive context for later texts, but they never explain them directly. There is never an instance when an earlier text will cite a later text and offer commentary on it. Rather, what we find is that later texts make explicit reference to earlier texts and provide explanations for them. New Testament priority simply recognizes this fact. Earlier passages provide the context for later passages, but later passages explain earlier ones.[8] Therefore, we need to allow later revelation in the Bible to explain earlier revelation, rather than insisting on our own uninspired interpretations of earlier revelation.

[7] Nehemiah Coxe and John Owen, *Covenant Theology from Adam to Christ*, ed. Ronald D. Miller, James M. Renihan, and Fransisco Orozco (Palmdale, CA: Reformed Baptist Academic Press, 2005), 36.

[8] This is no different from how we might read any book. When you begin to read a novel, you're still learning the characters and the setting, but later on, things that happened earlier begin to make sense. Mysteries are resolved as the story progresses. Earlier conversations between characters take on new significance as the story unfolds.

In opposition to New Testament priority, John MacArthur claims that to make "the New Testament the final authority on the Old Testament denies the perspicuity of the Old Testament as a perfect revelation in itself."[9] Of course, MacArthur's claim is easily reversed. One might argue that to suggest that the New Testament is not the final authority on the Old Testament denies the perspicuity of the New Testament as perfect revelation in itself. Moreover, the Old Testament recognizes that its own prophecies can be difficult to understand because they are given in riddles (Numbers 12:6–8). The New Testament too acknowledges that the Old Testament is not always clear. It tells us that there were "mysteries" yet to be revealed (Colossians 1:26). The meaning of the Old Testament "shadows" (Hebrews 10:1) and "types" (Galatians 4:24) only become clear after Christ comes. The Second London Baptist Confession 1.7 accurately declares, "All things in Scripture are not alike plain in themselves." MacArthur's critique of New Testament priority is not consistent with what the Bible teaches about the Old Testament's "shadowy" character.[10]

If we reject Dispensationalist presuppositions and instead allow the New Testament to explain the Old Testament, we find that the Old Testament consistently points to its own fulfillment in the Lord Jesus Christ.[11] The writings of the Old Testament prophets pointed to Christ, even though the prophets themselves were not always aware of it.[12] For example, when Hosea 11:1 says, "Out of Egypt I have called my son," Hosea is not speaking merely of national Israel as the Old Testament context seems to indicate; rather, he's also speaking of an ultimate fulfillment in Christ (Matthew 2:14). Similarly, when Jeremiah 31:15 says, "A voice was heard in Ramah, weeping and loud lamentation, Rachel weeping for her children; she refused to be comforted because they are no more," Jeremi-

[9] John MacArthur, "Why Every Self-Respecting Calvinist is a Premillennialist," a sermon delivered at the Shepherd's Conference in 2007.

[10] For an extensive treatment of John MacArthur's dispensationalism, see Samuel E. Waldron, *MacArthur's Millennial Manifesto: A Friendly Response* (Owensboro, KY: Reformed Baptist Academic Press, 2008). For a short critique of Dispensationalism's hermeneutic in general, see Kim Riddlebarger, *A Case for Amillennialism: Understanding the End Times* (Grand Rapids, MI: Baker, 2003), 33–40.

[11] Many passages of the New Testament clearly indicate that Christ is the center of the whole Old Testament: John 5:39, 46; Acts 3:18, 24; 7:52; 10:43; 13:29; 26:22–23; and 28:23.

[12] The Old Testament tells us that Daniel and Zechariah, for example, did not fully understand the visions God revealed to them (Daniel 8:27; Zechariah 4:13). Thus, it is not inconsistent with the Old Testament's understanding of its own revelation to say that further light may be shed upon it by future revelation.

ah is not merely speaking of Judah's deportation to Babylon and longing for restoration, which is what we would conclude if we only looked at the Old Testament context. Rather, Jeremiah is ultimately referring to Herod's effort to destroy Christ (Matthew 2:18). From the perspective of the New Testament, Psalm 22 is about the crucifixion of the Messiah, but that would not have been clear to the original audience. We know that Psalm 16 is about Christ's resurrection only because Christ has fulfilled it. It's clear now that Isaiah 7 is about the virgin birth of our Lord, but no one would have concluded that when Isaiah originally wrote it. The New Testament shows us that the Old Testament is intensely Christ-centered and that He is its ultimate fulfillment. We can only see clearly that the Old Testament is about Christ because of the revelation of the New Testament.

To illustrate how this principle of New Testament priority affects our theology, consider the example of Dispensationalists and Paedobaptists. Both Dispensationalists and Paedobaptists wrongly allow the Old Testament to have priority over the New Testament. For example, both systems of interpretation read the promise of a seed in Genesis 17:7 as a promise of physical offspring. In Genesis 17:7, God says, "And I will establish my covenant between me and you and your offspring after you."

Dispensationalists think Genesis 17:7 establishes an everlasting promise to national Israel and they read that understanding into the New Testament, convinced that God has future plans for ethnic Jews. But Paedobaptists, on the other hand, think the promise in Genesis 17:7 is a covenant of grace with believers and their physical offspring, which leads to the baptism of infants and to churches intentionally mixed with believers and unbelievers.[13] Both systems insist that Genesis 17:7 is finally about Abraham's physical offspring.

If, however, we allow the New Testament to interpret Genesis 17:7, then we will avoid both errors. Galatians 3:16 says, "Now the promises were made to Abraham and his offspring. It does not say, 'And to offsprings,' referring to many, but referring to one, 'And to your offspring,' who is Christ." Note well that Galatians 3:16 explicitly denies a plural offspring. The promise is to one Offspring only, not to many. Therefore, in view of the clear teaching of the New Testament, we must conclude that both Dispensationalists and Paedobaptists misinterpret the Old Testament at this point. Both think the promise to Abraham's seed is a promise to all of his physical descendants, rather than to Christ. The error leads Paedobaptists to tend to over-emphasize a visible church of natural gener-

[13] For an excellent critique of Reformed paedobaptism, see Fred A. Malone, *The Baptism of Disciples Alone: A Covenantal Argument for Credobaptism Versus Paedobaptism* (Cape Coral, FL: Founders, 2003, revised and expanded, 2007).

ation in their reading of Scripture, and it leads Dispensationalists to over-emphasize national Israel, when the New Testament clearly teaches us to emphasize Christ. The promise is to Christ, not to men.[14] The promise is centered on Christ, not men.[15]

Preachers need to learn how to interpret and explain the Scriptures from the Scriptures themselves. When they interpret the Bible biblically, they will be Christ-centered interpreters and preachers.

3. Covenant Theology

If we accept the principle of New Testament priority, as do all the children of the Protestant Reformation, then we will arrive at the theological superstructure of covenant theology, which is intensely Christ-centered. That is, when we allow the New Testament to form our understanding of the biblical framework of history, then we will conclude that there is a "covenant of works" and a "covenant of grace." A "covenant" is a promise from one person to another or among people. Rich Barcellos helpfully describes a covenant as "a divinely sanctioned commitment or relationship."[16] In the covenant of works, God promises life to Adam and his posterity for perfect obedience to the law and threatens death for violation. In the covenant of grace, God promises life to Christ and His elect people because of Christ's perfect obedience to the law, by which He both satisfied the law's penalty of death and procured the law's blessing of life. When a preacher sees that the Bible is put together this way, he will inevitably view any particular text in light of Adam's sin and Christ's redemption.

Consider how the book of Romans frames the whole of Scripture along the lines of these two great overarching covenants. Romans chapters 1–3a are about the law or covenant of works. These chapters show that the law condemns all human beings, both Jews and Gentiles, because all have

[14] To see this argument worked out more thoroughly, see Fred A. Malone, "Biblical Hermeneutics & Covenant Theology" in *Covenant Theology: A Baptist Distinctive*, ed. Earl M. Blackburn (Birmingham, AL: Solid Ground Christian Books, 2013), 63–87.

[15] This position does not entail a denial of any collective aspect to seed; rather, it recognizes that the seed is Christ and that by saving union with Him, the elect are also seed in Him. Galatians 3:7, 14, 29. Thus, all the promises made to Abraham in Genesis 17:7 were made to Christ and to all who are savingly united to Christ, Jew and Gentile alike.

[16] Richard Barcellos, "Getting the Garden Right: From Hermeneutics to the Covenant of Works" in *By Common Confession: Essays in Honor of James M. Renihan*, ed. Ronald S Baines, Richard C. Barcellos and James P. Butler (Palmdale, CA: Reformed Baptist Academic Press, 2015), 197.

sinned. The "work of the law" is written on the hearts and consciences of all human beings (Romans 2:15). Romans 3:9 says, "We have already charged that all, both Jews and Greeks, are under the power of sin." Romans 3:19–20 concludes that both Jews and Gentiles are condemned under the law: "Now we know that whatever the law says it speaks to those who are under the law so that every mouth may be stopped, and the whole world may be held accountable to God. For by works of the law no human being will be justified in his sight, since through the law comes knowledge of sin." The law brings condemnation to every human being because no one can keep it perfectly and because everyone has broken it. The double curse of the "covenant of works" is the total corruption of heart (Romans 1:21) and legal condemnation (Romans 3:19). We have to wait until chapter 5 to see clearly how the condemnation and corruption of all men is tied to Adam's sin in the garden covenant of works.

In Romans 3b–5a, Paul preaches the precious promises of the gospel or the covenant of grace. The Second London Baptist Confession 20.1 says, "The covenant of works being broken by sin, and made unprofitable unto life, God was pleased to give forth the promise of Christ, the seed of the woman, as the means of calling the elect, and begetting in them faith and repentance; in this promise the gospel, as to the substance of it, was revealed, and [is] therein effectual for the conversion and salvation of sinners." The heart of the gospel is that Jesus Christ died for poor sinners and fulfilled all righteousness that they may be justified by faith alone. In Romans chapters 3b–5a, Paul explains that we "are justified by his grace as a gift, through the redemption that is in Christ Jesus" (Romans 3:24) and that "one is justified by faith apart from the works of the law" (Romans 3:28). Romans 4:5 says, "And to the one who does not work, but trusts him who justifies the ungodly, his faith is counted as righteousness." Romans 5:1 explains the goal of justification: "Therefore, since we have been justified by faith, we have *peace* with God through our Lord Jesus Christ." Then in Romans 5:5, Paul shows that the gospel changes our sinful hearts: "God's love has been poured into our hearts through the Holy Spirit who has been given to us." One of the most magnificent statements of the gospel in the Bible is found in Romans 5:6–11:

> For while we were still weak, at the right time Christ died for the ungodly. For one will scarcely die for a righteous person-though perhaps for a good person one would dare even to die-but God shows his love for us in that while we were still sinners, Christ died for us. Since, therefore, we have now been justified by his blood, much more shall we be saved by him from the wrath of God. For if while we were enemies we were reconciled to God by the death of his Son, much more, now that we are reconciled, shall we be saved by his life. More than that, we also rejoice

> in God through our Lord Jesus Christ, through whom we have now received reconciliation.

Just as the covenant of works had a double curse, total corruption of heart and legal condemnation, so also the covenant of grace has a double blessing. First, Christ cancels our condemnation and justifies us (Romans 5:1) and second, He reverses our total corruption of heart by regenerating us (Romans 5:5). This double blessing of the "covenant of grace" overturns the double curse of the "covenant of works."

When we come to the final half of Romans 5, Paul zooms out of the details, and he shows us the big picture. He sets up a contrast between Adam and Christ who are the two federal, or covenant, heads of all humanity. Paul says, "Adam was a type of the one who was to come" (Romans 5:14). Adam is a type, and Christ is the anti-type. Anti-types give us more information about their typical antecedents.[17] That is, if we want to understand Adam's responsibilities in the garden, we need to understand Christ's responsibilities during His earthly life. Romans 5:21 speaks of Christ's covenant when it says, "even so grace would reign through righteousness to eternal life through Jesus Christ." In other words, Jesus Christ had to obey God's law perfectly, to fulfill all righteousness, in order to obtain eternal life. Adam was therefore responsible to do the same in his original garden arrangement, but Adam failed. Adam sinned in the garden and did not obtain the promise of life, while Christ perfectly obeyed God's law during His earthly life and He obtained the promise of life.

These are the two major covenants, or "promises," in the Bible. They frame the theological superstructure of the canon. Romans 5:18–19 further elucidates the contrast between the covenant of works with Adam and the covenant of grace with Christ: "Therefore, as one trespass led to *condemnation* for all men, so one act of righteousness leads to *justification* and life for all men. For as by the one man's *disobedience* the many were made sinners, so by the one man's *obedience* the many will be made righteous." Adam sinned against his covenant; therefore, he and his posterity were cursed with death. Christ obeyed His covenant; so, He and His people are blessed with life. These are the two major covenants, a "covenant of works" with Adam and a "covenant of grace" with Christ.

The Bible shows that the gracious covenant with Christ is really two distinct covenants. A "covenant of redemption" was eternally made between the Father and the Son about the salvation of the elect, which Christ accomplished in time by His obedience and death for their redemption (2 Timothy 1:9–10; Hebrews 10:5–7). The "covenant of grace" is the promise

[17] Barcellos, "Getting the Garden Right," 213.

of salvation made to the elect on the basis of what Christ did in the covenant of redemption (Hebrews 9:15–17). The covenant of grace with the elect was established immediately after the fall when God promised that the seed of the woman would crush the serpent and his seed (Genesis 3:15). That same promise is repeated throughout the Scriptures (Ephesians 2:12; Galatians 3; Jeremiah 31:31–34, 32:40; Isaiah 54:10, 55:3, 61:8; Ezekiel 16:60, 24:25; Hebrews 8:8–10, 13:20). The promise finds its highest expression in the establishment of the new covenant (Hebrews 9:15–16).[18] The Second London Baptist Confession 7.3 rightly says:

> This covenant is revealed in the gospel; first of all to Adam in the promise of salvation by the seed of the woman, and afterwards by farther steps, until the full discovery thereof was completed in the New Testament; and it is founded in that eternal covenant transaction that was between the Father and the Son about the redemption of the elect; and it is alone by the grace of this covenant that all the posterity of fallen Adam that ever were saved did obtain life and blessed immortality, man being now utterly incapable of acceptance with God upon those terms on which Adam stood in his state of innocency.

The hermeneutic of New Testament priority leads to the superstructure of covenant theology. When preachers have this covenantal framework as their biblical hermeneutic, and they apply it properly, they will inevitably preach Christ-centered sermons. They will find in every text evidence of the fall of man (the covenant of works), the hope of a Savior (the covenant of redemption), and salvation in Him (the covenant of grace). Where they do not find all these things in a particular text, they know the Bible's wider context always supplies them.

Covenant theology reads the Bible as a story about how Christ reverses the curse of Adam. "For as in Adam, all die, so also in Christ shall all be made alive" (1 Corinthians 15:22).[19] Christ in the covenants of redemption and grace makes right what Adam destroyed in the covenant of works. Scripture goes so far as to say that Christ is Himself God's gracious covenant. The Father tells the Son, "I will give you as a covenant for the

[18] For a wonderful description of the biblical doctrine of the covenant of grace, see Pascal Denault, *The Distinctiveness of Baptist Covenant Theology: A Comparison Between Seventeenth-Century Particular Baptist and Paedobaptist Federalism* (Birmingham, AL: Solid Ground Christian Books, 2013). For a fine collection of essays on Baptist covenant theology, see *Covenant Theology: A Baptist Distinctive*, ed. Earl M. Blackburn (Birmingham, AL: Solid Ground Christian Books, 2013).

[19] This verse means that all *in Adam* die and that all *in Christ* are made alive. It does not mean that every single person is made alive in Christ.

people, a light for the nations" (Isaiah 42:6; cf. 49:8). Jesus is the covenantal Savior of sinful human beings. He is the Hero of Scripture. He is our much-needed King. He is the Prophet who reveals God to our ignorance. He is the Priest who sacrifices Himself for His enemies and prays for them. He gives dead men eternal life.

The preacher's hermeneutic, therefore, determines whether he will preach Christ in all his sermons. If he accepts the grammatical-historical-theological hermeneutic with New Testament priority, which leads to covenant theology, then he will see that the theological center of the Bible is Jesus Christ Himself, and if he is consistent with these principles when he studies any passage of Scripture, he will preach Jesus from all the Scriptures.

The Biblical Mandate For Christ-Centered Preaching

Not only do the principles of biblical hermeneutics require our preaching to be Christ-centered, but Scripture provides explicit examples of Christ-centered preaching and commands that teach us to preach Jesus Christ in all our sermons. We find this mandate throughout the New Testament. In this section, therefore, we will work from the Gospels to the Epistles to see what the Scriptures say about preaching Christ.

1. Christ's Own Christ-Centered Preaching

The Lord Jesus Christ preached Himself. He was at the center of His own message. He called men to Himself. He offered Himself as the only hope of eternal life.

Matthew

In the Gospel of Matthew, Jesus preaches five sermons or discourses. His first sermon is about discipleship in His kingdom (Matthew 5–7). In this sermon, Jesus demonstrates that He is the authoritative giver of God's law. In the Old Testament, Moses ascended Mount Sinai and received the law from God. Now, Christ ascends a mountain and preaches a sermon in which He gives the law *as* God. Christ repeatedly hands down authoritative interpretations of divine commandments, declaring "but *I* say to you" (Matthew 5:22, 28, 32, 34, 39, 44). His sermon points to Himself as the lawgiver and the law's final interpreter. Later in the sermon, Jesus declares that He will be the Judge of all on the last day: "On that day, many will say to me, Lord, Lord, did we not prophesy in your name, and cast out demons in your name, and do many might works in your name? And then I will declare to them, I never *knew* you; depart from me you workers of lawlessness" (Matthew 7:22–23, italics are mine). The only way to pass on Judgment Day, according to Jesus, is to "know" Christ. Christ preached Himself.

In Christ's second discourse in Matthew, He exhorts His disciples to preach the gospel publicly. Jesus teaches them to preach an explicitly Christ-centered message. He says, "So, everyone who *acknowledges me* before men, I also will acknowledge before my Father who is in heaven, but whoever *denies me* before men, I also will deny before my Father who is in heaven" (Matthew 10:32–33, italics are mine). All are to "acknowledge" Jesus. In this sermon, Christ says, "Whoever loves father or mother more than me is not worthy of me" (Matthew 10:37). Everything is about Jesus, acknowledging Him, and loving Him. Christ was Christ-centered.

In Matthew 13, Christ preaches His third sermon in light of rising opposition to His ministry. He speaks in parables. Christ's main point in each parable is that He is the King of the promised kingdom. He is the Messiah who has come to establish the kingdom of God. In Matthew 13:44, Jesus compares the kingdom to a treasure buried in the field. To have the kingdom, you have to joyfully sell all you have to buy the field and obtain the treasure. In Matthew 13:35, He compares the kingdom to a pearl of great price. He says that when a merchant finds a valuable pearl, he will sell all he has to obtain the pearl. That's the only way people may obtain the kingdom and its King. People must die to themselves and give themselves to Christ and His teaching. Here again, the center of Christ's preaching was Himself.

Christ's fourth sermon is found in Matthew 18. He preaches this message in the face of even more polarization and conflict. Here we find another series of parables in which Christ tells sinners to "receive" Him personally (Matthew 18:5). Christ's final parable is about the unforgiving servant. He teaches His disciples to forgive because they have been forgiven. The master says to his servants, "And should you not have had mercy on your fellows servant, as I had mercy on you?" (Matthew 18:33). This is a clear allusion to forgiveness in Christ and the obligation of His subjects to forgive their fellow men. Christ preached Himself in this parable.

Christ's final sermon in the gospel of Matthew is found in chapters 23–25, which is about divine judgment to come. In this sermon, Christ declares that He will personally arrive in judgment (Matthew 24:29–31). He tells the parable of the virgins, who should eagerly anticipate the return of the bridegroom (Matthew 25:1–13). These warnings are personal to Jesus, never moralistic or legal. Jesus is not telling His disciples to be morally good so that they can avoid judgment. He is telling them to anticipate His personal return. Matthew 25:31–33 says, "When the Son of Man comes in his glory, and all the angels with him, then he will sit on his glorious throne. Before him will be gathered all the nations, and he will separate people one from another as a shepherd separates the sheep from the goats. And he will place the sheep on his right, but the goats on the left." Once again, the center of Christ's sermon is Christ Himself. Jesus will sort the goats from the sheep. Jesus is the ruling and judging King.

So it is clear from every sermon in the book of Matthew that Christ was a Christ centered preacher. The same is true in the other two Synoptic Gospels. Now, let us consider the Gospel of John.

John

Jesus preaches seven sermons in the Gospel of John. His first sermon is about the new birth (John 3:1–21). He preached His own crucifixion: "And as Moses lifted up the serpent, so must the Son of Man be lifted up" (John 3:14). He also famously declared, "For God so loved the world that he gave his only Son, that whoever believes in him should not perish, but have eternal life" (John 3:16). Christ proclaimed Himself as the only hope of salvation for the world.

Christ's second discourse in the Gospel of John is about the water of life (John 4:1–42). He preaches to the woman at the well and tells her, "Whoever drinks of the water that I will give him will never be thirsty forever. The water that I will give him will become in him a spring of water welling up to eternal life" (John 4:14–15). Later, the woman asks Him, "I know that the Messiah is coming (he who is called Christ). When he comes, he will tell us all things" (John 4:25). Jesus responds to the woman in no uncertain terms: "I who speak to you *am he*" (John 4:26). Christ preached Himself in an extended personal discourse with the woman at the well.

Christ's third sermon in John declares that He is the divine Son (John 5:19–47). Preaching to Jews who wanted to kill Him, Jesus said, "For as the Father raises the dead and gives them life, so also the Son gives life to whom he will. The Father judges no one, but has given all judgment to the Son *that all may honor the Son just as they honor the Father*. Whoever does not honor the Father does not honor the Son who sent Him" (John 5:21–23, italics are mine). Christ declares that the Scriptures do not give life; rather, He gives life. "You search the Scriptures because you think that in them you have eternal life: and *it is they that bear witness about me*, yet you refuse to come to me that you may have life" (John 5:39–40, italics are mine). Christ, therefore, preached Himself as the end goal of all the

Scriptures. He proclaimed that He should be honored just as the Father is honored.

In Christ's fourth sermon, He declares that He is the bread of life (John 6:22–66). This is an intensely Christ-centered sermon. He says, "Do not labor for the food that perishes, but for the food that endures to eternal life, which the Son of Man will give to you" (John 6:27). He proclaims, "I am the bread of life; whoever comes to me shall not hunger, and whoever believes in me shall never thirst" (John 6:35). In one of His most intensely Christ-centered statements of this sermon, Jesus says, "Truly, truly, I say to you, unless you eat the flesh of the Son of Man and drink His blood, you have no life in you" (John 6:53). Jesus preaches Himself as the only food that gives life to poor sinners.

In Christ's fifth sermon in John, He speaks of the life-giving Spirit (John 7:1–52). He proclaims, "Whoever *believes in me*, as the Scripture has said, 'Out of his heart will flow rivers of living water.' Now this He said about the Spirit" (John 7:38–39, italics are mine). Christ did not say that in order to have life, you must first believe in the Spirit. Rather, He taught that to have the Spirit, you must first come to Me, and I will give you the Holy Spirit. Christ called sinners to believe in Him to have the life of the Spirit.

In Christ's sixth sermon in the Gospel of John, He declares that He is the light of the world (John 8:12–59). Christ exclaims, "If the Son sets you free, you will be free indeed" (John 8:36). He says, "Truly, truly, I say to you, if anyone keeps my word, he will never see death" (John 8:51). And then, "Truly, truly, I say to you, before Abraham was, I am" (John 8:58). Throughout this whole discourse, Jesus points to Himself as the only hope for sinners, who need Him for life because He is the eternal God of life.

In Christ's seventh and final sermon, He declares that He is the Good Shepherd (John 10:1–42). Jesus says, "I am the door. If anyone enters by me, he will be saved and will go in and out and find pasture" (John 10:9), and "I am the good shepherd. The good shepherd lays down his life for the sheep" (John 10:11). He preaches, "I am the good shepherd, I know my own and my own know me, just as the Father knows me and I know the Father, and I lay down my life for the sheep" (John 10:14, 15). Christ is preaching that He is the true overseer of His people who not only dies for them, but also leads and provides for them every day.

In each of Christ's sermons, He preaches Himself as the patent center of God's revelation to men. He is the goal of all of His discourses. Jesus preached Himself because life is only found in Him and the goal of all His preaching was to impart life to men.

2. Christ-Centered Preaching in Acts

Christ's Apostles learned how to preach from Jesus Himself. They understood that the center of all their sermons should be the Lord Jesus Christ because all of Christ's sermons were centered on Himself. The book of Acts both declares that the Apostles preached Jesus and provides examples of the Apostles's sermons, all of which were Christ-centered.

Consider the great number of instances in which Acts explicitly says that the Apostles preached or proclaimed Christ. I've italicized the relevant portion of the following verses.

- Acts 4:2 says, "they were teaching the people and *proclaiming in Jesus the resurrection from the dead*."
- Acts 5:42 says, "And every day, in the temple and from house to house, they *did not cease teaching and preaching that the Christ is Jesus.*"
- Acts 8:5 says, "Philip went down to the city of Samaria and *proclaimed to them the Christ*."
- Acts 8:12 says, "But when they believed Philip as he preached good news about the kingdom of God and *the name of Jesus Christ*, they were baptized, both men and women."
- Acts 9:20 says of Paul, "And immediately *he proclaimed Jesus* in the synagogues, saying, "He is the Son of God."
- Acts 10:36 says, "As for the word that he sent to Israel, *preaching good news of peace through Jesus Christ*."
- Acts 11:20 says Peter declared, "But there were some of them, men of Cyprus and Cyrene, who on coming to Antioch spoke to the Hellenists also, *preaching the Lord Jesus*."
- Acts 14:3 speaks of Paul and Barnabus that "They remained for a long time, *speaking boldly for the Lord*, who bore witness to the word of *his grace*."
- Acts 17:3 says that Paul was "explaining and proving that it was necessary for the Christ to suffer and to rise from the dead, and saying, "*This Jesus, whom I proclaim to you, is the Christ*."
- Acts 17:18 says, "Some of the Epicurean and Stoic philosophers also conversed with him. And some said, "What does this babbler wish to say?" Others said, "He seems to be a preacher of foreign divinities"—because *he was preaching Jesus and the resurrection*."
- Acts 28:31 says that Paul was "proclaiming the kingdom of God

and *teaching about the Lord Jesus Christ* with all boldness and without hindrance."

Such statements clearly demonstrate that the Apostles were Christ-centered preachers. But that is not all. All of the sermon summaries in the Book of Acts are Christ-centered. There are no exceptions.

- Peter's sermon at Pentecost declares that Christ's coming, death, and resurrection ushered in the Spirit, which fulfills Joel's prophecy (Acts 2:14–40).
- Peter then preached to the crowds at the temple, calling them to repent for crucifying the Messiah (Acts 3:12–26).
- Peter preached at the Sanhedrin and reminded them that Jesus healed the crippled man (Acts 4:5–12).
- Stephen preached at the Sanhedrin, reviewing redemptive history, charging the Jews with guilt for crucifying Jesus and for failing to grasp that He is the very presence of God (Acts 7).
- Peter preached to the Gentiles in Acts 10:28–47 and taught them that they are saved though Christ the same way the Jews are. He said, "To Him all the prophets bear witness that everyone who believes in him receives forgiveness of sins through his name" (Acts 10:43).
- In Acts 11:4–18, Peter preached to the church at Jerusalem and declared that food and people are clean because of the work of Jesus Christ (Acts 11:4–18).
- Paul preached to the synagogue at Antioch and taught that Jesus is the Messiah who fulfills Old Testament prophecies (Acts 13:16–41).
- Peter preached to the Jerusalem council and declared that salvation by grace in Christ is available to all (Acts 15:7–11). He proclaimed, "We believe that we will be saved through the grace of the Lord Jesus, just as they will" (Acts 15:11).
- Paul and Silas preached Christ to the prison guard after an earthquake: "Believe on the Lord Jesus Christ and you will be saved, you and your household" (Acts 16:31).
- Paul preached Christ to the Areopagus in Athens (Acts 17:22–35). Paul preached Christ to the Ephesian elders (Acts 20:17–35): "testifying both to Jews and Greeks of repentance toward God and of faith in our Lord Jesus Christ" (Acts 20:21).

- Paul gave testimony to a crowd at Jerusalem of his conversion to Christ and calling to preach Christ to the Gentiles (Acts 22:1–21).
- Paul preached to Felix in Caesarea that "the Way" of Christ is anchored in the Hebrew Scriptures and is not a sect (Acts 24:10–21).
- Paul preached to King Agrippa and declared his conversion to Christ and zeal for the gospel (Acts 26:2–23).
- Paul preached to the Jewish leaders at Rome, declaring that Jesus fulfills the law of God (Acts 28:17–20): "From morning till evening, he expounded to them, testifying to the kingdom of God and trying to convince them about Jesus both from the Law of Moses and from the Prophets."

The evidence in the book of Acts shows that the Apostles consistently preached Christ in all their sermons. He was the hinge of all their messages. There isn't a single instance of a sermon in Acts in which the Apostles failed to preach Jesus as a part of the very essence of their message.

3. Christ-Centered Preaching in the Epistles

We not only have a good deal of evidence that the Apostles consistently preached Christ in the book of Acts, but we also see explicit references to preaching Christ throughout the Epistles of the New Testament.

Paul speaks of preaching Christ in Romans. When Paul considers his own calling, he explicitly speaks of preaching Christ: "I make it my ambition to preach the gospel, not where Christ has already been named" (Romans 15:20). In Romans 16:25, Paul tells us that he seeks to strengthen the Christian church by the preaching of Christ: "Now to him who is able to strengthen you according to my gospel and the preaching of Jesus Christ." Paul is not talking about preaching the gospel to unbelievers, but to the church. The church is strengthened according to the gospel and the preaching of Jesus Christ.

In 1 Corinthians, Paul makes the famous statement, "we preach Christ crucified, a stumbling block to Jews and folly to Gentiles" (1 Corinthians 1:23). He also says, "For I decided to know nothing among you except Jesus Christ and him crucified" (1 Corinthians 2:2). In 1 Corinthians 15:12, Paul declares, "Christ is proclaimed as raised from the dead." Paul explains that his preaching is only valuable because of the resurrection of Christ: "And if Christ has not been raised, then our preaching is in vain and your faith is in vain" (1 Corinthians 15:14).

In 2 Corinthians, Paul says, "The Son of God, Jesus Christ, whom we proclaimed among you, Silvanus and Timothy and I, was not Yes and No, but in him it is always Yes" (2 Corinthians 1:19). And, "I came to Troas to preach the gospel of Christ" (2 Corinthians 2:12). Finally, "What we proclaim is not ourselves, but Jesus Christ as Lord" (2 Corinthians 4:5).

In Galatians, Paul says, "The gospel that was preached by me is not man's gospel" (Galatians 1:11). He then specifies that his gospel is the "gospel of Jesus Christ" (Galatians 1:7). In Ephesians, Paul explains that his calling is "to preach to the Gentiles the unsearchable riches of Christ" (Ephesians 3:8) In Philippians, he shows that Christ can be preached with wrong motives: "Some indeed preach Christ from envy and rivalry, but others from good will" (Philippians 1:15). In Colossians, Paul sets forth the substance and goal of all his preaching: "Him we proclaim, warning everyone and teaching everyone with all wisdom, that we may present everyone mature in Christ." (Colossians 1:28). In 2 Timothy, Paul urges Timothy to "Remember Jesus Christ, risen from the dead, the offspring of David, as preached in my gospel" (2 Timothy 2:8).

In addition to all of these explicit references to the preaching of Christ, the epistles are saturated with many references to Christ. The epistles begin with the doctrine of Christ and they end with applications that honor Christ. The epistles were meant to be read in a single sitting in the churches. That means none of the doctrines in the Epistles were ever isolated from Christ who fills and gives life to them all. Today's preachers should follow the example set in the Epistles. They should determine to preach any particular Christian doctrine in light of Christ, just as it is done in the Epistles.

4. Christ-Centered Preaching in the Book of Hebrews

The book of Hebrews is a sermon.[20] Fred Malone writes, "There is general agreement among scholars that the literary form of Hebrews is that of a well-constructed homily."[21] I would add that the book of Hebrews is a consistently Christ-centered homily, or sermon. This sermon was written to a group of confessing believers who were being tempted to return to the ritual worship of the Old Covenant. The preacher's main burden in his sermon is to show that Christ is superior to the Old Covenant.

[20] Donald Hagner says, "The literary genre of Hebrews is an exhortatory sermon." Donald A. Hagner, *Hebrews*, New International Biblical Commentary: New Testament Series, ed. W. Ward Gasque (Peabody, MA: Hendrickson, 1983), 12.

[21] Fred Anderson Malone, "A Critical Evaluation of the Use of Jeremiah 31:31–34 in the Letter to the Hebrews" (PhD diss., Southwestern Baptist Theological Seminary, 1989), 18.

Jesus fulfills the types and shadows of the Old Testament (Hebrews 10:1), which is the church of the Hebrews should not turn to Old Testament worship. The Christ-centered character of this sermon to the Hebrews is seen in two ways. First, Hebrews handles the Old Testament in a Christ-centered way. Second, all of the themes of Hebrews are Christ-centered.

First, the way the preacher of Hebrews handles Old Testament texts is always Christ-centered. Though there is not enough space here to provide an extensive analysis of the manner in which Hebrews deals with Old Testament passages, I will provide a few examples from the first few chapters. Beginning in Chapter 1, the preacher cites numerous passages of the Old Testament (Hebrews 1:5–13) and ties them all to Christ. He then immediately applies his Christ-centered message to the souls of his hearers by warning them against drifting from the message of Christ (Hebrews 2:1–3). In Chapter 2, the preacher quotes an Old Testament passage about the humiliation and exaltation of mankind (Hebrews 2:6–8). He then ties it to Christ's own humiliation and exaltation (Hebrews 2:9–13). Finally, he makes application to his hearers by offering them comfort in Christ (Hebrews 2:14–18). In Chapter 3, the preacher compares Moses to Christ and says that Christ is superior (Hebrews 3:3–6). Then he cites warning from Psalm 95 and tells his readers that just as the people of Israel were not to have hard hearts, so also those who confess Christ must not harden their hearts against Him (Hebrews 3:7–14). Such examples could be multiplied. The sermonic pattern of Hebrews is that the preacher interprets a passage, shows its connection to Christ, and then makes pastorally wise Christ-centered application to his hearers. This is a pattern that all Christian preachers would do well to follow.

Second, all of the themes of Hebrews are Christ-centered. Chapter 1 declares that Jesus Christ is God, worthy of worship and submission. Chapter 2 shows us that Jesus is truly a man, who died to take away our fear of death. Chapters 3–4 are about how Jesus is superior to Moses and Joshua, that they were God's servants, but Jesus is God's son, who brings His people into final rest. Chapters 5–7 teach us that Jesus is superior to the Old Testament priesthood because His priesthood is perfect and eternal. Chapter 8 proclaims that Christ's covenant is superior to the old covenant because His covenant is effectual to the salvation of all within it. Chapters 9–10 shows us how Christ is superior to the Old Covenant tabernacle and temple, that Christ's offering secures "eternal redemption" (Hebrews 9:12) for all who belong to Him. Chapter 11 shows the lives of the faithful Old Testament saints who trusted the gospel promise and endured to the end whether they triumphed in this life or were martyred. Chapter 12 exhorts the saints to run the race of faith, looking to Jesus, the founder and perfecter of our faith" (Hebrews 12:2). Finally, Hebrews

13 provides practical moral directives about how to live in light of such a great Savior.

In conclusion, the book of Hebrews is a magnificently Christ-centered sermon. It is the only full length sermon we have recorded in the Scriptures. It is a model to all preachers, who should follow its example in preaching Christ as the patent center of every sermon. Charles Bridges wrote:

> Determine to know nothing among your people, but Christ crucified. Let his name and grace, his spirit and love, triumph in the midst of all your sermons. Let your great end be, to glorify him in the heart, to render him amiable and precious in the eyes of his people, to lead them to him, as a sanctuary to protect them, a propitiation to reconcile them, a treasure to enrich them, a physician to heal them, an advocate to present them and their services to God, as wisdom to counsel them, as righteousness to justify, as sanctification to renew, as redemption to save. Let Christ be the diamond to shine in the bosom of all your sermons.[22]

The Trinity and Christ-Centered Preaching

Some have criticized Christ-centered preaching as theologically flawed because they claim that centering on Christ somehow obscures or diminishes our view of the other two persons of the Trinity. But this objection misunderstands what it means to be "Christ-centered." To be Christ-centered is not to neglect the other persons of the Trinity in the least. All three persons of the Trinity are co-equal and co-eternal, each sharing the fulness of God's glory. But Christ-centered preachers believe the Triune God's greatest revelation of Himself to men is found in Christ alone. In other words, if you want to know what the Father is like, you must look at His Son, and if you look at the Holy Spirit, He will direct your eyes to the Son. Christ-centered preachers are trying to pay attention to the Bible's own teaching about *how* God makes Himself *known* to men. They believe that Jesus makes God known; therefore, we must preach Jesus, if we want men to see the one true God of the Bible and to respond to Him in faith and worship and all of life.

Christ had a discussion about this with His disciples. He said, "I am the way and the truth and the life. No one comes to the Father, except though me. If you had *known* me, you would have *known* my Father also. From now on you do *know* him and have *seen* him" (John 14:6–7, italics are

[22] Charles Bridges, *The Christian Ministry: With an Inquiry into the Causes of its Inefficiency* (Carlisle, PA: Banner, 1958), 258.

mine). Christ is not claiming to be superior to the Father, nor is He suggesting that the Father be obscured. Instead, Jesus is teaching His disciples the only way that the Father can be truly *known* and *seen*. The Father is only *known* and *seen* in Jesus. Therefore, far from obscuring the knowledge of the Father, a Christ-centered theology is the only way the Father can be truly known or seen.

Christ's teaching does not, however, satisfy Philip. "Philip said to him, 'Lord, show us the Father, and it is enough for us'" (John 14:8). Philip is uncomfortable believing that to see and know Christ is to see and know the Father. He wants to see the Father directly. But Jesus rebukes Philip and says, "Have I been with you so long, and you still do not know me Philip? Whoever has seen me has seen the Father. How can you say, 'Show us the Father?' Do you not believe that I am in the Father and the Father is in me?" (John 14:9–10). This is called "perichorisis," or the interpenetration of the persons of the Trinity. The persons mutually indwell one another. Jesus is telling us that the only way to see the Father is to look upon Him. Jesus is exactly what the Father is like. If we try to see the fullness of the Father in any way other than looking upon Jesus, then we will fail to see Him clearly.

Just a couple of chapters later in the book of John, Jesus explains His relationship to the Holy Spirit. He says, "When the Spirit of truth comes, he will guide you into all truth, for he will not speak on his own authority, but whatever he hears he will speak and he will declare to you the things that are to come" (John 16:13). That means the Holy Spirit will reveal the Word of God to the apostles. And then Jesus says, "He will glorify me, for he will take what is mine and declare it to you" (John 16:14). That is a very important verse because it teaches us the relationship between Christ and the Holy Spirit. It tells us that the Holy Spirit is Christ-centered. The Spirit glorifies Christ. When believers study the Word of God, the Spirit uses those words, originally written by the apostles and prophets, and points us to Jesus. Therefore, when we read the Bible and hear it preached correctly, the Holy Spirit adds His blessing to His people by fixing their eyes upon Jesus. If we look directly at the Spirit speaking in the pages of Scripture, we find Him telling us to look at Christ. Scripture calls the Holy Spirit "the Spirit of Christ" (Romans 8:9, 1 Peter 1:11).

All of this shows us in what manner we are to be "Christ-centered." Far from obscuring the knowledge of the Trinity, focusing on Christ is the only way we can know what the Trinity is like. Jesus most fully reveals the character and purposes of the whole godhead. Hebrews 1:3 tells us that Jesus is "the radiance of the glory of God and the exact imprint of His nature." Colossians 1:15 says, "He is the image of the invisible God" and Colossians 2:9 says, "For in Him the whole fullness of deity dwells bodily."

If you want to know what the Triune God is like, you see Him most fully in the person of Jesus Christ.

Faithful preachers are committed to preaching God to men, which means they must preach Christ to men. Preachers should never think that by centering on Christ they neglect the Father or the Holy Spirit. Quite the opposite is true. The only way to see the Father is to see the Son. And if we look at the Spirit, He sets us upon Jesus. Therefore, preachers should preach the Bible as centered on Jesus Christ with all confidence that they are preaching the whole godhead.

Conclusion

In conclusion, the Bible requires Christ-centered preaching. The Bible's hermeneutic leads to the conclusion that Jesus Christ is the center of God's revelation to men. Jesus Christ preached Himself and taught His apostles to do the same. The Book of Acts and the Epistles mandate Christ-centered preaching. The only full-length sermon in the Bible, Hebrews, is intensely Christ-centered. Jesus Christ reveals the whole Trinity. Therefore, Christian preachers must preach the Lord Jesus Christ in every sermon.

This is the only way for sinners to be saved and saints to be edified. Churches and individual Christians can only grow in a balanced way, when Christ is faithfully set before their eyes from all the Scriptures. God's people will only have strength to believe in Christ every day, to seek Him faithfully, to commune with Him continually, and to submit to His good commands in their homes, churches, communities and workplaces, if Christ is central in their thinking and in their souls. The final goal of Christ-centered preaching is the salvation and sanctification of God's chosen people to His great glory.

3

Exalting Christ by Preaching Him and Him Crucified

Michael McKelvey

The subject of homiletics occupies an important place in the curriculum of seminaries, the discussions of ministers, and the work of churches and denominations. Many books have been written on the topic, ranging from styles of preaching, to methods of preaching, to theologies of preaching.[1] Much of what has been written provides very helpful insight into the central task of the minister. However, much of what has been written is not. Perhaps, this is because so much of preaching is caught rather than taught. We learn much by seeing and doing, as opposed to studying and reading about preaching. Yet taking the time to purposefully evaluate the method, manner, and rudiments of preaching is a vital undertaking in shaping both the preacher and his preaching. Thankfully, that is not the task of this essay!

[1] See, e.g., Bryan Chapell, *Christ-Centered Preaching: Redeeming the Expository Sermon* (Grand Rapids: Baker, 2002); T. David Gordon, *Why Johnny Can't Preach* (Phillipsburg, NJ: P&R, 2009); Syndey Greidanus, *Preaching Christ from the Old Testament: A Contemporary Hermeneutical Method* (Grand Rapids: Eerdmans, 1999); John Carrick, *The Imperative of Preaching: A Theology of Sacred Rhetoric* (Carlisle, PA: Banner of Truth, 2002); Dennis E. Johnson, *Him We Proclaim: Preaching Christ From All the Scriptures* (Phillipsburg, NJ: P&R, 2007); Samuel T. Logan, Jr., ed., *The Preacher and Preaching: Reviving The Art in the Twentieth Century* (Phillipsburg, NJ: P&R, 1986); D. Martyn Lloyd-Jones, *Preaching and Preachers* (Grand Rapids: Zondervan, 1972).

The design of this paper is to consider preaching with respect to the theme of Jesus Christ and Him crucified. Notably, this is not the only theme to consider within the subject of preaching (hence the other essays in this book), but it may be valid to argue that this theme is the primary goal of biblical preaching, and if preaching lacks this Christ-centered aspect, it falls short of the scriptural ideal. This may be a weighty claim, but hopefully we will see that the essence of biblical preaching is Christ crucified.

At the outset, it is worth stating that preaching Christ and Him crucified does not mean simply presenting the gospel of salvation so that someone may become a Christian. Rather, it is the center-point or wellspring out of which all of life and practice flows. If someone does not begin and continue to drink from the well of Jesus Christ and Him crucified, then he will not know God (salvation) or understand the implications of living in communion with God (sanctification). The reality of Christ crucified touches upon everything for the believer, because the whole counsel of God radiates through knowing the person and work of Jesus Christ.

To understand this, we will investigate the biblical idea of preaching Jesus Christ and Him crucified (which I understand to be synonymous with the concepts of Christ-centered preaching, preaching Christ, etc.).[2] Then, since Christ crucified is the central message of the Bible, we will consider principles for preaching this message. The necessity of this message will then be addressed, followed by analyzing the relationship of the preacher to the message. In the end, I hope that this essay will help us become more resolved to preach the wonders of our Risen Lord.

Paul's Message to Corinth

In Paul's first letter to the church in Corinth, he is concerned for the Corinthians. He writes to a church in the throes of quarreling over the various teachers to which they identify: "What I mean is that each one of you says, 'I follow Paul,' or 'I follow Apollos,' or 'I follow Cephas,' or 'I follow Christ'" (1 Corinthians 1:12). The church had fallen into the common and subtle trap of following people, and developed a sectarian spirit, notably not over doctrine but over men. Exalting men or women can become a type of idolatry, whether intentional or not. As Paul points out, "Is Christ divided? Was Paul crucified for you? Or were you baptized in the name of Paul?" (1 Corinthians 12:13).

[2] See Greidanus, *Preaching Christ*, 1–15, for his discussion of the meaning of "Preaching Christ."

Christ alone is Savior and Lord, and the church at Corinth must follow Him. Even in following apostolic teaching, they must follow *the God* of the doctrine and not merely the human vessel who teaches the doctrine (1 Corinthians 11:1, "Be imitators of me, as I am of Christ"). Only God, in Jesus Christ, can save the church at Corinth, sanctify them, sustain them, and preserve them to the end. Paul argues that they are not united to Him or Apollos or Cephas. They are united to Jesus. They are in Christ.

They are also united to each other "in him," and therefore, factionalism surrounding human personalities actually divides Christ's body, the very body he came to unite. So Paul's goal in this initial part of the epistle is to logically and powerfully show the utter folly of following and elevating men (i.e. man worship). Interestingly, he emphasizes the peculiar manner in which God saves sinners—not by man or man's wisdom or man's personality, but through the foolishness of preaching.

At the center of his argument, Paul states,

> For since, in the wisdom of God, the world did not know God through wisdom, it pleased God through the folly of what we preach to save those who believe. For Jews demand signs and Greeks seek wisdom, but we preach Christ crucified, a stumbling block to Jews and folly to Gentiles, but to those who are called, both Jews and Greeks, Christ the power of God and the wisdom of God. For the foolishness of God is wiser than men, and the weakness of God is stronger than men (1 Corinthians 1:21–25).[3]

The message preached is unexpected. To the Greek mind, a crucified God was irrational, and the resurrection from the dead was simply nonsense. To the Jews, a crucified Messiah was a stumbling block. They expected a victorious Messiah who would restore the kingdom to Israel with signs and wonders. The message that Christ died, rose from the dead on the third day, and ascended to heaven was vastly different than Jewish expectations. The Jew anticipated an earthly kingdom, not a spiritual kingdom.

However, in God's wisdom, "Christ crucified" is the very message that God uses to save sinners, both Jew and Greek. Paul explains,

> But God chose what is foolish in the world to shame the wise; God chose what is weak in the world to shame the strong; God chose what is low and despised in the world, even things that are not, to bring to nothing things that are, so that no human being might boast in the presence of God. And because of him you are in Christ Jesus, who became to

[3] Unless otherwise noted, all Scripture quotations are from the ESV.

> us wisdom from God, righteousness and sanctification and redemption, so that, as it is written, "Let the one who boasts, boast in the Lord" (1 Corinthians 1:27–31).

Paul makes clear that salvation is a sovereign gift of God. Note His words in v. 30: "And because of him you are in Christ Jesus." The eloquence of men (or lack thereof) has no bearing upon the salvation of a sinner, nor does the strength of personality. The simple message of the gospel brought into the heart by the Spirit of God is the only manner in which those who believe are saved. This is why the message of Christ crucified is so central to Paul's life and ministry, and it must remain central to the church's life and ministry.

This message was so crucial for Paul that his purpose among the church in Corinth was shaped by it. He concludes,

> And I, when I came to you, brothers, did not come proclaiming to you the testimony of God with lofty speech or wisdom. *For I decided to know nothing among you except Jesus Christ and him crucified.* And I was with you in weakness and in fear and much trembling, and my speech and my message were not in plausible words of wisdom, but in demonstration of the Spirit and of power, so that your faith might not rest in the wisdom of men but in the power of God. (2 Corinthians 2:1–5, emphasis added)

The significance of Paul's decision expressed in v. 2 should not be overlooked or interpreted as hyperbolic expression. It provides the very essence of Paul's argument of the previous chapter in summary fashion. He yearns for the church to know and exalt Christ, and be united together "in him" instead of being divided by a sectarian spirit based upon the cult of personality. From beginning to end, his ultimate goal is that Christ and His work would perpetually affect the life and practice of the church. Paul's own life and ministry among them was not the result of human wisdom or strength, but the power of God through the Spirit's exaltation of Jesus Christ and Him crucified.

The Scope of this Message

What does Paul's phrase "Jesus Christ and Him crucified" signify? As implied above, it is the whole counsel of God radiating and rightly understood through the person and work of Jesus Christ. As Ciampa and Rosner indicate, "For Paul, *Christ crucified* is more than just the means of forgiveness and salvation; rather it informs his total vision of the Christian life and ministry."[4] It cannot be simply reduced to a gospel presentation nor can it be exhaustively outlined in a systematic theology, and yet, it must permeate, undergird, and propel both. It is the means through which we truly know God and His Word, and live out the salvation He gives.

"Jesus Christ and Him crucified" is a wonderful expression that encompasses both Christ's *person* and *work*. These two subjects are not mutually exclusive, and must never be divided in the grand scheme.[5] However, it is worth briefly considering these two topics individually in order to see the vastness upon which they touch. First, the name "Jesus Christ" highlights His person as both God and man. All that God is, He is. The fullness of deity dwells in Him (Colossians 1:19; 2:9). The One who created all things, sustains all things, ordains and overrules all things, reveals Himself by His Word, judges mankind, and saves sinners is the One who became flesh and dwelt among us (John 1:14). The sheer wonder of the incarnation lies beyond the finite mind to fully grasp, and yet, we may truly know the God-man and glory in His person. He displayed both His divinity and humanity for the world to see, so that we may know the answer to the question, "Who then is this …?" (Mark 4:41). The fullness of His humanity is wonderfully displayed in His being sent "in the likeness of sinful flesh and for sin" to condemn "sin in the flesh" (Romans 8:3) and by His perfect obedience to the law of God: "For we do not have a high priest who is unable to sympathize with our weaknesses, but one who in every respect has been tempted as we are, yet without sin" (Hebrews 4:15). His death and resurrection further display His perpetual human nature. He is *fully* God and *fully* man in *one* person, and the only One in whom sinners meet God, and dwell with God forever.

Here we see the intimate connection between His *person* and His *work* as Creator, Redeemer, Savior, Prophet, Priest, and King. His life of perfect righteousness, substitutionary death, resurrection from the dead, and ascension to heaven are all contained in the phrase "and Him crucified." The accomplishment of eternal salvation for His people is at the heart of His work as He glorifies His Father in heaven. This salvation has past, present, and future realities. He has accomplished once for all the salvation of His church through the cross and resurrection. He has poured out the Holy Spirit upon His people, who unites them to Christ, sanctifies them,

[4] Roy E. Ciampa and Brian S. Rosner, *The First Letter to the Corinthians* (PNTC; Grand Rapids: Eerdmans, 2010), 114.

[5] See Sinclair B. Ferguson, *The Whole Christ: Legalism, Antinominaism, and Gospel Assurance—Why the Marrow Controversy Still Matters* (Wheaton, IL: Crossway, 2015), in which Ferguson warns of the dangers of separating the benefits of Christ's work from Christ Himself. I cannot recommend this book too highly!

and prepares them for the glory to come. Christ builds His church by the preaching of "Jesus Christ and Him crucified." He will come again to judge the living and the dead. He will gather His bride into the new heavens and new earth, and the wicked He will cast away into the place where there is "weeping and gnashing of teeth" (Matthew 24:51).

This brief consideration of the person and work of Christ is by no means exhaustive, but perhaps it begins to flesh out the fullness of the phrase "Jesus Christ and Him crucified." This is what Paul determined to know among the church at Corinth (and certainly all the churches he served), because he knew that this subject in some way encapsulates the whole counsel of God. And to support his perspective, Paul frequents the Old Testament Scriptures.

The Message of Scripture

Paul's perspective is not new. While he certainly received new revelation from Christ and wrote under the inspiration of the Spirit, he stood upon the ancient texts of the Hebrew Bible. Paul understood that "Jesus Christ and Him crucified" is at the heart of the message of the OT Scriptures, and he makes this case throughout his writings. He especially highlights Christ as both Creator and Redeemer, two roles uniquely attributed to Yahweh in the OT.

Creation

When Paul saw God's purposes in creation, he saw Christ. He writes in Colossians 1:15–17,

> He is the image of the invisible God, the firstborn of all creation. For by him all things were created, in heaven and on earth, visible and invisible, whether thrones or dominions or rulers or authorities—all things were created through him and for him. And he is before all things, and in him all things hold together.

Paul was not the only one to see this. The author the Hebrews writes,

> Long ago, at many times and in many ways, God spoke to our fathers by the prophets, but in these last days he has spoken to us by his Son, whom he appointed the heir of all things, through whom also *he created the world*. He is the radiance of the glory of God and the exact imprint of his nature, and he *upholds the universe by the word of his power*" (1:1–3a, emphasis added).

Also, the apostle John waxes with theological profundity in John 1:1–3,

> In the beginning was the Word, and the Word was with God, and the Word was God. He was in the beginning with God. *All things were made through him, and without him was not any thing made that was made"* (emphasis added).

Each of these passages (and many more) establishes that God the Son is the agent of creation, and the creating purposes of God cannot be understood apart from Him.

Redemption

Additionally, when Paul saw God's purposes in redemption, he saw Christ. In the great tome of Romans, he wrote, "For I am not ashamed of the gospel, for it is the power of God for salvation to everyone who believes, to the Jew first and also to the Greek" (1:16). Again, he states in Romans 3:23–25b, "For all have sinned and fall short of the glory of God, and are justified by his grace as a gift, through the redemption that is in Christ Jesus, whom God put forward as a propitiation by his blood, to be received by faith." Having explained the "redemption of our bodies" in the coming resurrection (Romans 8:18–25), Paul climaxes with Christ's centrality in this ultimate redemption: "For those whom he foreknew he also predestined to be conformed to the image of his Son, in order that he might be the firstborn among many brothers" (Romans 8:29). In other words, ultimate redemption is to be conformed to the image of Christ. Furthermore, in Galatians the apostle shows that God's redemptive purposes in the OT, namely through Abraham, are realized in Jesus: "Christ redeemed us from the curse of the law by becoming a curse for us—for it is written, 'Cursed is everyone who is hanged on a tree'—so that in Christ Jesus the blessing of Abraham might come to the Gentiles, so that we might receive the promised Spirit through faith" (Galatians 3:13–14).

Paul was not alone in his convictions. Luke records the actions of the prophetess Anna who saw the incarnate God as a babe in the temple: "And coming up at that very hour she began to give thanks to God and to speak of him to all who were waiting for the redemption of Jerusalem" (Luke 2:38). Notably, the author of Hebrews emphasizes how Christ as both high priest and sacrifice is the fulfillment of the OT sacrificial system. He is the once-for-all sacrifice needed for the redemption promised in the OT: "But when Christ appeared as a high priest of the good things that have come, then through the greater and more perfect tent (not made with hands, that is, not of this creation) he entered once for all into the holy places, not by means of the blood of goats and calves but by means of his own blood, thus securing an eternal redemption" (Hebrews 9:11–12). Each of these passages (and many more) establish that God the Son is the agent of redemption, and the saving purposes of God cannot be understood apart from Him.

Jesus' Perspective

It would be detrimental to move on without considering Jesus' own confirmation of the centrality of His person and work in the OT. Four penetrating texts will suffice. In the Sermon on the Mount, Jesus clarifies His relationship to the Hebrew canon: "Do not think that I have come to abolish the Law or the Prophets; I have not come to abolish them but to fulfill them. For truly, I say to you, until heaven and earth pass away, not an iota, not a dot, will pass from the Law until all is accomplished" (Matthew 5:17–18). Secondly, after His resurrection, Jesus challenges two of His perplexingly despondent disciples regarding their understanding of the Messiah's work:

> And he said to them, 'O foolish ones, and slow of heart to believe all that the prophets have spoken! Was it not necessary that the Christ should suffer these things and enter into his glory?' And beginning with Moses and all the Prophets, he interpreted to them in all the Scriptures the things concerning himself" (Luke 22:25–27).

Thirdly, several verses later, Luke records that Christ appears among his disciples. He writes, "Then [Jesus] said to them, 'These are my words that I spoke to you while I was still with you, that everything written about me in the Law of Moses and the Prophets and the Psalms must be fulfilled.' Then he opened their minds to understand the Scriptures" (Luke 24:44–45). Finally, Jesus gives the Jews a lesson on hermeneutics from the OT, and His words are utterly profound. As He explains that the Father bears witness of Him through His Word, Jesus states, "You search the Scriptures because you think that in them you have eternal life; and it is they that bear witness about me, yet you refuse to come to me that you may have life" (John 5:39–40). Each of these passages (and many more) establish that God the Son is the One to whom all the Scriptures point, and He is to be seen (in one way or another) in all the Scriptures.

God's intent through the Word of God is to reveal Himself to the creatures that He made in His image and to restore them from their fallen estate. Jesus *is* the revelation of God to man (Hebrews 1:1–4; John 1:1–4, 14; 1 John 1:1–5). God the Son is the agent through whom the Father reveals Himself. So the Scriptures are given to us from the Father, through the Son, and by the inspiration of the Holy Spirit. This is a Trinitarian act, in which God makes Himself known through the person and work of Jesus Christ. This fact should elevate our consideration of, and sensitivity to, what should characterize our preaching.

Jesus Christ and Him crucified must be the paradigm through which we understand God, His promises, and His purposes. Many Bible-believing Christians will agree with this to some degree. However, it is one thing to say this, and another thing to actually *believe* this and have it transform your life and ministry. The same is true when it comes to preaching. It is one thing to *say* we must be Christ-centered in preaching, and it is another thing to actually *be* Christ-centered in preaching. Moreover, since preaching is the central "means of grace" through which God is made known in Christ, the paradigm of Jesus Christ and Him crucified remains absolutely vital for the ministry of the Word.

Preaching the Message

Perhaps it goes without saying, but preaching Jesus Christ and Him crucified is not simply mentioning Christ, His death, and His resurrection. Preaching elementary evangelistic sermons either occasionally or every service does not sufficiently qualify as Christ-centered preaching. These presentations have their place, and the Holy Spirit may powerfully use them in the lives of sinners. But to approach preaching Christ solely in this manner woefully stops short of the intent of preaching. Preaching needs to be doctrinally rich, but even doctrinal preaching must get to Christ in some manner in each particular message. Also, preaching entire sermons without even mentioning the name of "Jesus" or asking, "how shall we then live?" in the light of the gospel, falls short of the intent of preaching. To preach a sermon, especially from the OT, and not even speak of Jesus seems to go against the entire thrust of the apostles and the New Testament.

Every truth of Scripture (OT and NT), whether doctrinal or practical, can only be fully understood in the light of Jesus Christ and Him crucified. And we can never assume that our hearers are able to make this connection on their own. One of the main roles of preachers is to instruct their hearers how to read, interpret, trust, and apply God's Word to themselves in the light of the person and work of their Savior. Preachers must show their listeners how the paradigm of Christ crucified affects their lives.

Preaching Responsibly

It must be emphasized that preaching in this way must be done legitimately and responsibly. For instance, allegorizing or spiritualizing a text of the Bible is not an appropriate way to get to Christ. For instance, allegorizing is looking for hidden/symbolic meanings in parts of the text that do not clearly point to Christ.[6] An example of allegory appears in the following interpretation of 2 Kings 6:1–7. In that passage, Elisha throws a stick into the river to retrieve the borrowed axe head that the borrower lost. This act delivers the responsible party from the consequences of losing the axe head. To say that the stick actually points to the cross that delivers us from the consequences of our sins is allegory. Both the stick and the cross are a means of deliverance. Both are made of wood. Both take away consequence. Therefore, the stick clearly points to the cross of Christ, and that is how we can get to Christ from this passage. This interpretation, however, is allegorical, and does not do justice to the meaning of the OT passage. It is a dangerously subjective hermeneutical approach that leaves the actual "meaning" of the text in the hands of the individual interpreter, and does not grasp the point of the text in its original setting.

However, the passage does show us the amazing and miraculous power of God to help his people in their time of need (even with small things like an axe head), and that God cares about the small things in their lives. With this principle, we are then able to move on to see how Jesus Christ and Him crucified is the greatest expression of God's loving help and concern for His people. God the Son became man, and He Himself experienced the big and small issues of life. He knows what it is like to experience the trials of this fallen world. In Christ, we see that God's care for us is unceasing, and that He understands our weaknesses and needs. "For we do not have a high priest who is unable to sympathize with our weaknesses, but one who in every respect has been tempted as we are, yet without sin. Let us then with confidence draw near to the throne of grace, that we may receive mercy and find grace to help in time of need" (Hebrews 4:14–15). From here, application of the love of God for us in Christ can then be further elaborated. Admittedly, this is not the only way to preach this text and its message, while bringing it to bear on our lives in the light of the gospel, and the direction a preacher will take will largely differ from preacher to preacher. But it is a way that upholds the meaning of the text and applies it in the light of the gospel. In the end, careful and faithful exegesis, and application in view of the Savior, should be the goal of every preacher.

[6] See the discussion on allegorical interpretation in Greidanus, *Preaching Christ*, 70–90.

Preaching Powerfully

With that said, preaching Christ crucified consistently from all the Scriptures is necessary because it is both the power of God *for salvation* and the power of God *for obedience*. "For I am not ashamed of the gospel, for it is the power of God for salvation to everyone who believes" (Romans 1:18). "For the word of the cross is folly to those who are perishing, but to us who are being saved it is the power of God" (1 Corinthians 1:18). "And there is salvation in no one else, for there is no other name under heaven given among men by which we must be saved" (Acts 4:12). Only through Jesus is there power for salvation. Additionally, only in Christ crucified is there the power to obey God's commands. Note Christ and His work at the center of Paul's prayer for sanctification for the church in Ephesus:

> For this reason I bow my knees before the Father, from whom every family in heaven and on earth is named, that according to the riches of his glory he may grant you to be strengthened with power through his Spirit in your inner being, so that Christ may dwell in your hearts through faith—that you, being rooted and grounded in love, may have strength to comprehend with all the saints what is the breadth and length and height and depth, and to know the love of Christ that surpasses knowledge, that you may be filled with all the fullness of God. Now to him who is able to do far more abundantly than all that we ask or think, according to the power at work within us, to him be glory in the church and in Christ Jesus throughout all generations, forever and ever. Amen.
> (Ephesians 3:14–20)

And Jesus Himself wonderfully notes the believer's need of Him to persevere: "Abide in me, and I in you. As the branch cannot bear fruit by itself, unless it abides in the vine, neither can you, unless you abide in me. I am the vine; you are the branches. Whoever abides in me and I in him, he it is that bears much fruit, for apart from me you can do nothing" (John 15:4–5). Powerful preaching (i.e. power that truly saves people and sanctifies them) does not originate in the preacher. It comes solely from Christ and Him crucified.[7]

[7] Note Paul reasoning regarding this truth: "And I was with you in weakness and in fear and much trembling, and my speech and my message were not in plausible words of wisdom, but in demonstration of the Spirit and of power, so that your faith might not rest in the wisdom of men but in the power of God" (1 Corinthians 2:3–5).

Preaching Comprehensively

The question may be asked, "If we always focus upon Christ, will we be guilty neglecting other things or emphasizing one thing more than another?" This is a good question, and it largely depends on understanding how to be Christ-centered. If we only talked about the basics of the gospel, then yes, we will neglect other crucial issues of the Bible. However, if Christ crucified is the theological *thrust, pulse, spirit* of our preaching, then whatever we teach or address will have the flavor of the person and work of the Savior. We must preach comprehensively, i.e. the whole counsel of God in all the Scriptures, and in doing so, our union with the Risen Lord provides the basis through which we understand the whole counsel of God.

Another question may be, "What about the other persons of the Trinity? If we center on Christ, do we risk neglecting God the Father and God the Holy Spirit?" The Scriptures themselves help us to answer this question. The Father's purpose is to reveal *Himself* to us in His Son; Jesus is Immanuel, "God with us" (Isaiah 7:14; Matthew 1:23). Two passages will suffice to highlight God the Father's purpose to make Himself known through Jesus. The book of Hebrews begins by this truth. It states,

> Long ago, at many times and in many ways, God spoke to our fathers by the prophets, but in these last days he has spoken to us by his Son, whom he appointed the heir of all things, through whom also he created the world. *He is the radiance of the glory of God and the exact imprint of his nature*, and he upholds the universe by the word of his power. After making purification for sins, he sat down at the right hand of the Majesty on high …" (Hebrews 1:1–3, emphasis added)

In the Scriptures, "the glory of the Lord" often refers to the manifest presence of God, especially in the OT (see, e.g., Exodus 40:34–38; 1 Kings 8:10–11; Ezekiel 3:12, 23; 10:1–5, 18–19; 43:4–5).[8] So the writer of the epistle makes unequivocally clear that Christ reveals God the Father to us.[9] Secondly, and perhaps even more pointedly, Jesus made shocking statements to Philip in John 14:8–14. Philip tells Jesus to show the Father to the disciples and that will be sufficient for them. To this request, Jesus replies, "Have I been with you so long, and you still do not know

[8] For more discussion on "the glory of the Lord" as the manifest presence of God in the OT, especially in Ezekiel, see Michael G. McKelvey, "Ezekiel" in Miles V. Van Pelt, ed., *An Expositional Introduction to the Old Testament: The Gospel Promised* (Wheaton, IL: Crossway, 2016), 310–313, 316–318.

[9] See also John 1:1–3, 14; Colossians 1:15–20.

me, Philip? Whoever has seen me has seen the Father. How can you say, 'Show us the Father'?" (14:9). Christ proceeds to explain that He is in the Father and the Father is in Him.[10] To see Jesus is to the see the Father. So when Christ is proclaimed, it is the Father we see. In Jesus Christ and Him crucified, God's character, nature, love, mercy, power, sovereignty, patience, wisdom, justice, etc., are all wonderfully revealed! Rather than neglecting the Father, preaching Christ *exalts* the Father![11]

What about the third person of the Trinity? The Holy Spirit's purpose is to exalt Christ:

> Nevertheless, I tell you the truth: it is to your advantage that I go away, for if I do not go away, the Helper will not come to you. But if I go, I will send him to you. And when he comes, he will convict the world concerning sin and righteousness and judgment: concerning sin, because they do not believe in me; concerning righteousness, because I go to the Father, and you will see me no longer; concerning judgment, because the ruler of this world is judged. I still have many things to say to you, but you cannot bear them now. When the Spirit of truth comes, he will guide you into all the truth, for he will not speak on his own authority, but whatever he hears he will speak, and he will declare to you the things that are to come. *He will glorify me, for he will take what is mine and declare it to you.* All that the Father has is mine; therefore I said that he will take what is mine and declare it to you. (John 16:7–15, emphasis added)

The Holy Spirit uses the one who preaches Christ to exalt Christ. Rather than neglecting the Holy Spirit, preaching Christ *honors* the Holy Spirit![12] We must be Trinitarian in our theology, life, and practice. Christ-

[10] See also John 10:22–39.

[11] "Whoever has my commandments and keeps them, he it is who loves me. And he who loves me will be loved by my Father, and I will love him and manifest myself to him" (John 14:21); "If anyone loves me, he will keep my word, and my Father will love him, and we will come to him and make our home with him" (John 14:23); "For the Father himself loves you, because you have loved me and have believed that I came from God" (John 16:27); "Whoever receives me receives the one who sent me" (John 13:23).

[12] "And such were some of you. But you were washed, you were sanctified, you were justified in the name of the Lord Jesus Christ and by the Spirit of our God" (1 Corinthians 6:11); "If you are insulted for the name of Christ, you are blessed, because the Spirit of glory and of God rests upon you" (1 Peter 4:14); "By this you know the Spirit of God: every spirit that confesses that Jesus Christ has come in the flesh is from God" (1 John 4:2); "This is he who came by water and blood—Jesus Christ; not by the water only but by the water and the blood. And the Spirit is the one who testifies, because the Spirit is the truth" (1 John 5:6).

centered preaching not only exalts the Triune God, it reflects with the Trinity's economy of work in revealing God through the Son by the power of the Holy Spirit.[13]

The Point

Admittedly, preaching Jesus Christ and Him crucified can be difficult to explain and outline since it is a broad subject in which there are different ideas and opinions (hence, the many contemporary books on Christ-centered preaching!).[14] The above principles are not meant to be exhaustive. There are always questions that could be asked, or more precise definitions or parameters or principles given regarding this issue.

However, it ultimately comes down to this. We all likely know what it is like to sit under preaching that exalts Christ, as opposed to preaching that does not. This type of preaching stirs the mind and heart, and fills us with the wonder of God in Jesus. We may picture two different preachers, preaching on the same topic or text. And all things being equal, they are both very able expositors and speakers, and they are godly men who essentially address the primary issues faithfully and in an orthodox manner. However, with one preacher, we come away thinking, "That was very good, interesting, articulate, illuminating, helpful, faithful, clear, etc." With the other, we come away thinking, "What a glorious Savior! O Father in heaven, by the power of the Holy Spirit, help me to love and obey you for the love that you have shown me in Christ!" The *thrust, pulse, spirit* of the second type of preaching was Christ *Himself*, and by God's grace, we the saw the LORD!!! This is preaching Jesus Christ and Him crucified. It is like good art. I may not be able to always explain what is good art or fully define it, but I know good art when I see it. Likewise, we know Christ-centered preaching when we *hear* it!

[13] See Greidanus, *Preaching Christ*, 177–182.

[14] On this note, ministers should not only consult contemporary works on preaching. Great benefit can be had from older authors who often speak more plainly and clearly about preaching since they were not necessarily addressing the same trends or questions of our time. See, e.g., Charles Bridges, *The Christian Ministry* (Carlisle, PA: Banner of Truth, 2001), 222–339; William M. Taylor, *The Ministry of the Word* (Grand Rapids: Baker, 1975); Charles P. McIlvaine, *Preaching Christ* (Carlisle, PA: Banner of Truth, 2003); James Stalker, *The Preacher and His Models* (Birmingham, AL: Solid Ground Christian Books, 2003).

The Need of this Message

Perhaps all Bible-believing ministers will agree on the essential necessity of this message. In fact, there is no message more needed for the dire situation of our world. Only the preaching of Jesus Christ and Him crucified will convert men, women, boys, and girls to God. No other message can or will raise dead souls to find eternal life in Jesus. Benevolence, education, stability, etc., (even though they have a place) will not deliver human beings from the wrath to come. There is only one Savior, one mediator between God and man, and how will the world know him unless He is preached?

Note Paul's logic: "How then will they call on him in whom they have not believed? And how are they to believe in him of whom they have never heard? And how are they to hear without someone preaching? And how are they to preach unless they are sent? As it is written, 'How beautiful are the feet of those who preach the good news!'" (Romans 1:15–16). The Great Commission of Jesus Christ is a call to "make disciples" and teach them to observe everything that *He* (i.e. Christ) commanded—His doctrine. At its heart, the commission is Christ-centered, and He Himself has promised to be with His church to the end of the age (Matt. 28:18–20). The reason and motive for, as well as the message of, evangelism and missions rest entirely upon the person and work Jesus Christ. Without "Jesus Christ and Him crucified," these proselytizing endeavors become humanistic labors that may improve present circumstances of human beings in a materialistic manner, but they will not bring them eternal life by seeing "the light of the knowledge of the glory of God in the face of Jesus Christ" (2 Corinthians 4:6).

Discipleship is deeply rooted in the message as well. The truth of Christ crucified is not just the means to convert sinners, but to sanctify them and preserve them to the end. In Paul's epistles, all of His instructions on duty and obedience are grounded in the doctrinal truth that believes are justified by grace alone, through faith alone, in Christ alone. (For example, note the structure of the book of Ephesians where chapters 1–3 address the doctrinal truths of the gospel and chapters 4–6 expound the practical implications of the gospel). Their union with Christ provides the atmosphere in which they now live for God. To consider the Christian life apart from the enveloping nature of union with Jesus will stagnate the growth of a believer, bring him frustration in pursuing holiness, incite pride in his progress, or even poison his faith altogether.[15] Christians need

[15] See Ferguson, *The Whole Christ*, 57–73.

to be consistently shown that the life they now live is lived by "faith in the Son of God, who loved me and gave himself for me" (Galatians 2:20).

From the early New Testament period, to the Reformation, to today, the church has been built upon Jesus Christ and Him crucified, and it will continue to be! All religious endeavors are in vain apart from Him. Only when Christ is lifted up, will He draw all people unto Himself (John 12:32); the Father Himself will draw His elect to His Son (John 6:37, 44, 65); and the Spirit will convict the world of sin and righteous and judgment (John 16:8–11). And when all the elect are gathered from the four corners of the earth, then Christ will come again, and every knee will bow, "in heaven and on earth and under the earth, and every tongue confess that Jesus Christ is Lord, to the glory of God the Father" (Philippians 2:10–11).

In the new heavens and the new earth, creation itself will ring with the glory of Jesus Christ and Him crucified. Every creature will declare, "Worthy is the Lamb who was slain, to receive power and wealth and wisdom and might and honor and glory and blessing! … To him who sits on the throne and to the Lamb be blessing and honor and glory and might forever and ever!" (Revelation 5:12–13). And a thunderous cry will be heard saying, "Hallelujah! For the Lord our God the Almighty reigns. Let us rejoice and exult and give him the glory, for the marriage of the Lamb has come, and his Bride has made herself ready; it was granted her to clothe herself with fine linen, bright and pure" (Revelation 6–8). Then, "The earth will be filled with the knowledge of the glory of the Lord as the waters cover the sea" (Habakkuk 2:14). The glory of God is the great goal, and that "light of the knowledge of the glory of God" is seen in the face of his Son (2 Corinthians 4:9).

This is why we must preach Jesus Christ and Him crucified: For the salvation of sinners, the sanctification and preservation of the people of God, the expansion of the kingdom of God and the building of the church, and ultimately, for the glory of the Most High.

The Message for the Preacher

Before preaching Jesus Christ and Him crucified, a preacher himself must see that this message is for him. Even before he is a preacher, he is a sinful man in need of the merciful and mighty Savior.[16] Christ himself must be the preacher's treasure (Philippians 1:21–23, 3:7–11; Colossians 3:1–4), not the praise of men or the successes of ministry. All the minister's

[16] For splendid work that briefly addresses the preacher himself and his work, see Geoff Thomas, *Preaching: The Man, the Message and the Method* (Greenville, SC: Reformed Academic Press, 2001).

preaching, teaching, and shepherding must be for Jesus. Since He is our life, we must bring every thought captive to Him (2 Corinthians 10:5). And it is the love of Christ that compels us in all things (2 Corinthians 5:14), especially preaching.

Why do you preach Christ? Because you love *Him*. You have seen that He first loved you (1 John 4:10) and He loved you to the end (John 13:1). His everlasting love for your soul has so captivated and overwhelmed you (even perplexed you) that you cannot help but reciprocate that love. So you lovingly serve Him, and you want others to know your Savior. So whether preaching systematically through books, or topically on doctrines, or teaching a catechism in a children's Sunday School class, you want your hearers to see the wonder and beauty of Christ. *He* fuels your message. *He* is the one you want others to see. *He* is the one you want to glorify.

As preachers, we may be accused of many things, and some of it may be legitimate. We may be accused of not being the best speakers. So be it. We may be accused of not being as intelligent, or even as well studied, as we should be. Fair enough. We may be accused of having blind sides and weaknesses. No argument here. However, if there is one thing that can be positively said about us, may it be this: We did not fail to preach Jesus Christ and Him crucified, to the glory of God the Father, relying on the power of the Holy Spirit.

4

Exalting Christ by Preaching The Law and the Gospel

Raymond Perron

The Law and the Gospel (Ralph Erskine)[1]

The law supposing I have all,
Does ever for perfection call;
The gospel suits my total want,
And all the law can seek does grant.

The law could promise life to me,
If my obedience perfect be;
But grace does promise life upon
My Lord's obedience alone.

The law says, Do, and life you'll win;
But grace says, Live, for all is done;
The former cannot ease my grief,
The latter yields me full relief.

The law will not abate a mite,
The gospel all the sum will quit;

[1] Stephen H. Tyng, *Lectures on the Law & the Gospel* (Birmingham, AL: Solid Ground Christian Books, 2008), preface.

There God in thret'nings is array'd
But here in promises display'd.

The law excludes not boasting vain,
But rather feeds it to my bane;
But gospel grace allows no boast
Save in the King, the Lord of Hosts.

The law brings terror to molest,
The gospel gives the weary rest;
The one does flags of death display
The other shows the living way.

The law's a house of bondage sore,
The gospel opens prison doors;
The first me hamer'd in its net,
The last at freedom kindly set.

An angry God the law reveal'd
The gospel shows him reconciled;
By that I know he was displeased,
By this I see his wrath appeased.

The law still shows a fiery face,
The gospel shows a throne of grace;
There justice rides alone in state,
But here she takes the mercy-seat.

Lo! in the law Jehovah dwells,
But Jesus is conceal'd;
Whereas the gospel's nothing else
But Jesus Christ reveal'd.

Introduction

It has been said rightly and repeatedly that Christ Himself is the key that unlocks the riches of Scriptures. There is no way of having a right apprehension of the Old Testament without seeing it in the light of the coming Messiah. One of the best demonstrations of this reality is the incident found in Luke's narrative concerning two disciples on the road to Emmaus who were heartbroken over the death of their master in whom they had put all their hopes. Their real problem, though, was not their master's death; it was rather their lack of understanding of the Old Testament. This is indeed what Jesus pointed out after joining them on the road and inquiring about their conversation; He provided them with a gentle rebuke and teaching: "O foolish ones and slow of heart to believe in all that the prophets have spoken! Ought not the Christ to have suffered these things and to enter into His glory? And beginning at Moses and all the Prophets, He expounded to them in all the Scriptures the things concerning Himself."[2] This simply means that the law and the Prophets, in other words, the Old Testament, were preparing for the coming of Christ, the Savior.

In this chapter, we will use the term *law* to refer to the moral law, namely the Ten Commandments, the rule of perfect obedience, the guide written in man's heart at creation, reiterated under Moses and rewritten in the heart of those who are regenerated. This is to say that the Decalogue, far from being the enacting of a new law, is rather an external proclamation of it. And it is only in the light of the strict requirements of this very law that the Gospel takes all its meaning, that it becomes good news. If the law does not humble, the gospel cannot comfort. In fact, it could be said that every Scripture is either law or gospel and, as we will see, both of them are exalting the majestic Person of our Lord and Savior Jesus Christ. In this matter, we could not agree more with Dr. Fred Malone who poured out his pastoral heart as he wrote: "If I could do one thing to improve the effectiveness of pastoral preaching and pastoral care in the church, it would be to call all pastors to understand the doctrine of the Law and the Gospel in Scripture."[3]

So the humble intent of this article is to be a reminder of this fundamental truth of the interconnection between Law and Gospel and of the importance of preaching both to the glory of Christ. We need anew to lend an attentive ear to this most wise 19th century's advice from the pen of Charles Bridges:

> The mark of a minister 'approved unto God, a workman that needeth not to be ashamed,' is, that he 'rightly divides the word of truth.' This implies a full and direct application of the Gospel to the mass of his unconverted hearers, combined with a body of spiritual instruction to the several classes of Christians. His system will be marked by Scriptural symmetry and comprehensiveness. It will embrace the whole revelation of God, in its doctrinal instructions, experimental privileges, and practical results. This revelation is divided into two parts — The Law and the Gospel —

[2] Luke 24:25–27.

[3] Fred Malone, "The Law and the Gospel," *Founders Journal* (Fall 2004), 7–12.

> essentially distinct from each other; though so intimately connected, that an accurate knowledge of neither can be obtained without the other.[4]

The Nature of the Law

The first affirmation that must be made is that the law is spiritual. This is such an inclusive expression. The very fact that God is Spirit means *de facto* that His law is of the same nature. We can, to a certain extent, appreciate the plurality of perspectives on the law of God in the variety of expressions found in Psalm 119 in reference to it: statutes, commandments, testimonies, judgments, precepts and law. All through this Psalm, we are told that the law of God is a delight, an object of love, the embodiment of truth, a means of peace and liberty and a unique unmatched treasure. In the same line of thought, the benefits, the blessings bestowed upon us through this law are so numerous according to Psalm 19:7–11.

> The law of the Lord is perfect, converting the soul; the testimony of the Lord is sure, making wise the simple; the statutes of the Lord are right, rejoicing the heart; the commandment of the Lord is pure, enlightening the eyes; the fear of the Lord is clean, enduring forever; the judgments of the Lord are true and righteous altogether. More to be desired are they than gold, yea, than much fine gold; sweeter also than honey and the honeycomb. Moreover by them Your servant is warned, and in keeping them there is great reward.

In Paul's statement in Romans 7:14 to the effect that the law is spiritual, the apostle contrasts our human sinfulness with God's law whose perfection is described in the terms of v 12 "… the law is holy, and the commandment is holy and just and good." The law is holy, deriving from God and bearing the marks of its unmistakable origin and authority. It is also just in its merciful and not burdensome requirement of men. Thirdly, the law of God is good in that it is intended for men's benefit. Calvin comments:

> … the law itself and whatever is commanded in the law, is holy, and therefore to be regarded with the highest reverence, —that it is just, and cannot therefore be charged with anything wrong, —that it is good, and hence pure and free from everything that can do harm.[5]

[4] Charles Bridges, *The Christian Ministry with an Inquiry into the Causes of its Inefficiency* (Banner of Truth, reprinted 1997) 222.

[5] John Calvin, *Calvin's Commentary* (Grand Rapids, MI: Baker Book House, 1989), 19.257.

The moral law, to quote one of our Quebec politicians referring to the Bible, is "*la charte universelle du genre humain*."[6] It talks about its ultimate authority as it stands as "a transcript and publication" of God's holy and perfect mind. It is nothing less than a reflection of God's character. In the words of the Puritan Thomas Goodwin: "The Word of God is a glass… that revealeth God, or rather, what the image of the mind of God is."[7] This law, which proceeds from the Spirit of God, is not only addressing our external conduct, but appeals to the internal obedience of the heart. We could say, with some nuances, that the whole Scripture is a commentary on the law, an exhortation as well as a warning with respect to our obedience or transgression of it.

In fact, the moral law within man's heart is a part of his being *imago Dei*. Thus the statement of Paul concerning man "created according to God, in true righteousness and holiness."[8] The words of Ernest F. Kevan as he summarizes the Puritan view of the law are most appropriate: "A Law emanating from the Divine reason, and given in so direct a manner by God Himself, and for so blessed an end, was held by the Puritans to be nothing less than the very transcript of the glory of God. Man has been made in God's image, and so the moral Law written within him must be part of that very image itself."[9] It is to say that the law fits human nature as well as God's nature so that we cannot escape the conclusion that human beings are structured to live accordingly. So we can join Ezekiel Hopkins in saying: "The law which is our rule on earth shall become our nature in heaven."[10]

Obviously, this law which is a revelation of the will of God to man is a grace, a gift from God. God Himself told His people that they should be proud of the law He gave them: "And what great nation is there that has such statutes and righteous judgments as are in all this law which I set before you this day?"[11] The New Testament expresses this same reality under the pen of John in his Gospel: "And of His fullness, we all received, and grace for grace. For the law was given through Moses, but grace and truth

[6] "The universal Charter of humankind." Speech of Jean Temblay, Mayor of Saguenay, Quebec, Canada.

[7] Thomas Goodwin, *The Works of Thomas Goodwin* (USA: Tanski Publications vol. 4, reprinted 1996), 323.

[8] Ephesians 4:24.

[9] Ernest F. Kevan, *The Grace of the Law, a Study of Puritan Theology*. (Grand Rapids, MI: Baker Book House 1976), 62.

[10] Ezekiel Hopkins, *An Exposition of the Ten Commandments* (Birmingham, AL: Solid Ground Christian Books, 2009), 19.

[11] Deuteronomy 4:7.

came through Jesus Christ."[12] The preposition ἀντί carries the meaning of one after another[13] as rendered by the NASV "For of His fullness we have all received, and grace upon grace," which means that we are constantly receiving grace in the place of grace.

It goes without saying that this law of God is eternal. For it to be changed, altered or abolished, God would have to change, alter or abolish Himself. The law, being the eternal and unchangeable expression of God's holiness and justice cannot but be permanent, eternal. In relation to man, this law was there in his very constitution at the beginning and will remain there as long as man is man, namely, the image of God. Thomas Gouge gives a good synthesis of this reality:

> A Law of Universal Obedience written in his heart, which by his Fall was much obliterated and defaced: Yet all Mankind have some Fragments of it remaining in their hearts; such as make the very Gentiles, who have not the written Law, inexcusable for their Transgressions.[14]

Kevan, commenting on the subject, writes: "A Law so related to the Divine reason, conveyed by so Divine an action, and embodying such Divine glory cannot pass away."[15]

The Requirements of the Law

Curtis Grenshaw captures the real significance of the word *law* in the title of his book *Not Ten Suggestions*.[16] A law, by definition, carries requirements. So, what can be said about the demands of God's law? First of all, the crystal clear teaching of the Bible concerning human's status is that man is not autonomous but imperatively *theonomous* (not to be conflated with theonomist). As a matter of fact, man is a covenant creature who transgressed the covenant and God, in His sheer mercy, made a new covenant in Christ Jesus; it gave the historical synthetic triad of creation/fall/redemption. It is to say that we need to interpret the Holy Scriptures by way of covenants.

The Second London Confession of Faith provides us with the essentials on this subject:

[12] John 1:16–17.

[13] *NIV Greek Dictionary* in Accordance Bible Software.

[14] Kevan, *The Grace of the Law*, 47.

[15] Ibid., 66.

[16] Curtis I. Crenshaw, *Not Ten Suggestions* (Spring, TX: Footstool Publications, 2010).

> God gave to Adam a law of universal obedience written in his heart, and a particular precept of not eating the fruit of the tree of knowledge of good and evil; by which he bound him and all his posterity to personal, entire, exact, and perpetual obedience; promised life upon the fulfilling, and threatened death upon the breach of it, and endued him with power and ability to keep it. The same law that was first written in the heart of man continued to be a perfect rule of righteousness after the fall, and was delivered by God upon Mount Sinai, in ten commandments, and written in two tables, the four first containing our duty towards God, and the other six, our duty to man.[17]

Man at creation, as soon as he came out from the hand of God, was accountable to his creator. John Murray accurately writes:

> Man is created in the image of God and the demand, the inescapable postulate of that relation that man sustains to God as responsible and dependent creature, is that he be conformed in the inmost fibre of his moral being and in all the conditions and activities of his person to the moral perfection of God. 'Ye shall be holy, for I am holy'.[18]

As an image of God, Adam had been created with the law of God within and this law represented all the conditions of his covenant relationship. As we read in the Epistle to the Romans,[19] the first man, not only stood as the natural head of mankind, but also as its federal representative; then, we cannot avoid the conclusive consequence that Adam's sin is our sin and that every single human being born from Adam is a covenant transgressor; everyone is still under this first covenant obligation and curse.

What kind of obedience or to what extent should man obey the law of God? It is of the utmost importance to acknowledge the fact that the law requires perfection not approximation. Calvin discards all kinds of half-measures in this respect:

> For God has not promised the reward of life for particular works but he only declares that the man who does them shall live [Lev. 18:5], leveling that well-known curse against all those who do not persevere in all things [Deut. 27:26; Gal. 3:10]. The fiction of partial righteousness is abundantly refuted by these statements, where no other righteousness than complete observance of the law is allowed in heaven.[20]

[17] LCF 1689, 19.1–2.

[18] John Murray, *Collected Writings of John Murray*, vol. 1 (Carlisle, PA: The Banner of Truth, 1976), 196.

[19] Romans 5:12–21.

[20] John Calvin, *Institutes of the Christian Religion* (1559) translated by F. L. Battles (Louisville, KY: Westminster John Knox Press), 3.14.13.

All of this tells us that we are still under the same obligation of a perfect obedience to the law. Fred Malone articulates it this way:

> All of biblical history can be summarized under the outworking of this dual headship in Adam and in Christ. The Covenant of Law-works in Adam and the Covenant of Grace in Christ continues today as the reason for the condemnation of all men in Adam and the only hope of redemption in Christ. This theology of the two covenant heads is found historically in the theology of the Law and the Gospel, championed by Luther, Calvin, and the great confessions. Therefore, all men are either in Adam or in Christ.[21]

This is to say that the covenant of law-work is still in effect. In his excellent work, Pascal Denault, in an economy of words, provides this clear statement:

> Under the Covenant of Works, eternal life cannot be given freely, it must be earned. But now, because of sin, the Covenant of Works is ineffective in giving life; it can only bring death. Reformed theologians considered that the Covenant of Works remained in effect after the fall…[22]

It is impossible to imagine how it could be otherwise. What is the source of our apprehension of purity and holiness if not the law of God? And it is the same with our notion of justice. So, since our God is absolutely pure, holy and just, we need to be perfectly conformed to His law in order to be in communion with Him. Tyng goes in the same direction as he writes:

> It requires entire submission to the will of the Creator; and is obligatory upon Gentiles as upon Jews: —and as binding in heaven, as upon earth.…It is in its principles and precepts, but a copy in words, of the will and character of God. A perfect conformity to its commands, would be a perfect conformity to the holy character of God.[23]

We just cannot think for a moment that our God would ever lower the holy demands of His righteous law or that He would divest himself of His glory in allowing his creatures to violate His will. As He Himself is unchangeable, so is His law that expresses His own mind and character whereby the unalterable and eternal obligation to love Him with undivided affection.

[21] Class notes 2008, Quebec City, Canada.

[22] Pascal Denault, *The Distinctiveness of Baptist Covenant Theology, a Comparison Between Seventeenth-Century Particular Baptist and Paedobaptist Federalism* (Birmingham, AL: Solid Ground Christian Books, 2013).

[23] Tyng, *Lectures*, 42.

Another aspect of the law that should not be passed over in silence is this: When the law forbids a single transgression, it equally forbids everything that could lead to its commission; it means that it also makes appeal to the realm of thoughts. The Sermon on the Mount comes immediately to our mind as Jesus shows the extent of the requirements of the law, not limited in the action itself, but including what is going on in the inner man. This is what Douma labels *rules for interpretation*:

> A proper treatment of the Ten Commandments is possible only with the context of the whole Scripture. We no longer stand at the foot of Sinai, but we live after Christ. For this reason, we cannot read the Ten Commandments without taking into account the Sermon on the Mount.... We cannot confine ourselves simply to the letter of the Ten Commandments. They must be apprehended in all their depth and breadth...[24]

Two last elements must also be mentioned before leaving this subject and they are also related to the interpretation of the law. First, the negative commandments always imply their positive side and vice versa. Second, in the words of Douma, "Each commandment must be interpreted 'per synecdoche', which means that where one sin is mentioned, the commandment intends to cover the entire range of related sins."[25]

The Threefold Use of the Law

Contrary to the common saying, ignorance is not bliss. In fact, there is no greater curse or misery than ignorance since it leads to eternal doom. Jesus Himself shows the primary importance of knowledge as it paves the way to salvation: "And this is eternal life, that they may know You, the only true God, and Jesus Christ whom you have sent."[26] The Heidelberg Catechism echoes our Lord's words in what we label the triple knowledge. After having established, in the first question, that our only comfort is the assurance of belonging to Christ, question number two goes like this:

> How many things are necessary for thee to know, that thou, enjoying this comfort, mayest live and die happy? Answer: Three; the first, how great my sins and miseries are; the second, how I may be delivered from all my sins and miseries; the third, how I shall express my gratitude to God for

[24] J. Douma, *The Ten Commandments, Manual for the Christian Life* (Phillipsburg, NJ: Presbyterian and Reformed Publishing, 1996), 12.

[25] Ibid., 12.

[26] John 17:3.

> such deliverance.[27] And question number three that follows goes right to the point: "Whence knowest thou thy misery? Answer: Out of the law of God.[28]

And the two following questions of the catechism teach us how the law makes us acquainted with our misery.

It is then crystal clear that the law of God is providing us with most important knowledge. As we have already seen, the law is the expression of God's most holy character; and as we know God through His law so are we becoming conscious of our condition as His creatures. Since the Reformation, we have come to express or synthesize the knowledge flowing from the law by the traditional expression that comes from John Calvin, *the threefold knowledge of the law*. Though it has been expressed in different ways, it is generally agreed in all reformed milieu. These three uses of the moral law can be summarized as follows: (1) The elenctic or pedagogical use which consists in driving sinners to despair of their own righteousness; (2) the civil use, that is the refraining of evil and (3) the didactic or normative use; in this last one, law serves as a guide for the believer in revealing what is pleasing to God.[29]

Let's see first the pedagogical use of the law that has been often compared to a mirror as it highlights our weakness in order to send us seeking strength in Christ. This is to say that the law is for all nations for by the law is the knowledge of sin (Romans 3:20), though not everybody who looks at the law will come to Christ.

This pedagogical character of the law is also expressed in the famous passage of Paul's Epistle to the Galatians 3:23–24 "But before faith came, we were kept under guard by the law, kept for the faith which would afterward be revealed. Therefore, the law was our tutor to bring us to Christ, that we might be justified by faith." Luther's comments on this passage are worth quoting:

> This simile of the schoolmaster is striking. Schoolmasters are indispensable. But show me a pupil who loves his schoolmaster. How little love is lost upon them the Jews showed by their attitude toward Moses. They would have been glad to stone Moses to death. (Ex. 17:4.) You cannot expect anything else. How can a pupil love a teacher who frustrates his desires? And if the pupil disobeys, the schoolmaster whips him, and the

[27] Zacharias Ursinus, *Commentary on the Heidelberg Catechism* (Phillipsburg, NJ: Presbyterian and Reformed Publishing), 20.

[28] Idem.

[29] Richard A. Muller, *Usus legis* in *Dictionary of Latin and Greek Theological Terms* (Grand Rapids, MI: Baker Book House, 1985), 320.

> pupil has to like it and even kiss the rod with which he was beaten. Do you think the schoolboy feels good about it? As soon as the teacher turns his back, the pupil breaks the rod and throws it into the fire. And if he were stronger than the teacher he would not take the beatings, but beat up the teacher. All the same, teachers are indispensable; otherwise the children would grow up without discipline, instruction, and training... The Law is such a schoolmaster. Not for always, but until we have been brought to Christ. The Law is not just another schoolmaster. The Law is a specialist to bring us to Christ. What would you think of a schoolmaster who could only torment and beat a child? Yet of such schoolmasters there were plenty in former times, regular bruisers. The Law is not that kind of a schoolmaster. It is not to torment us always. With its lashings it is only too anxious to drive us to Christ. The Law is like the good schoolmaster who trains his children to find pleasure in doing things they formerly detested.[30]

We can say that the law of God instructs us but does not reform our hearts. It informs us about God's requirements and consequently makes us aware of our utter inability to meet them. It is to say that the law brings our depravity into light and, consequently, it shows us the judgment that is awaiting us. Listen to Calvin:

> ...what was the instruction or education of this schoolmaster? First, the law, by displaying the justice of God, convinced them that in themselves they were unrighteous; for in the commandments of God, as in a mirror, they might see how far they were distant from true righteousness."[31] There can be no real conviction of sin without an adequate conception of the demands of the law we are accountable for. The law sweeps away all our rationalistic excuses that shelter our self-righteousness and brings us face to face with our guilt: "O wretched man that I am! Who will deliver me from this body of death?" (Rom 7:24). And this desperation leads us to look for mercy and to take refuge in Christ. In the words of a famous nineteenth century divine: "The principal means of conviction is the law, the law of God in its purity, spirituality, and power... The law in its holy commandment, the law in its curse, the law in its spiritual nature, as reaching the heart... the law in its condemning power, whereby every mouth must be stopped, and all the world must become guilty before God.[32]

[30] Martin Luther, *Commentary on the Epistle to the Galatians* (1535), translated by Theodore Graebner (Grand Rapids, MI: Zondervan Publishing, 1949), 141.

[31] John Calvin, *Calvin's Commentary* (Grand Rapids, MI: Baker Book House, 1989), 21:108.

[32] James Buchanan, *The Office and Work of the Holy Spirit* (Birmingham, AL: Solid Ground Christian Books, reprinted in 2016), 63.

The second use of the law is to restrain evil. When you drive on a highway and you see a speed limit sign, you tend to lift your foot off the accelerator. Not that your heart is changed but the possibility of having to pay a sizeable fine represents somewhat of a deterrent. The idea is well expressed by Douma: "Traffic signs do not so much restrict travel, as provide for its safe and orderly movement."[33]

This second function of the law is aiming at restraining, by fear of punishment, sinners who are indifferent to justice and righteousness. Let's appeal to Calvin again: "But they are restrained not because their inner mind is stirred or affected, but because, being bridled, so to speak, they keep their hands from outward activity, and hold inside the depravity that otherwise they would wantonly have indulged."[34] This keeps in step with Proverbs 29:18 "Where there is no revelation, the people cast off restraint." In other words, when God's commandments are kept before people, they produce moral restraint as well as protection from one another. Paul writes along the same line "... the law is not made for a righteous person, but for the lawless and insubordinate, for the ungodly and for the sinners, for the unholy and profane, for murderers of fathers and murderers of mothers, for manslayers, for fornicators, for sodomites, for kidnappers, for liars, for perjurers, and if there is any other thing that is contrary to sound doctrine."[35]

We come to the third use of the law that is more in relation with the believers. In this case, the law no longer represents God as Judge, but instead as Father. This is the very same law but in the hands of a Mediator or administered by a Mediator, and it tells us that if we are not justified by the observance of the law, we are nevertheless not without law. It keeps us from the errors of legalism and antinomianism. This is well expressed by Ernest Reisinger: "The law, like Christ, has always been crucified between two thieves—antinomianism on the one side and legalism on the other."[36]

What is more precisely this third function of the law? Paul calls it the law of Christ (1 Corinthians 9:21). The Lord Himself exhorts his disciples to be mindful of the observance of the commandments, equating them with the way they should express their love for him: "If you love Me, keep My commandments" (John 14:15). The law is instructing us on what is pleasing to God. In fact, a Christian delights in the law as God Himself delights in it since he has received the same Spirit. In reality, only those who are saved take pleasure in the law of God; only they can progressively submit to this law. It is only at conversion that we begin to pursue God's

[33] Douma, *The Ten Commandments Manual*, 11.

[34] John Calvin, *Institutes*, 20.8.10.

[35] 1 Timothy 1:9–10.

[36] Ernest C. Reisinger, *The Law and the Gospel* (Phillipsburg, NJ: Presbyterian and Reformed Publishing, 1997), xvi.

law. At regeneration God writes afresh His law on the heart; this is the same as saying that He gives a heart for the law that stands as a rule of life for Christians who are already justified. There is a whole world of difference between "do this and you shall live" and "because you live, do this". In fact, the law in Christian life is the very essence of the new covenant: "Behold, the days are coming, says the Lord, when I will make a new covenant with the house of Israel and with the house of Judah… I will put My law in their minds, and write it on their hearts: and I will be their God, and they shall be My people."[37] These words of Samuel Bolton represent a fit conclusion to the matter: "The law sends us to the Gospel for our justification; the Gospel sends us to the law to frame our way of life."[38]

The Fulfillment of the Law in the Gospel

After this succinct survey of the Law, we will look at its fulfillment in the gospel through the perfect life and the unique sacrifice of our Lord and Savior Jesus Christ and how He is exalted by their preaching. In the *Evangelical Dictionary of Theology*, R.H. Mounce begins his entry with the following rhetoric:

> The English word 'gospel' (from the Anglo-Saxon god-spell, ie God-Story) is the usual translation of the Greek euangellion. According to Tyndale, the renowned English Reformer and Bible translator, it signified 'good, mery, glad and ioyful tydinge, that maketh a mannes hert glad, and maketh hym synge, daunce, and leepe for ioy'. While this definition is more experiential than explicative, it has touched that inner quality which brings the word of life. The gospel is the joyous proclamation of God's redemptive activity in Christ Jesus on behalf of man enslaved by sin.[39]

First of all, let us be clear as to what is meant by Gospel. We certainly do not mean, as has sometimes been the case in history, that the Law was set aside in order to make room for the reconciliation of the sinners with God. Michael Horton observes:

> In much of medieval preaching, the Law and Gospel were so confused that the 'Good News' seemed to be that Jesus was a 'kinder, gentler Mo-

[37] Jeremiah 31:31, 33.

[38] Samuel Bolton, *The True Bounds of Christian Freedom* (Carlisle: The Banner of Truth Trust, reprinted in 2001), 11.

[39] R.H. Mounce, *Gospel* in *Evangelical Dictionary of Theology*, ed. Walter A. Elwell (Grand Rapids, MI: Baker Book House, 1984), 472.

> ses', who softened the Law into easier exhortations, such as loving God and neighbor from the heart. The Reformers saw Rome as teaching that the Gospel was simply an easier 'Law' than that of the Old Testament."[40]

It is of the utmost importance to keep in mind, once more, that the Law requires perfection, not approximation. Walt Chantry aptly points out: "Righteousness described under the Covenant of Grace is precisely the same code of conduct prescribed under the Covenant of Works."[41] It is to say that for the gospel to be Good News, it needed, at all cost, to fully meet the requirements of the law for there is no other way of justice. To put it simply, salvation is by works and this is the reason why it is inaccessible to sinners like us. Salvation is by works and the Good News is that we have a Mediator who did it, namely who provided an active righteousness for us who believe.

The very fact that Christ came under the Law is meaningful. The apostle Paul wrote to the Galatians: "But when the fullness of time had come, God sent forth His Son, born of a woman, born under the law, to redeem those who were under the law."[42] Christ came into the world not to abolish or lessen the Law but in order to fulfill it, that is to bring it to its completion; and it comes out clearly from the terminology used by our Lord Himself (Matthew 5:17) "Do not think that I came to destroy the Law or the Prophets. I did not come to destroy but to fulfill." The word translated by fulfill is πληρόω and here is the definition provided by the *NIV Greek Dictionary*: to fulfill, make full; (pass.) to be filled, full, complete (often used with reference to the fulfillment of the OT Scriptures). So the goal of the incarnation was that "the righteous requirements of the law might be fully met."[43] This is what is signified by the declaration that "Christ is the end (τέλος: the goal and end of divine purposes)[44] of the law for righteousness to everyone who believes."[45]

The gospel, then, far from ignoring or discrediting the law, is exalting it. And when the law is thus magnified, Christ, the second Person of the

[40] Michael Horton, *The Law & The Gospel*. https://www.whitehorseinn.org/resources/free-articles/180-horton-law-gospel.

[41] Walt Chantry, *The Covenants of Works And of Grace in Covenant Theology, A Baptist Distinctive*, ed. Earl M. Blackburn (Birmingham, AL: Solid Ground Christian Books, 2013), 105.

[42] Galatians 4:4–5.

[43] Romans 8:4.

[44] *The New International Dictionary of New Testament Theology*, ed. Colin Brown, vol. 2 (Grand Rapids, MI: Zondervan 1986), 52.

[45] Romans 10:4.

Trinity whose law it is, is also exalted. The gospel is indeed honoring the law, bringing into a new light, its holiness and authority. This is what led Charles Bridges to write about the harmony of the law with the Gospel:

> "Though distinct, they are not opposite. As coming from the same source, they must ultimately meet in the same plan, and subserve the same end. Like the seemingly opposite of perfections or their glorious Author, they harmonize in mutual subserviency in the Christian system. The provisions of the Gospel are fully commensurate with the demands of the law. Its righteousness fulfils the law as a covenant; its grace obeys it as a rule. Both have a commanding and condemning power."[46] And a few pages later he adds: "Thus also, the grace of the Gospel 'establishes the law' in its twofold character. What the doctrine of faith reveals, the grace of faith applies; both for acceptance, as exposed in the penalty of the covenant; and for ability to exercise that love, which is the fulfilling of the law."[47]

It could be said that the law prepares the ground for the sowing of the gospel. Commenting on Ephesians 6:19, Gurnal said: "The field is not fit for the seed to be cast into it, till the plough hath… broken it up; nor is the soul prepared to receive the mercy of the Gospel, till broken with the terrors of the law."[48] It simply means that the preaching of the law cannot be dissociated from the preaching of the gospel and vice versa. Preaching the gospel in the absence of the law is utterly meaningless. In a certain way, if I can borrow from the neo-orthodox theologian Richard Niebuhr, it would be like preaching "A God without wrath who brought men without sin into a Kingdom without judgment through the ministrations of a Christ without a cross."[49] This is the pairing of the law and the gospel that is producing a genuine spirit of humiliation, the sense of sin and misery linked to the hope of mercy. This is to say that there is a fundamental revelation in the law; as an instrument of conviction, it reveals the price paid by the Gospel so that we might enjoy grace. It means that we imperatively need this very conviction of the law in order to appreciate the preciousness of the Gospel. The incident that Luke the evangelist is reporting in the 7th chapter of his gospel is certainly an illustration of this truth as we see the contrast between Simon the Pharisee and the woman who anointed Jesus' feet; Simon whose conscience was not the least troubled by the law treated

[46] Bridges, *The Christian Ministry*, 231.

[47] Ibid., 237.

[48] Ibid., 234.

[49] Richard Niebuhr, http://www.goodreads.com/author/quotes/41386.H_Richard_Niebuhr

Jesus in a most cavalier way while the woman, under strong conviction, ministered in a bold, costly and loving manner to Jesus.[50]

The Bible itself provides us with the best synthesis of the fulfillment of the law in the gospel as we read in Psalms 85:10 "Mercy and truth have met together; Righteousness and peace have kissed".

Christ, the Righteousness of the Law

Now, let us have a closer look at the way the gospel is the perfect fulfillment of the righteousness that the law requires; this immaculate righteousness has a name, Jesus Christ. Ernest Kevan encapsulates in a masterful way the whole matter: "Sin is the transgression of Law, the death of Christ is the satisfaction of Law, justification is the verdict of Law…."[51]

One of the best summaries the Bible provides with regard to God's modus operandi in His redemption project comes from Paul's pen in Romans 10:4, "For Christ is the end of the law for righteousness to everyone who believes". Everything in the Jewish religion, the sacrifices, the priesthood, the religious festivals, the temple and the covenants of promise, everything was pointing to the coming Messiah. The law clearly reminded them they were sinners in need of a Savior. Nevertheless, instead of letting the law lead them to Christ, they rather worshipped the law and rejected the Savior. And this was their drama for there is no accepted justice in the sight of God but *the justice of God.*

We cannot overemphasize the importance of this text to guilty man as it presents us with the full scheme of divine redemption. Robert Haldane gives this very plain exposition:

> What the end of the law is, Paul shows, Rom vii. 10, when he says, 'it was ordained to life', namely, that the man who doeth all that it commands, should live by it. And what is it that, in the present state of human nature, the law cannot do? It cannot justify, and so give life, because it has been broken. How then did God act? He sent His Son in the likeness of sinful flesh, and condemned sin in the flesh. And why has He done this? The answer is given, ch. viii. 4, 'that the righteousness of the law might be fulfilled in us' who are in Him.[52]

Simply said, it means that Christ is Himself the righteousness of the law for man. And in order to accomplish His mission as our Mediator, He

[50] Luke 7:36–50.

[51] Kevan, *The Grace of the Law*, 21.

[52] Robert Haldane, *Romans* (Carlisle, PA: The Banner of Truth Trust, reprinted 1996), 502.

had, first of all, to become a man. This is to say that because of His incarnation He could act as our substitute so that whoever received Him and His vicarious work, might possess the perfect righteousness required by the law. In fact, Jesus, the second Person of the Triune God became man, or more accurately our "*theanthropic*" Mediator. Let us listen to Calvin:

> … it was also imperative that he who was to become our Redeemer be true God and true man. It was his task to swallow up death. Who but the Life could do this? It was his task to conquer sin. Who but very Righteousness could do this? It was his task to rout the powers of world and air. Who but a power higher than the world and air could do this? Now, where does life or righteousness, or lordship and authority of heaven lie but with God alone? Therefore our most merciful God, when he willed that we be redeemed, made himself our Redeemer in the person of his only-begotten Son.[53]

We have already briefly mentioned the meaning of the word "end" (τέλος) in this verse; it conveys the idea of completion, fulfillment. Tyng brings out the main elements of this passage.[54] First, ***Christ is the end to which the law as a dispensation was designed to lead.*** As we said earlier, everything in the Jewish religion was pointing to Christ and His work. Jesus Christ is the answer to Isaac's old question as he was accompanying his father Abraham to Mount Moriah: "My father… look, the fire and the wood, but where is the lamb"?[55] And after many centuries, the answer came from the mouth of John the Baptist: "The next day John saw Jesus coming toward him, and said, 'Behold! The Lamb of God who takes away the sin of the world."[56]

Second, ***Christ is the end in whom all the demands of the law are actually accomplished.*** It means that by His active as well as His passive perfect obedience, Christ fully satisfied the law. By His active obedience, He acquired a justice that is imputed to the one who receives it by faith; and by His passive[57] obedience, He made atonement for all the believer's sins. And the purpose of Christ thus becoming the end of the law was *for righteousness to everyone who believes*. As our Great High Priest, He offered the only sacrifice fully acceptable to God. "But Christ came as High Priest of

[53] Calvin, *Institutes*, 13.2.

[54] Tyng, *Lectures*, 114–125.

[55] Genesis 22:7.

[56] John 1:29.

[57] The use of the word *passive* should not be understood in opposition to *active* but in the sense of the first meaning of the word: paqew (to suffer) that has given the word *passion* (suffering).

the good things to come, with the greater and more perfect tabernacle not made with hands, that is, not of this creation. Not with the blood of goats or calves, but with His own blood He entered the Most Holy Place once for all, having obtained eternal redemption."[58]

Space constraints prevent me from expounding on many other pericopes affirmative of this fundament truth. For example: "For He made Him who knew no sin to be sin for us, that we might become the righteousness of God in Him."[59]

Conclusion

In the light of what we have said, it is not without reason that the gospel is called "*The gospel of the glory of Christ.*"[60] The gospel represents certainly a window displaying the glory of our Lord and Savior Jesus Christ. At the same time, since the law cannot be divorced from the gospel, Christ is also exalted in His law as we contemplate its beauty, its sanctity, its power, its wisdom and its authority. The Law is the Law of God, the Law of Christ and it shows His perfect character. The Law is magnified in the Gospel as we see that no human being can fulfill it because of sin. The Gospel is magnified in the Law as it brings full satisfaction to every single requirement of the Law.

Christ is obviously exalted in the Law and the Gospel. He is the author of the first and the Mediator of the second. Only He could live up to the perfection of the Law and thus accomplish our salvation as our substitute.

Christ is indeed exalted in the nature of the law as well as in its role as it restraints evil, brings sin into light so as to lead the convicted sinner to Christ and shows the believer how to express his gratitude to his Savior.

In the same manner, Christ is greatly exalted in the gospel that displays His attributes like sacrificial love, abundant mercy. It also reveals His amazing humility and willingness. How can we fail to marvel at His resurrection, His ascension, His sitting at the right hand of God, His intercession for us!

In closing this chapter, I would like to give place to Charles Haddon Spurgeon who preached on 2 Corinthians 4:4, at the Metropolitan Tabernacle, Sunday morning, March 31, 1889.[61] He opens his sermon with

[58] Hebrews 9:11–12.

[59] 2 Corinthians 5:21. See also Romans 3:22; Philippians 3:9, etc.

[60] 2 Corinthians 4:4

[61] Charles Haddon Spurgeon, *The Gospel of the Glory of Christ* (Newington: Metropolitan Pulpit, No 2077, 1889).

these words: *"Shining in the center of the verse, like a pearl in its setting, you find these words. Literally and accurately translated, they run thus — "The light of the Gospel of the glory of Christ".* The essence of his message includes the following elements: (1) The glory of Christ lies in His Person. (2) The glory of Christ lies in His love. (3) The glory of Christ is further seen in His atoning sacrifice.

"O Calvary, whose base is eternal justice
and whose spirit is eternal love."[62]

Solus Christus

---

[62] Cited in Reisinger, *The Law and the Gospel*, xiii.

Bibliography

Bible: The New King James Version

Articles:

Horton, Michael S. "The Law & The Gospel" https://www.whitehorseinn.org/resources/free-articles/180-horton-law-gospel

Horton, Michael S. "Calvin on Law and Gospel" http://www.wscal.edu/resource-center/calvin-on-law-and-gospel

Malone, Fred A. "The Law and the Gospel" *Founders Journal* (Fall 2004): 7-12.

Malone, Fred A. Class notes, 2008.

Perron, Raymond. "La loi de Dieu et le chrétien." Unpublished article.

Books:

Blackburn, Earl, editor. *Covenant Theology, A Baptist Distinctive*. Birmingham, AL: Solid Ground Christian Books, 2013.

Bolton, Samuel. *The True Bounds of Christian Freedom*. Carlisle, PA: Banner of Truth Trust, reprinted 2001.

Bridges, Charles. *The Christian Ministry, with An Inquiry into the Causes of its Inefficiency*. Carlisle, PA: Banner of Truth Trust, reprinted 1997.

Buchanan, James. *The Office and Work of the Holy Spirit*. Birmingham, AL: Solid Ground Christian Books, reprinted in 2016.

Calvin, John. *Institute of the Christian Religion*. Vol. I, John T. McNeil, editor. Louisville: Westminster John Knox Press.

Chantry, Walter. *Today's Gospel, Authentic or Synthetic*. Carlisle, PA: The Banner of Truth Trust, reprinted 1989.

Denault, Pascal. *The Distinctiveness of Baptist Covenant Theology*. Birmingham, AL: Solid Ground Christian Books, 2013.

Douma, J. *The Ten Commandments, Manual for the Christian Life*. Nelson D. Kloosterman, translator. Phillipsburg, NJ: Presbyterian & Reformed Publishing, 1996.

Fairbain, Patrick. *The Revelation of Law in Scripture*. Phillipsburg, NJ: Presbyterian & Reformed Publishing ,1996.

Fisher, Edward. *The Marrow of Modern Divinity*. New York: Westminster Publishing House.

Goodwin, Thomas. *The Works of Thomas Goodwin*, Vol IV. California: Tanski Publications, 1996.

Grenshaw, Curtis I. *Not Ten Suggestions*. Spring, TX: Footstool Publications, 2010.

Hopkins, Ezekiel. *An Exposition of The Ten Commandments*. Birmingham, AL: Solid Ground Christian Books, 2009.

Kevan, Ernest F. *The Grace of the Law, a Study of Puritan Theology*. Grand Rapids, MI: Baker Book House, 1976.

Muller, Richard. *The Unaccomodated Calvin, Studies in the Foundation of a Theological Tradition*. Oxford: Oxford University Press, 2000.

Murray, John. *Collected Writings of John Murray*, Vol. I. *The Claims of Truth*. Carlisle, PA: The Banner of Truth Trust 1976.

Poythress, Vern. *The Shadow of Christ in the Law of Moses*. Brentwood, TN: Wolgemuth & Hyatt Publishers, 1991.

Reisinger, Ernest C. *The Law and the Gospel*. Phillipsburg, NJ: Presbyterian & Reformed Publishing, 1997

Tyng, Stephen H. *Lectures on the Law & the Gospel*. Birmingham, AL: Solid Ground Christian Books.

Commentaries:

Calvin, John. *Calvin's Commentaries*, Acts 14-18; Romans 1-16. Vol. 19. Grand Rapids, MI: Baker Book House, reprinted 1989.

Calvin, John. *Calvin's Commentaries*, Galatians-Philemon. Vol. 21. Grand Rapids, MI: Baker Book House, reprinted 1989.

Haldane, Robert. *Romans*. Carlisle, PA: The Banner of Truth Trust, reprinted 1996.

Luther, Martin. *Commentary on the Epistle to the Galatians* (1535), Theodore Graebner, translator. Grand Rapids, MI : Zondervan Publishing, 1949.

Ursinus, Zacharias. *Commentary on the Heidelberg Catechism*. Phillipsburg, NJ: Presbyterian & Reformed Publishing, ND.

Dictionaries:

Brown, Colin. editor. *The New International Dictionary of New Testament Theology*, Vol. 2. Grand Rapids, MI: Zondervan, 1986.

Elwell, Walter A. editor. *Evangelical Dictionary of Theology*. Grand Rapids, MI: Baker Book House, 1984.

Ferguson, Sinclair B., Wright, David F., Packer, J.I. editors. *New Dictionary of Theology*. Downers Grove, IL: IVP, 1988.

Muller, Richard A. *Dictionary of Latin and Greek Theological Terms*. Grand Rapids, MI: Baker Book House, third printing, 1985.

Sermons:

Bédard Paulin. "L'accomplissement de la loi en Jésus-Christ. Église réformée de Beauce," 2001

Spurgeon, Charles. "The Gospel of the Glory of Christ." Sermon No 2077. Newington: Metropolitan Tabernacle, March 31, 1889.

5

Exaltng Christ by Exegeting His Word

A Case Study from the Bread of Life Discourse in John 6

Stephen Murphy

Stephen Kim is surely correct when he observes: "The literary structure of the Fourth Gospel makes it one of the most carefully crafted pieces of literature in the Bible."[1] This carefully crafted structure facilitates the author of the Fourth Gospel[2] addressing, in both depth and nuance, some of the key issues of the early Christian community. These are woven into a highly developed series of repeating occurrence throughout the gospel, with a richly stylized selection of incidents from the life and ministry of Jesus to develop and drive home his key theme: "these are written that you may believe that Jesus is the Christ, the Son of God, and that believing you may have life in His name (John 20:31)."[3]

Nowhere is this more evident than in the "Bread of Life Discourse." Here we have something that is both unique in John, and yet representa-

[1] Stephen Kim, S., "The Christological and eschatological significance of Jesus' Passover signs in John 6," *Bibliotheca Sacra* (2007), 164 (655), 307.

[2] I hereafter refer to "John" —without prejudice to the voluminous debate on the authorship of the Fourth Gospel.

[3] Quotations in this chapter, unless otherwise specified, are from The Holy Bible: New King James Version. Copyright (c) 1982 by Thomas Nelson, Inc. All rights reserved. Used by permission.

tive of the Fourth Gospel's style and its key theme. It is unique in that it combines a key incident from the synoptics—the feeding of the five thousand—with the extended teaching that Jesus subsequently gives. It is representative in that it addresses the heart of the Fourth Gospel's agenda: the identity and mission of Jesus of Nazareth.

It will be the purpose of this chapter to locate the discourse within the Fourth Gospel and show how John uses its discursive nature to address and develop two key ideas: (1) namely that Jesus is the Messiah; and (2) as such is the prophesied "Son of Man" to whom a unique and decisive eschatological role has been entrusted. All this is done in an intensely Jewish context. The argument of the discourse in both substance and style, as we shall see, reflect this.

The Place of the Miracle and the Discourse in the Fourth Gospel

Given the highly stylized and systematic nature of the Fourth Gospel, we would expect the placing of this incident to be significant. It occurs at the season of Passover—probably the first third of Jesus ministry. Commenting on the setting of the sign, Keener points out the almost incidental detail of the flourishing grass, as further if unintended support to the reality of the Passover coincidence.[4] Passover allusions can be noted in both John's account and the parallel in the Synoptics (Jesus' warning to beware of the leaven of the Pharisees, for example in Mark 8:14ff.). The Passover Lamb had to be eaten by the Israelites as a central part of the divinely given plan for their redemption from Egypt and their ultimate establishment in a New Land. Is Jesus linking this to His eschatological role as the true and decisive redeemer—the one who leads not into a new land but a new eternal reality—when He states that eating his flesh is required? Certainly a Passover context is helpful in understanding an otherwise perplexing statement.

The miracle of the feeding and the subsequent discourse are linked by a further miracle—the miraculous display of Jesus power over the waters of the Lake of Gennesaret. Here again the links to the Exodus and Passover are telling. In the Exodus the parting of the Red Sea follows the salvific feast and the eating of the lamb—which as I have stated already, Jesus likely is referring to in the later discourse. The Christological significance of this cannot be underestimated — indeed a strong allusion to specific deity may also be involved here. The Old Testament reminded God's people

[4] C. S. Keener, *The Gospel of John: A Commentary*, Vol. 2. (Peabody, MA: Hendrickson, 2003), 667.

that "He alone spreads out the heavens, and treads on the waves of the sea" (Job 9:8). Stephen Kim is again helpful in this regard:

> Thus the Evangelist's references to the Passover Feast are more than just time indicators. The two sign-miracles in chapter 6—Jesus feeding the five thousand and his walking on the water—contribute significantly to John's aim to present Jesus as the promised Messiah and the Son of God.[5]

The idea of "Cycles" as a systematic literary mechanism in the Fourth Gospel, has been advanced by Kim among others. He suggests that the themes of the gospel are elaborated by these cycles:

> Whereas the "Cana Cycle" reveals Jesus as the Messiah who grants life and emphasizes the importance of believing in Him to receive that life, the "Festival Cycle" develops the theme of increasing opposition by the Jewish leaders to the One who grants life.[6]

If that indeed is the case, we see in this Passover linked miracle and subsequent discourse, the continuation of the idea of Jesus as the life giver. The claim is in fact brought into sharper focus by John's record of Jesus' words and actions, as well as the Jewish opposition, and Jesus' rebuttal of it.[7]

The role of questioning, debate and discourse are observable key literary devices in the Fourth Gospel, and are of course key devices in the explication of the feeding miracle and its significance. They are used as recurring devices to expose the paucity of spiritual understanding among Jesus' hearers—sympathetic and hostile alike. They also enable either him directly, or the evangelist as narrator, the opportunity to elaborate on the deeply spiritual significance of the event in question. So Rusch comments:

> In studying John's Gospel one finds oneself working through a series of interrelated and interlocked patterns. The shaping of one account mirrors that of another. The difficulty Nicodemus has in understanding Jesus' words (3:2, 4, 9) has a counterpart in the crowd's quizzing of Jesus in Capernaum after the feeding of the five thousand (6:25, 30–31, 34). The Samaritan woman's literal response to Jesus' talk of water that ends all thirst (4:15) matches that of the crowd when Jesus talks of the bread that "comes down from heaven and gives life to the world" (6:33–34). This

[5] S. Kim, "The Christological and eschatological significance of Jesus' Passover," 311.

[6] Ibid., 311.

[7] John Ashton's work on the identity of "The Jews" as Jesus' antagonists in the Fourth Gospel is helpful here. See: J. Ashton, "The identity and function of the *Ioudaioi* in the Fourth Gospel." *Novum Testamentum* (1985), 27 (1), 40–75.

> literalness in dealing with Jesus is one of the repeated problems displayed by his hearers in the Fourth Gospel. It is a problem of "seeing but not believing," of eyeing the externals, the visible, but never catching sight of the confronting reality, the spiritual.[8]

Nowhere is this problem more acutely seen and directly addressed than in the "Bread of Life" discourse.

The Case for the Discourse as Internal Jewish Polemic

The discursive method highlights another key aspect of the fourth gospel; that it is intensely Jewish in character. The "Jewishness" of the fourth gospel is now widely acknowledged.[9] The setting and nature of the miracle as well as the subsequent teaching and confrontation regarding it, all display characteristics that would be immediately recognised as Jewish by a contemporary audience. Jesus choosing a wilderness environment to enact a sign miracle that inevitably recalls the feeding of Israel by God with the Manna in the desert is a case in point.

In his "The Jewishness of John's Use of the Scriptures in John 6:31 and 7:37–38," Glenn Balfour gives extensive examples of this distinctly Jewish form of argument employed by Jesus in the Fourth Gospel.[10] With particular reference to the disputation he states (quoting Peder Borgen):

> Borgen, who has thoroughly explored the background of John 6:31–58, suggests this since the passage can then be seen as based on a homily in the haggadic tradition in which a main text from the Torah is followed by a subordinate one from the Prophets or Writings (here John 6:45). This best explains the exegesis involved in John 6:32–33, 36, and provides a context in which 'bread' and 'murmuring' both occur.[11]

[8] F. A. Rusch, "The signs and the discourse : the rich theology of John 6," *Currents In Theology And Mission* (1978), 5 (6), 386.

[9] "Jewish terms and usages are sometimes explained in the Fourth Gospel, but knowledge of Judaism is assumed. We are hardly through the Prologue when we meet with priests, Levites and Pharisees, a reference to Elijah, and a quotation from Isaiah, all without any explanation. There are unexplained allusions to Rabbinic doctrines, and interpretations of the Old Testament." (Dodd, *The Background of the Fourth Gospel* 1935), 334.

[10] G. Balfour, "The Jewishness of John's Use of the Scriptures in John 6:31 and 7:37–38." *Tyndale Bulletin* (1995), 46 (2), 357–380.

[11] Peder Brogen, quoted in G. Balfour. "The Jewishness of John's Use of the Scriptures in John 6:31 and 7:37–38," *Tyndale Bulletin* (1995), 46 (2), 361.

If that is the case—and Balfour makes a good argument for it—then much of what we see happening between Jesus and the disputing Jewish authorities is more easily understood. It is not anti-Jewish polemic as we would understand it, but rather a fierce yet not unrepresentative internal polemic within Judaism that contests one of its key ideas; the identity and role of the Messiah. Also, the kernel of the teaching—the imperative to believe—following upon signal demonstrations of salvific and providential care, mirror one of the great themes of the Exodus itself. Israel's recurring failure to do precisely that, is recapitulated by John's summary of the reception of Jesus teaching by Israel's contemporary leaders: "But although He had done so many signs before them, they did not believe in Him" (John 12:37).

Contrasting Moses and Jesus

The development of this internal Jewish polemic largely centres on the identity of Jesus' claim to be the Christ. This is specifically seen in contrast to Moses whom the Jewish leadership claim as the source of their authority. For the Jewish authorities, Jesus' claims are continually measured against, and seen to be largely in conflict with the received traditions from Moses—the undisputed lawgiver.[12] So, as we shall see, the measure and significance of the feeding miracle is contrasted with Moses in the desert. John carefully builds up a counter narrative in which Jesus fulfils the role of Moses prophesied successor. But not only that, as the Messiah He superlatively excels the role of even Moses himself. If the Law indisputably came by Moses, grace and truth came by Jesus the Messiah. He is the one of whom Moses and all the prophets spoke. Moses healing of the nation in the desert with the brazen serpent was a type of Jesus self-sacrifice for the people. Moses writings foretold his coming, etc.[13]

Jesus however is not only shown as the prophet that is "like Moses,"[14] for, while Moses spoke to God "face to face" and he "sees the form of the LORD" and God spoke to him "plainly;"[15] Jesus as the Word was eternally with God "πρὸς τὸν θεὸν and indeed Jesus as the pre-incarnate Word, was God "θεὸς ἦν ὁ λόγος."[16]

The subsequent signs and discourse develop, elaborate and anchor this truth in both the narrative of Jesus ministry and the Old Testament

[12] See John 9:28–29, for example.

[13] John 1:17;45; 3:14; 5:46.

[14] Deuteronomy 18:15,18.

[15] Numbers 12:8.

[16] John 1:1.

scripture, which the evangelist sees it supremely exemplify and fulfil. Craig Keener captures the superlative aim of John's contrast between Jesus and Moses with particular reference to John 6:

> This the feeding miracle in John points to a deeper Christological interpretation: Jesus is not merely a new Moses providing a sample of a new manna, but he is heaven's supply for the greatest need of humanity.[17]

This—the superlative aspect of Jesus identity and mission—will be repeatedly reinforced by the audacious language that He will use. His intent is to impress upon His hearers the existential necessity of belief in Him. Life itself is contingent on feeding upon the Son of Man.[18]

The Christological Climax

All of this brings us to the substance of the discourse itself. "Comfortably filled with the loaves Jesus has provided, the multitude challenge him to provide a permanent supply of bread."[19] It is likely that the reaction of the multitude to this sign was a call for some further sign or word from Him that He would permanently supply them with bread like, but no doubt exceeding the Exodus miracle. Jesus responds however with a challenge to seek spiritual food.[20] Linked to that challenge is an explicit claim that He personally is the dispenser of this food and has been authoritatively and uniquely commissioned by God the Father for this role.[21] When challenged by the Jews as to what constituted works acceptable to God, Jesus replies with a further challenge that again focuses upon Himself as the divinely required locus of faith.[22]

This counter challenge of Jesus—not to labour for food that perishes, is followed up by the crowd asking what are the works that God requires. This is typical of the contemporary Jewish mind-set. It betrayed a fragmented, legalistic view of God's requirements. It is evidenced by the rich young ruler who, confronted by the attractiveness of Jesus and challenged to follow him, asks "...what do I still lack?"[23] In the Bread of Life discourse

[17] C. S. Keener, *The Gospel of John: A Commentary*, Vol. 2, 663.

[18] John 6:48–51, 53–56, 58.

[19] L. Morris, *The Gospel According to John* (Grand Rapids, MI: Willliam B. Eerdmans, 1971), 361.

[20] John 6:26–27.

[21] John 6:32–33.

[22] John 6:35.

[23] Matthew 19:20.

Jesus, in contrast to legalistic expectations, conflates all of God's moral requirements into personal faith in Him. This of course firmly equates Jesus with the Law itself. He is claiming to be the embodiment of the Law. It is an unambiguous claim to deity.

This, and the subsequent challenge by His hearers for a sign, frame the resulting discourse with its difficult allusions and disputed meaning. It is crucial to note then that this dispute regarding the identity of Jesus is quintessentially Christological. Surely then we can legitimately understand what happens in the unfolding discourse and dispute as a heightening and explication of these Christological claims? So when, for example the Jews, begin to contrast unfavourably Jesus claims and the sign upon which they are made with Moses; He retorts with a contextualising of Moses role as an agent of God with His own role as the "the true bread from heaven..."[24] In the reply to this claim they ask for "this bread always" in a manner that is initially reminiscent of the woman in John 4. But the "repeated problem of literalness" as Rusch reminds us (see footnote 8 above) soon reasserts itself.

Jesus deals with this literalness by using even deeper spiritual allusions and ironically is less understood and provokes even more hostility. Yet even this is accounted for in His self -revealing rationale. He reminds them that the Messiah's claims will be understood by those who are spiritual—those drawn by the Father to Him.[25] His rejection as the Christ by the crass literalists is further proof that He is indeed the Son of Man. Jesus repeatedly reasserts the claim—indeed He expands it and interlaces it with a profound eschatological significance all pointing decisively to Himself.[26] Embedded in this claim is also the eschatological certainty of His having and retaining a people,[27] all of which are claims to be none other than Israel's Messiah.

The Eschatologically "Expectant" Environment

That the Fourth Gospel is laden with eschatological allusions is widely accepted. Dodd expresses this in his introduction to his commentary:

> The kerygma is essentially a proclamation of the facts about Jesus in an eschatological setting, which indicates the significance of the facts. It is prefaced, or accompanied, by the announcement that the prophecies are

[24] John 6:32–33.
[25] John 6:43–45.
[26] John 6:35–40.
[27] John 6:37 & 40.

> fulfilled in these facts, which must consequently be regarded as inaugurating a new age, and a new order of relations between God and man; and it is attested by an appeal to the experience of the Spirit in the Church.[28]

The building up of these claims and the reaction to them reach an intense crescendo in the sixth chapter. The expectation among the Jews was indeed for a Messiah who would provide heavenly Manna, though there were, needless to say differences as to what that would be like. Some were actually inclined to spiritualise the Manna. Balfour again is helpful here.

> This tendency to "spiritualise" the manna was developed by Philo who in a number of places allegorises it. The real development, however, was in its becoming a symbol of the new (messianic) age. So, for example, the Mekilta on Exodus 16:25 reads, "You will not find it [the manna] in this world but you will find it in the world to come."[29]

This idea persisted into later 1st century and even 2nd century Judaism as Jewish pseudepigraphical texts such as 2 Baruch attest: "And it will happen at that time the treasury of manna will come down again from on high, and they will eat of it in those years because these are they who will have arrived at the consummation of time."[30] So the dispute that Jesus enters into here is on spiritual territory quite familiar to a first century Jewish audience. With this in mind it is time to turn to the development of Jesus' specific claims and the language He uses to underpin them.

The "Son of Man" References

Six times in the passage Jesus is referred to as "Son". He claims in John 6:27 to be the "Son of Man" who, with the Father's authority, can dispense "the food which endures to everlasting life". In verse 40 he refers to Himself as "the Son" (likely in reference to the One who sent Him). Here He makes a specific eschatological claim to be the one who can raise the believer in Him "on the last day." In verse 42 however the Jews incredulously ask: "Is not this Jesus, the son of Joseph, whose father and mother we know? How is it then that He says, 'I have come down from heaven'?" In verse 53 He makes life contingent upon eating "the flesh of the Son of Man" and drinking "His blood." In verse 62, responding to the unbelief of even some of the disciples, He states: "What then if you should see the

[28] C. H. Dodd, *The Interpretation of the Fourth Gospel* (Cambridge: Cambridge University Press, 1953), 6.

[29] G. Balfour, "The Jewishness of John's Use of the Scriptures," 366.

[30] 2 Baruch 29:8.

Son of Man ascend where He was before;" finally Peter confesses in verse 69: "We have come to believe and know that You are the Christ, the Son of the living God."

In Jesus' own statements, in the Jewish reaction and in Peter's affirmation of them a common theme is present: the identity of Jesus. Whether this claim is accepted or rejected, it is clear that it refers to the expected "Son of Man" who as the Messiah would restore Israel and bring life for the righteous dead.[31] There can be little doubt that among those who accept or reject him,[32] this idea of the Son of Man is a reference back to the great eschatological and apocalyptic figure from the Book of Daniel. To Him, judgement and everlasting universal dominion, has been entrusted by God Himself.[33] At that time—the culmination of history itself—"many of those who sleep in the dust of the earth shall awake."[34] It is hardly coincidental then that Jesus frames His own claims and the promises associated with them—as the giver of life and restorer of life on "the last day"—in exactly these terms.[35] It is to the promises associated with this momentous figure that He invites—summons even, His hearers.

This building up of Jesus' claims is seen particularly though not exclusively in the Fourth Gospel. The healing in chapter five, for example, is followed by an unambiguous assertion of the rights of Jesus as the "Son of God."[36] Echoing Daniel's prophecy that the Son of Man will give life to many who sleep in the dust (see above), Jesus now asserts this personally for Himself. It is likely picked up and amplified from the synoptics where healing miracles are followed by the judicial role of the "Son of Man" to forgive sin on earth (Matthew 9:6; Mark 2:10; Luke 5:24). This claim is of course challenged vigorously by the Jewish authorities. All of these claims

[31] John Gill the 18th century commentator has decisively demonstrated that this was a common expectation. Gill quoting Talmudic sources states "That the Jews expect the resurrection of the dead, when the Messiah comes, appears from their Targums, Talmuds and other writers; so the targumist on Hos xiv 8 (T. Bab. Sanhedrin, fol. 92.1; T. Hieros. Kilaim, fol.32.3.). They shall be gathered from their captivity, they shall sit under the shadow of their Messiah, and the dead shall live and good shall be multiplied in the land." J. Gill, *An Expositon of the New Testament*, Vol. 5. (Grand Rapids, MI: Baker Book House, 1852, 1980), 658.

[32] As the dispute intensifies the Jews challenge his authority for making what to them are outrageous, blasphemous claims. It is telling that the Jews do not question the idea of "The Son of Man" but rather Jesus' interpretation of the role and His applying it to Himself.

[33] Daniel 7:13–14.

[34] Daniel 12:2.

[35] John 6:33, 39, 54.

[36] John 5:17–30.

climax in the Fourth Gospel with the raising of Lazarus, and the attendant claim of Jesus not only to give life, but to personally *be* "the resurrection and the life" (John 11:25).

Yet even as Jesus unhesitatingly claims that He is the personal fulfilment of the expectations that the Old Covenant generated, He does so in ways that do not seek to accommodate themselves to the traditional accretions that have grown up in rabbinic and popular minds. Herman Ridderbos rightly observes: "It is clear that John the Evangelist does not aim to characterize or define Jesus' messiah-ship from the perspective of specific Jewish expectations."[37] It is partly, if not largely, this divergence that generates the conflict, and it is seen in the most stark terms in the dispute that His claim of the necessity of " eating his flesh" will generate.

"Unless you eat..."

The divergence among interpreters on the significance of Jesus statements in John 6:48–51, 53–56, 58 broadly breaks down into sacramental or non-sacramental understandings of His words. It is hard not to see among the advocates of a sacramental position a reading into the words of Jesus the concerns of a much later ecclesiastical tradition. So Culmann can state, for example, that John's objective was to link the Jesus of history with the living Christ who was truly present in the church's liturgy, a real presence "not in terms of substance but experience."[38]

Bultmann, on the other hand, in his desire to refute any sacramental significance surely over compensates when he assumes the entire section is the work of a later ubiquitous[39] ecclesiastical redactor. Hermann Ridderbos is no doubt nearer to the mark when he observes:

> If anywhere, the basic principle of the structural-analytic exegesis applies here, namely that of the synchronic approach: We should explain the term from within its own semantic frame of reference (here that of the bread discourse) and not derive its meaning (diachronically) from an externally adduced semantic context (sacramental language).[40]

[37] H. N. Ridderbos, *The Gospel accoring to John*, J. Vriend, trans. (Grand Rapids, MI: William B.Eerdmans, 1991), 216.

[38] O. Culmann, *Early Christian Worship* (London: SCM, 1953), 101. Dodd and Culmann are representative exponents of this position.

[39] Bultmann also assigns chapters 3, 6 &19 to the "ecclesiastical redactor." It seems a rather convenient "out."

[40] Ridderbos, *The Gospel accoring to John*, 235 fn.

The language of feeding upon the Son of Man can indeed be understood without a resort to an imposed sacramental template. Can it not be a metaphor—a deeply powerful one no doubt—that is describing the personal focus, depth of intensity and transforming intimacy of faith in Jesus? Its results—eternal life—are already and subsequently clearly ascribed to faith in Jesus as the Son of Man (John 6:40, 47;11:25, 26).

Furthermore, this "feeding" upon Jesus results in the mirroring, in human experience, of the life that He has with the Father. This is the life that He has come to impart, as the Messiah, to those who believe in Him. This of course is a favourite theme in Johannine writings.[41] It parallels the statements Jesus has already made regarding His mission from the Father and the benefit that accrues to those who "believe" (v. 29 & 40) who "come to" Him (v. 35, 37 & 44). That the sacraments—specifically the Lord's Supper—refers back to, and signifies this same reality, is beyond dispute.[42] The coincidence of this Passover miracle and its teaching regarding believing/eating, and the final Passover at which Jesus uses bread and the command to eat, has blurred the distinction for many. Calvin who denied that the discourse was intended to teach anything about the Lord's Supper could not however evade any connection as Eleanor Hanna points out,

> Despite Calvin's explicit rejection of a sacramental meaning for this passage, there is no denying that his exegesis of this pericope has eucharistic overtones because of his language. For example, he claimed that Christ's sacrifice of his flesh "would be no use to us ... if we did not now feed upon that sacred feast." That he immediately followed this claim with a polemical reference to the Roman Mass suggests that thoughts of the Lord's Supper were in his mind even though he denied the connection.[43]

A better resolution is to say that the sacrament, as sign and seal of faith, preserves vividly in the church's life the same Christological and eschatological focus that the "Bread of Life" discourse anticipates and toward which it directs attention.

It is worth noting too that the objection of the Jews was not so much directed at the presumed literalism of Jesus statement, as the personal focus upon Himself as the dispenser of eternal life and eschatological Son of

[41] See 1 John 1:1–4 for example.

[42] D.A. Carson states: "John 6 is not about the Lord's Supper; rather the Lord's Supper is about what is described in John 6" (Quoting Colin Brown, ed. NIDNTT 2 p535).

[43] E. B. Hanna, "Biblical Interpretation and Sacramental Practice: John Calvin's Interpretation of John 6:51–58," *Worship* (1999)," 73 (3), 228.

Man. "How can *this Man* (Πῶς δύναται οὗτος) [emphasis added] give us His flesh to eat?" It is a reemphasising of the statement earlier in verse 42: "Is not this Jesus, the son of Joseph, whose father and mother we know? How is it then that He says, 'I have come down from heaven'?" The incredulity is not in response to the idea of coming from heaven or the giving of flesh for life, so much as that Jesus would dare suggest that *He* had come from heaven or that *His* flesh was for the life of the world.

That the Jews—or at least some among them, understood the "eating " of the Son of Man in non-literal terms John Gill has shown.[44] So it is possible then that the objections of some of the Jews at least, was not on the basis of a merely crass literal understanding of His words—though that may have stumbled some, but that they were rejecting the Christological and eschatological claims He was so clearly enunciating.

Conclusion

The feeding miracle and the subsequent discourse occupy a central role in the message of the Fourth Gospel. Standing as they do at the turning point between Jesus' initial ministry and his final rejection they mark a crucial turning point. Using both occasion and language that inevitably recall both Israel's genesis and purpose, Jesus presents Himself as the personal fulfilment of her deepest expectations.

In a discourse that is intensely Jewish in both its matter and execution He deliberately ratchets up His claims to be the prophesied "Son of Man" in the face of bitter opposition on behalf of His confirmed enemies, and disturbing unexpected disbelief on behalf of many of His disciples. In a sense the claims to be the one, who, by the giving of His life would provide life for believers, becomes self-fulfilling. The Christological and eschatological claims that He makes, on foot of the signs that underpin them, open up the final act of the drama that these claims both predict and necessitate.

As the scene closes the section performs a further final and necessary function. The claims of Jesus as well as his elucidation and intensification

[44] "The phrase of eating the Messiah was a familiar one, and well known to the Jews; though these Capernaites cavilled at it, and called it an hard saying. Says Rab, the Israelites shall 'eat' the years of the Messiah: (the gloss on it is, the fullness which the Israelites shall have in those days:) says R. Joseph, it is certainly so; but who shall 'eat him?' 'shall Chellek and Billek' (two judges in Sodom) אכלי לה, 'eat him?' contrary to the words of R. Hillell, who says, Israel shall have no Messiah, for אכלוהו, 'they ate him in the days of Hezekiah'" T. Bab. Sanhedrin, fol. 98. 2. & 99. 1. Gill, *An Exposition*, 1852,1980, 661.

of them ultimately provide a clear if jarring contrast between faith and unbelief. The "manifesto" of the Fourth Gospel—"And truly Jesus did many other signs in the presence of His disciples, which are not written in this book; but these are written that you may believe that Jesus is the Christ the Son of God, and that believing you may have life in His name."[45] —is echoed by Jesus' question and Peter's reply: "Do you also want to go away? But Simon Peter answered Him, 'Lord, to whom shall we go? You have the words of eternal life. Also we have come to believe and know that You are the Christ, the Son of the living God.'"[46]

---

[45] John 20:30, 31.
[46] John 6:67–69.

Bibliography

Ashton, J. "The Identity and Function of the *Ioudaioi* in the Fourth Gospel." *Novum Testamentum* 27 (Issue 1, 1985): 40–75.

Balfour, G. "The Jewishness of John's Use of the Scriptures in John 6:31 and 7:37–38." *Tyndale Bulletin* 46 (Issue 2, 1995): 357–380.

Borgen, P. *Logos was the true light, and other essays on the Gospel of John.* Trondheim, Norway: Tapir, 1983.

Borgen, P. "The Christology of the Fourth Gospel: Its Unity and Disunity in the Light of John 6." *Journal Of Theological Studies* 49 (1998): 751–758.

Borgen, P. "Observations on the Midrashic Character of John 6." *ZNW* 54 (1963): 232–40.

Brown, R. "John 6 and the Jewish Passover." *Theological Studies* 21 (Issue 1, 1960): 144–145.

Bultmann, R. *The Gospel of John: A Commentary.* G. R. Beasley-Murray, translator. Philadelphia, PA: Westminster Press, 1971.

Calvin, J. *Commentary on the Gospel According to John.* Vol. 1. R. W. Pringle, translator. 1853, Grand Rapids, MI: Baker Book House, 1993.

Carson, D. A. *The Gospel According to John.* Leicester: Inter Varsity Press, 1991.

Culmann, O. *Early Christian Worship* . London: SCM, 1953.

Culpepper, R. A. *The Gospel and letters of John.* Nashville, TN: Abingdon Press, 1998.

Dodd, C. H. "The Background of the Fourth Gospel ." *BJRL* (Issue 19, 1935).

Dodd, C. H. *The Interpretation of the Fourth Gospel.* Cambridge: Cambridge University Press, 1953.

Gill, J. *An Expositon of the New Testament.* Vol. 5. 1852, Grand Rapids, MI: Baker Book House, 1980.

Hanna, E. B. "Biblical Interpretation and Sacramental Practice : John Calvin's Interpretation of John 6:51–58." *Worship* 73 (Issue 3, 1999): 211–230.

Hendriksen, W. *Exposition of the Gospel According to John.* 1953, Grand Rapids, MI: Baker book House, 2002.

Keener, C. S. *The Gospel of John: A Commentary.* 2 Volumes.. Peabody, MA: Hendrickson, 2003.

Kim, S. "The Christological and eschatological significance of Jesus' Passover signs in John 6." *Bibliotheca Sacra* 164 (Issue 655, 2007): 307–322.

Kóstenberger, A. J. *John.* Grand Rapids, MI: Baker Academic, 2004.

Michaels, J. R. *The Gospel According to John.* Grand Rapids, MI: William B. Eerdmans, 2010.

Moore, F. "Eating the flesh and drinking the blood : a reconsideration." *Anglican Theological Review* 48 (Issue 1, 1966): 70–75.

Morris, L. *Reflections on the Gospel of John.* 1986, Peabody, MA: Hendrickson, 2000.

Morris, L. *The Gospel According to John.* Grand Rapids, MI: Willliam B. Eerdmans, 1971.

Painter, J. "The christology of the Fourth Gospel: its unity and disunity in the light of John 6." *Journal Of Biblical Literature* 117 (Issue 1, 1998): 144–145.

Ridderbos, H. N. *The Gospel Accoring to John*. J. Vriend, translator. Grand Rapids, MI: William B.Eerdmans, 1991.

Rusch, F. A. "The signs and the discourse : the rich theology of John 6." *Currents In Theology And Mission* 5 (Issue 6, 1978): 386–390.

Rutland, V. "Sign and sacrament : John's bread of life discourse (Chapter 6)." *Interpretation* 18 (Issue 4, 1964): 450–462.

Von Wahlde, U. C. "Literary structure and theological argument in three discourses with the Jews in the Fourth Gospel." *Journal Of Biblical Literature* 103 (Issue 4, 1984): 575–584.

Westcott, B. F. *The Gospel According to John*. London: James Clarke, 1958.

Yeago, D. S. "The Bread of Life : Patristic Christology and Evangelical Soteriology in Martin Luther's Sermons on John 6." *St Vladimir's Theological Quarterly* 39 (Issue 3, 1995): 257–279.

6

Exalting Christ by Serving Him As a Steward of the Mysteries of God

Hearing the Voice of the Savior

Jim Renihan

It is a great pleasure to offer this essay in honor of Dr. Fred Malone. He has been a friend, colleague and example of godliness and humble service over the years. May the Lord continue to bless him.

A wise pastor has offered profound wisdom when he states "Ultimately, everything is disciplined by theology."[1] He is correct, though few recognize the significance of this assertion. Theology is the basis of everything in the Christian life. Its influence ought to profoundly shape each decision and action we take. When faced with a difficult circumstance (in reality any situation), before we ask the question "What shall I do?" we should ask and answer a far more basic question "What do I believe?" If we fail to approach life in this way, we face the danger of pragmatism or mysticism. Pragmatism will cause us to decide and act based on circumstance—the things we observe or the perceived pressing nature of the moment. At times, it will lead us to conclusions contrary to our faith, yet we justify them on the basis of necessity. Mysticism moves us to deeds based on feel-

[1] The quotation is from Pastor Tom Lyon of Providence Reformed Baptist Church, University Place, Washington.

ings and urges, dangerous territory in all cases. Seldom if ever does either of these lead us to the proper God-honoring decision.[2]

Sadly, this is not only true of the Christian life in general, but it is also true of many approaches to the Christian ministry. Entranced by the prospect of success, men allow the circumstances of the day, or the latest and greatest method to determine their approach to pastoral service. Rather than a principled commitment to the methodology of Scripture, they pursue trendy contemporary methods, or the scratch-where-you-itch pragmatism and mysticism of the culture around them. When I was a seminary student, there was much talk about a personal "philosophy of ministry." Each of us was urged to develop an approach to ministry that was individually useful and contextually beneficial. We read books that taught that one might work out a different approach based on any number of factors—personal preferences, cultural milieu, felt-needs etc. Various models were presented and analyzed for their potential utility and advantage. All of this made me exceedingly uncomfortable, as the discussion seldom if ever began with Scripture. A basic assumption seemed to be that the Bible spoke of the necessity of ministry, but did not contain direction as to the *how* of ministry. In fact, the phrase "philosophy of ministry" implies that there are many and varied ways to lead a church to fulfill its tasks.

This is the unhappy reality of Western ministry at the beginning of the 21st century. We must reply by asserting that understanding the doctrinal content of faith is essential to everything—and for the purposes of this essay—especially the Christian ministry. Before we begin to describe the acts of the Christian ministry, we need to identify and understand its divine basis. If indeed "everything is disciplined by theology," we may apply this principle to pastoral duties and responsibilities. This article is an attempt to begin to lay the groundwork for a theological approach to ministry. We should reject the phrase "philosophy of ministry" and its implications, and replace it with "theology of ministry."

What is requisite in a theology of ministry? I would suggest three things must be present:[3]

1. **Exegetically based.** In the first place, a theology of ministry must be exegetically based. This is easy to say, but much more difficult to ac-

[2] There are many treatments describing the sad state of the evangelical and/or "Christian" world in the West. For example, see Carl R. Trueman, *The Real Scandal of the Evangelical Mind* (Chicago: Moody Press, 2011); Michael S. Horton, *Christless Christianity: The Alternative Gospel of the American Church* (Grand Rapids: Baker, 2008); Russ Douthat, *Bad Religion: How We Became a Nation of Heretics* (New York: Simon and Schuster, 2012).

[3] This is not intended to be an exhaustive list.

complish. I recently listened to a sermon that unconsciously articulated a philosophy of ministry, ostensibly based on a text of Scripture. Sadly, the preacher imposed his own grid on that text, missing the fact that it quite explicitly contradicted the point he tried to make! He imported his view into the passage, ignoring a very clear point that would have countered his view. His fault lay in the fact that he uncritically read the text in the light of his own presuppositions, and this caused him to miss a statement that would have provided a very different conclusion.

This task of exegesis requires hard work. In order to have a proper exegetically based theology, we must consider all of Scripture. The Old Testament is preparatory; the New Testament is fulfillment. Since we live after Pentecost, our theology should seek to prioritize New Testament covenantal teachings. We know, for example, that Jewish ceremonial is ended; we have no tabernacle or temple, hereditary priesthood, or Levitical system. These things may have served as anticipatory, but they cannot and must not become the standard pattern. We see the roots of many New Testament practices in the Old (as good Biblical Theology reminds us), and it serves as an important inspired text for our theology, but our practices come from apostolic injunction. Patrick Fairbairn's observation is especially important: "There cannot be a surer canon of interpretation, than that *everything which affects the constitution and destiny of the New Testament Church has its clearest determination in New Testament Scripture.*"

2. **Intellectually coherent.** Secondly, a proper theology of ministry must be intellectually coherent. It must fit together well, reflecting the interconnection of exegesis and theology. Two ancient hermeneutical concepts help to explain my point here: the analogy of Scripture and the analogy of faith. The first of these may be defined as "the interpretation of unclear, difficult, or ambiguous passages of Scripture by comparison with clear and unambiguous passages that refer to the same teaching or event."[4] This principle reminds us that we must begin our process of building a theology of ministry from clear texts, and these are abundant. The second concept, the analogy of faith, may be defined as

> the use of a general sense of the meaning of Scripture, constructed from the clear and unambiguous *loci* …, as the basis for interpreting unclear or ambiguous texts. As distinct from the more basic *analogia Scripturae* …, the *analogia fidei* presupposes a sense of the theological meaning of Scripture.[5]

[4] Richard Muller, *Dictionary of Latin and Greek Theological Terms* (Grand Rapids: Baker, 1985), 33, s.v. *analogia Scripturae.*

[5] Muller, *Dictionary*, 33, s.v. *analogia fidei.*

This principle requires of us a careful theological interpretation. It reminds us that our theology of ministry must be placed within the larger context of Christian theology as a whole, ensuring consonance between the various *loci* and assuring that our practice of theology will reflect our theological commitments. As an example, if (based on our exegesis) we believe in the sovereignty of God and the necessity and priority of grace in salvation, then we must have a theology of ministry that reflects that same necessity and priority of grace. We ask questions such as "how does God dispense His grace?" and shape our theology of ministry based on the reply provided by Scripture. In this way, our practice will be molded by and fit beautifully with our theological commitments. Anything else is incoherent and contradictory.

3. **Historically informed.** The third factor that must be present is that our theology of ministry must be historically informed. We must not be guilty of the primacy of the present—the notion that our day is the best and final day in the history of the church, and thus that current ideas may push aside belief and practices of our predecessors. Since the data for building this theology of ministry is set down in final form and has been unchanged for 2000 years, a proper theological formulation must take into account both the thought and practice of our fathers in the faith. We must not suppose that we have superior ideas; we must not presume that any of our modern conclusions are best! We recognize that since all have had access to the data—Scripture—opportunity has been present to understand and practice the truth, and we humbly submit ourselves to experienced teachers from the past. Of course, everyone is a servant of his own time, and so are we. For this reason, we ought to check our conclusions against those that have been drawn before ourselves. The entire history of the church belongs to us, with its heights and depths. It may serve as both role model and deterrent example, in so far as its practice accords (or not) with careful exegesis and sound theology. We ignore both aspects of the past to our own peril. The imperialism of the contemporary is a plague to be avoided.

These three principles may be exceedingly useful in constructing a faithful theology of ministry. Starting with Scripture, carefully evaluating our theological conclusions and consulting the check and balance of Christ's activity in his church through the centuries, we may construct a perspective on ministry which reflects the fullness of our Confession of faith.

Stewards of the Mysteries of God

We have learned that we ought to place the ministry within a theological context. In reality, we must view all of life theologically, and must seek to bring all our thoughts captive to Christ and His word. Our tasks as ministers of the New Covenant are very specific, and come to us in a very important context. We are not clinicians, and our efforts are not attempts to be therapeutic—we are the servants of God. We interpret theological truths for the benefit of people, so that they might understand "how to glorify God and enjoy Him forever."

If we are to do this, we must have a correct understanding of the context of pastoral ministry. I openly repudiate any notion that our ministry resembles in any sense that of a social worker. I remember an ordination council I once sat on. The first question addressed by the candidate was his call to the ministry. As he spoke, it was obvious that he had no idea of what a scriptural call to the ministry included. He said that he wanted to be a pastor because he wanted to help people. I asked him how that differed from the "call" of a social worker. He had no clue how to answer.

We must do far better than this. Without a proper sense of our task—its theological context—we will be no better than clinicians. We are to be the servants of God, and ministers to people, and we must have a self-conscious understanding of our task.

How shall we view the ministry? It seems to me that the whole context of the covenants of the Bible provide for us a wonderful context. If our theology is truly integrative—and it surely must be—then there must be a theological foundation for our task.

A Theological Framework for Viewing the Ministry

One way to consider this is to think of the entire picture in a threefold schema:

Pactum Salutis

Historia Salutis

Ordo Salutis

These three terms are of immense importance, for they each describe an aspect of Christian theology. They are not the final answer for structuring our theological formulations, but they help us none the less. Consider them individually:

1. *Pactum Salutis.* Muller defines this as

> *covenant of redemption*; in Reformed federalism, the pretemporal, intratrinitarian agreement of the Father and the Son concerning the covenant of grace and its ratification in and through the work of the Son incarnate. The Son covenants with the Father, in the unity of the Godhead, to be the temporal *sponsor* of the Father's *testamentum* in and through the work of the Mediator. In that work, the Son fulfills his *sponsio* or *fideiussio*, i.e., his guarantee of payment of the debt of sin in ratification of the Father's *testamentum*. The roots of this idea of an eternal intratrinitarian *pactum* are clearly present in late sixteenth-century Reformed thought, but the concept itself derives from Cocceius's theology and stands as his single major contribution to reformed system. Although seemingly speculative, the idea of the *pactum salutis* is to emphasize the eternal, inviolable, and trinitarian foundation of the temporal *foedus gratiae*, much in the way that the eternal decree underlies and guarantees the *ordo salutis*."[6]

Robert Reymond has called the covenant of salvation a "theological convention"[7] and to be sure it is, but that does not undermine the truth of the matter taught in the concept. We believe that God is a covenanting God. The *pactum salutis* provides us with a solid basis for our theological inquiry. It is the context for all theological study.

2. *Historia Salutis.* The historia salutis refers to the actual events, in space and time, by which God brings salvation to His people. Creation, the fall, the flood, the call of Abraham, the exodus, the captivity, the life and death of Christ, Pentecost, all of these are events of the *historia salutis*. On the one hand, they are true events of cosmic history. They actually happened in space and time. But in another sense, they bear theological significance, because they come in order to fulfill—accomplish—the eternal decrees of God. We do not simply speak of abstract decrees of God, but of genuine historical events bearing a great theological significance. We believe that the Scriptures record the actual historical events of redemption, occurring over several millennia, from creation to consummation. The events recorded in Scripture, while real events in human history, bring into human history the decrees of God. They give substance and historical reality to these decrees. They provide the basis, in space and time, of our exegetical studies. Since even the most seemingly mundane parts of Scripture—e.g the genealogies or some of the Proverbs come to us through inspired authors writing as representatives of the history of redemption,

[6] Muller, *Dictionary*, 217, s.v. *pactum salutis*.

[7] Robert Reymond *A New Systematic Theology of the Christian Faith* (Nashville: Thomas Nelson, 1998), 337.

we give ourselves to exegetical study. But even these events are not the end. The third category concludes the act:

3. *Ordo Salutis*. The *ordo salutis* refers to the application of the great acts of God in the life history of the individual believer. Muller again:

> a term applied to the temporal order of causes and effects through which the salvation of the sinner is accomplished … because of their emphasis upon the eternal decree and its execution in time, the Reformed developed the idea of an ordo salutis in detail in the sixteenth century.[8]

Berkhof points us to the relationship between the *pactum salutis* and the *ordo salutis*:

> Reformed Soteriology takes its starting point in the union established in the *pactum salutis* between Christ and those whom the Father has given him, in virtue of which there is an eternal imputation of the righteousness of Christ to those who are His.[9]

While his definition of the *pactum salutis* does not exactly coincide with above (as he seems to speak of it only in the terms of the covenant of grace), the point is made. The *ordo salutis* is rooted in the *pactum salutis*. But we must also assert that the *ordo salutis* is rooted in the *historia salutis*, for it is there that the mighty acts of God are accomplished in space and time. That which is planned in eternity is accomplished in space and time, and applied in the life of each believer. In this way, the counsels of God are brought down to the personal level.

What does all of this have to do with the ministry? Just this: the task of the minister is to bring what was planned in eternity and accomplished in history and apply it to the life of the church. He is an important part of the outworking of the whole. Surely, the treasure is placed into earthen vessels so that the glory of God may be manifest—but let us not forget the earthen vessels. They seek to take the truth of Scripture and bring it to bear in the lives of individuals. They take theology and redemptive-history, and apply them to the people of their generation. They interpret events of the past—theological, redemptive-historical events—for the benefit of men, women and children. We do not abstract the *ordo* from the theological or exegetical, rather we ground it there. For this reason, we must view our ministries in the context of the theological and exegetical, rather than the psychological or clinical. We are the human instruments of bringing the

[8] Muller, *Dictionary*, 215, s.v. *ordo salutis*.

[9] Louis Berkhof, *Systematic Theology* (Grand Rapids: Eerdmans, 1938), 418.

eternal plan of God, accomplished *par excellence* in Christ, to the men and women around us. It is a glorious task.

This is how our Puritan fathers viewed their task. In the *Briefe Premonition* at the beginning of his *Marrow of Divinity*, William Ames says "if there be any who desire to have some practical things … more largely explained, we shall indeavour to satisfie them hereafter … in a particular treatise … touching questions which are usually called cases of conscience." A few pages later, he explains:

> Divinity is the doctrine of living to God … This practice of life is so perfectly contained in Divinity, that there is no precept universally true pertaining to living well, contained in the disciplines of household government, morality, political government or making Lawes, which doth not properly pertaine to Divinity … . There are two parts of Divinity, Faith and observance."[10]

Richard Baxter, in the preface to his *Christian Directory* says that that work must be viewed as a companion to another, *Methodius Theologiae*, and that its purpose may be summarized as "the reducing of theoretical knowledge into serious Christian practice."[11] That which we believe has much to say to the way that we live, and the task of the gospel minister is to make that transition for God's people.

Two relevant texts

This brings us to two texts to consider: 1 Timothy 3:14–16 and 1 Corinthians 4:1. Both of them speak of "mystery," a very important term in the NT.

Consider first 1 Timothy 3:14–16. The ESV text reads

> I hope to come to you soon, but I am writing these things to you so that, if I delay, you may know how one ought to behave in the household of God, which is the church of the living God, a pillar and buttress of the truth. Great indeed, we confess, is the mystery of godliness:

[10] William Ames, *The Marrow of Divinity* (London: Edward Griffin, 1642), unnumbered page 6 of the Briefe Premonition, 1–4.

[11] Richard Baxter, *A Christian Directory: Or, A Summ of Practical Theologie, and Cases of Conscience* (London: Robert White, 1673), unnumbered page 3 of the "Advertisements." Baxter modeled his work on Ames, stating "As *Amesius* his Cases of Conscience are to his *Medulla*, the second and Practical part of Theologie, so is this to a *Methodus Theologiae* …"

He was manifested in the flesh,
vindicated by the Spirit,
seen by angels,
proclaimed among the nations,
believed on in the world,
taken up in glory.[12]

Verses 14–16 serve as a discrete section, describing to us the purpose for Paul's writing this epistle. He wants Timothy to have in hand some practical instruction for the church to live by, should he be delayed in his efforts to come to them. This governs everything in the epistle, especially chapters 2:1–6:19. The epistle is about conduct in the church—the behavior of Christians.

Notice how verses 15 and 16 relate doctrine and duty. Verse 15 speaks to the necessity of conduct: Paul uses the indeclinable particle of necessity δεῖ. There is a way to live, in the context of the church. But it is based on a doctrinal truth—the mystery of godliness.

The text is really fascinating. The layout helps us to see that there is a descent/ascent motif present: Christ is manifest in flesh, vindicated by the Spirit, seen by angels: all themes relating to His humiliation, and He is proclaimed among the nations, believed on in the world, and received up in glory, themes relevant to his ascent.

The center of the text is the emphasis on the mystery of godliness. The copula καὶ connects verse 16 with verse 15 so that it should read "*and* confessedly great is the mystery of godliness."[13] What is the mystery of godliness? At this point we may say that it is something that is to be confessed. This adverb is important to notice. The NASB translation is helpful, "By common confession, great is the mystery of godliness." The church of the living God, the household of God, a pillar and buttress of the truth, is built upon this mystery, and must confess it. It is the common foundation for everyone in the church, and it is their task together to testify to its truth.

Mystery in itself is an important concept in the NT. It has reference to something that has been hidden but is now revealed, though to some it remains a mystery. Notice the grammar of the passage: μέγα ἐστὶν τὸ τῆς εὐσεβείας μυστήριον. The verb *to be* points to a present quality of this thing: the mystery is now great. But then notice the first strophe of the hymn: ὅς ἐφανερώθη—it has been revealed. It is a present mystery, though it has been revealed. But only those who are part of the house of God, the church

[12] *The Holy Bible: English Standard Version* (Standard Bible Society: Wheaton, 2001).

[13] My rendering of καὶ ὁμολογουμένως μέγα ἐστὶν τὸ τῆς εὐσεβείας μυστήριον.

of the living God, comprehend the nature of the mystery. Even though it is preached to the nations, many of them remain in the darkness of their unbelief.

What is the content of the mystery here? It is Christ as the fulfiller of the plan of God. That's the point of the text—the descent/ascent motif. He[14] was manifest in the flesh—who but the pre-existent One, the One who is the object of all of the revelation of the prophets, the Yea and Amen of the ages? And the mystery is great. It is profound—stunning—breath-taking—comprehensive—there are many senses to "great." The meeting of heaven and earth in the person of Jesus Christ is enough to make the angels of God marvel. This is what Paul says. And it is the basis for the necessity of a certain kind of behavior among God's people. They must conduct themselves in a certain way in order to live in consonance with this mystery. The revelation of the hidden impinges on the life of its recipients. Theology, in this case the revelation of the God-man, necessitates a certain type of ministry, one that calls the people of God to careful and godly living. The *pactum salutis, historia salutis* and *ordo salutis* come together wonderfully in this text. God's plan, accomplished in Christ, profoundly changes lives. Theology disciplines everything.

Now consider 1 Corinthians 4:1. The ESV text reads "This is how one should regard us, as servants of Christ and stewards of the mysteries of God. Moreover, it is required of stewards that they be found faithful."[15]

These words are found in the midst of the larger contextual section 3:18–4:5. But in order to think through the immediate context, we must catch the flow of thought up to this point in the epistle. After an initial greeting, Paul immediately in 1:10 begins to respond to the troubles afflicting the Corinthian church, most notably the divisions which have begun to evidence themselves in their midst. In Paul's mind, such schismatic behavior is far removed from that which ought to be present in the lives of Christians. It is this discussion of divisions in the church, and attendant issues, which influences Paul's thematic development in the first four chapters of the letter.

In 1:10–17, there is a frank discussion of the nature of the divisions, followed by a lengthy section in 1:18–2:16 in which Paul opens up the dif-

[14] There is a variant reading at the beginning of this line; some ancient manuscripts read "God" rather than "he." In either case, the referent is clearly Jesus Christ.

[15] *The Holy Bible: English Standard Version*. (Standard Bible Society: Wheaton, 2001), 1 Corinthans 4:1–2. The Greek text is Οὕτως ἡμᾶς λογιζέσθω ἄνθρωπος ὡς ὑπηρέτας Χριστοῦ καὶ οἰκονόμους μυστηρίων θεοῦ ὧδε λοιπὸν ζητεῖται ἐν τοῖς οἰκονόμοις ἵνα πιστός τις εὑρεθῇ, (NA27).

ference between the worldly wisdom exhibited in the Corinthians' behavior, and the other-worldly wisdom of God, considered foolishness by those who do not understand, but evidencing the power of God in the Gospel. The weakness of the cross demonstrates the wisdom of God, which is a musth,rion (2:7), hidden in the past but destined for the glory of believers before time. It is this wisdom of God which Paul calls "the mind of Christ" in 2:16, something that should have a deep and lasting influence on the thinking and behavior of the Corinthians.

At the beginning of chapter 3, Paul returns to the specific issue at hand, namely division in the church, and demonstrates that the actions of the Corinthians betray an understanding of the very basic principles of the gospel. It is highly inconsistent to profess knowledge of Christ, and then to act as if this made no difference in the outworking of church life. By their schismatic conduct, the Corinthians are acting as "mere men" (3:4). Especially egregious is the fact that these divisions are carried on under the names of prominent church leaders: Paul, Apollos, Cephas and even Christ. Such evidences of a party spirit belie the facts of the Christian message, and evidence a total misunderstanding of the nature of Christian leadership. Paul argues that the Corinthians need to stop and think about the essence of the ministries of these leaders. Are they not all simply servants of Christ? Paul's emphatic words in 3:21, "let no one boast in men"[16] (ESV), are intended to drive home the point. Do not boast in men, even if they are good men.

The Corinthians have badly misunderstood the role of Christ's servants. They are not rallying points for sectarian schisms, they are stewards, entrusted with the μυστηρίων θεοῦ, and must be reckoned as such. They are obligated to be faithful, for the Lord will one day judge them. If Paul is unwilling even to judge himself, why should the Corinthians enter in, even with a positive judgment, such as "I am of Paul?" To do so is to undermine the very nature of Paul's role as steward. He did not put himself forward, but God chose him for this role, and so he must answer to his master. The same is true for all other stewards in God's household. When the Corinthians exalt one and reject another, they in effect countermand God's design. They place their eyes on the earthly servant rather than on the heavenly Lord.

Raymond Brown points to an interesting parallel in the Qumran literature:

> The entrusting of mysteries to one man for the sake of others is nothing new. The Qumran psalmist (1QH 2:13–14) thanks God that He has set

[16] ὥστε μηδεὶς καυχάσθω ἐν ἀνθρώποις.

> him up as a banner for the elect, and the interpreter of knowledge in His marvelous mysteries, to test the men of truth. In other words, he is to interpret the mysteries of God for the sectarians who must accept his interpretation.[17]

Paul's idea is not new, but it is important. Ministers are simply the messengers, servants and heralds of the words of another, God Himself. They are sent on His behalf to instruct His people in His ways. For this reason, the eyes of the Corinthians ought not to be on the servant, but on the Master who sent that messenger.

The connection of μυστήριον with οἰκονόμους is important. Gordon Fee argues that both οἰκονόμους and the earlier ὑπηρέτας are parallel. He states that ὑπηρέτας is

> a more general term, but often refers to one who has the duties of administering the affairs of another. That this was Paul's intent is verified by the second word, oikonomos, which denotes a "steward" (often a slave) who has been "entrusted with" managing a household."[18]

A "servant of Christ" and a "Steward of the mysteries of God" is thus a person who must answer to his master, charged with the responsibility of managing and dispensing that which has been granted him by his lord. In this case, Paul as a steward is charged with the μυστήριων θεοῦ.

Verse 2 of 1 Corinthians 4 then makes an important point: a steward must be found faithful. The nature of his task impinges on his fulfilling that task: he dispenses the mysteries of God. He takes that which was hidden, that which was the object of even prophetic inquiry (1 Peter 1:10), and dispenses it to men and women. Thus, he is not his own master, he is but a servant. Once more we see how the *pactum salutis, historia salutis* and *ordo salutis* intersect. God's eternal purpose, His wisdom, is accomplished in the person and work of Jesus Christ, and then preached by His stewards. They simply proclaim the great things He has planned and accomplished, calling on people to believe, looking to God alone. Ultimately, it is all God's work, including the methods employed by the messengers.

This is why a theological perspective on the ministry is so foundational. We are, as ministers, first and foremost the servants of God. And as such, we labor with a theological perspective always in mind. All that we do must have reference to God's mystery now revealed: Christ has come in

[17] Raymond Brown, *The Semitic Background of the Term "Mystery" in the New Testament* (Philadelphia: Fortress Press, 1968), 44–5.

[18] Gordon Fee, *The First Epistle to the Corinthians*, New International Commentary on the New Testament (Grand Rapids: Eerdmans, 1987), 159.

fulfillment of the promises of all of the ages. He is Lord, and as such must be the subject of our proclamation. Once again we may quote our brother, "ultimately, everything is disciplined by theology."

Heralds and Ambassadors

We have already argued that our perspectives on the ministry must be theologically shaped. True ministers of the gospel are men who have been commissioned and sent by Jesus Christ. They must view themselves as the instruments in history of the accomplishment of certain aspects of the eternal plan of God. They are the means that God has ordained to bring the *pactum salutis* and *historia salutis* to the *ordo salutis*. But we need to consider this concept in much greater detail. What is the minister as a preacher? What should be his self-conscious identity? Or more directly, how does the Lord accomplish this eternal work?

The Herald

In Romans 10:14–15, we have one of the most important and amazing texts with regard to the nature of the preaching office.

Our text comes in the midst of chapters 9–11, a passage of great importance in the book of Romans. Paul has expounded his doctrine of justification by grace through faith and its attendant blessings in Romans 3:21–8:39, and anticipates a significant objection that will be made by many of his readers: what about the Jews? The fact that they are God's ancient people, and yet are condemned in unbelief, poses a perplexing matter for Paul's doctrine, and he knows that he must deal with it forthrightly. In so doing, he speaks to the nature of Israel's unbelief—though they were blessed with far more than any race of people in human history, they still missed what God had intended for them, because they had no faith. On the one hand, God's purpose was never that all of Israel according to the flesh would be saved—the very fact that two sons, born of the same mother and sharing the same womb could have such different destinies demonstrates this fact. God's purpose according to election must stand. But on the other hand, the failure is Israel's own fault. They did not believe. They pursued the law as if it were an instrument of salvation, failing to see that it was intended to point them to Christ. Romans 10:1–13 is a statement of the difference between two systems of obtaining salvation: works and faith. Paul concludes that salvation only comes by faith, "everyone who calls on the name of the Lord will be saved."

Romans 10:14–15 follows immediately after and carries through with the same theme. Paul's assertion that calling on the name of the Lord brings salvation begs a series of rhetorical questions that he presents to the reader in retrogressive order. William Hendriksen[19] argues that this regressive order is intended to point to the final element—the Lord who sends men to preach, so that men might hear and believe Him.

For our purposes, the exegesis of the passage is very important. Notice the structure of the text: there are four questions, each beginning with πῶς. The first has the postpositive οὖν, demonstrating that these thoughts open up an aspect of the previous material. The following questions have de., indicating that they are part of the series. The verse might be visually presented in this way:

Πῶς οὖν ἐπικαλέσωνται εἰς ὅν οὐκ ἐπίστευσαν;
Πῶς δὲ πιστεύσωσιν οὗ οὐκ ἤκουσαν;
Πῶς δὲ ἀκούσωσιν χωρὶς κηρύσσοντος;
Πῶς δὲ κηρύξωσιν ἐὰν μὴ ἀποσταλῶσιν;

How then shall they call on Him in whom they have not believed?
And how shall they believe Him whom they have not heard?
And how shall they hear without preaching?
And how shall they preach unless they are sent?

The pattern of the questions is the same, except for one variation in the third question. Each question takes the second verb from the previous question as its first verb, and incorporates by implication the modifying phrase attached to that verb in the previous question.

In the first question, the initial verb ἐπικαλέσωνται is in the middle voice. According to BDAG, when used in the middle voice it signifies "to call upon deity for any purpose."[20] Thus, the object of the verb is included in the verb itself, hence "how shall they call on him." The prepositional phrase εἰς ὅν does not modify ἐπικαλέσωνται, but rather belongs with the second verb, ἐπίστευσαν. This is a relatively rare occurrence in Paul, though familiar from John.

In the second question, εἰς ὅν is implied from the previous question, modifying πιστεύσωσιν. Thus, οὗ does not modify πιστεύσωσιν, as might seem initially apparent, but rather modifies ἤκουσαν. The second verb, ἤκουσαν, is unusual in that it takes the genitive rather than the accusative

[19] William Hendriksen, *New Testament Commentary: Exposition of Paul's Epistle to the Romans* (Grand Rapids: Baker, 1981), 349.

[20] Frederick William Danker, *A Greek-English Lexicon of the New Testament and other Early Christian Literature* Third Edition, Chicago: The University of Chicago Press, 2000, s.v. ἐπικαλέω.

case as object to denote the person who is heard. As Murray says, "There is no need to insert the preposition 'in' before 'him.' … A striking feature of this clause is that Christ is represented as being heard in the gospel when proclaimed by the sent messengers. The implication is that Christ speaks in the gospel proclamation."[21] The proper translation of this phrase is thus "And how shall they believe him whom they have not heard?" This is vital to understand.

In the third question, οὗ (or perhaps more precisely—the one referred to by οὗ) is implied from the previous question. Up to this point, the referents of the pronoun "they" have been the same. They are unbelievers. In the context, "they" are perhaps especially Jews, but certainly all unbelievers. But now, there is a change that must not be missed. Until now, Paul has completed the question with a finite verb—aorist active indicative. But at the end of the third question, he uses an anarthrous participle—the object of the preposition χωρὶς. This is different from the rest of the series. Two things need to be said about this: 1. Paul did not use the noun κῆρυξ which was available to him. He uses a verbal noun, probably to bring out a dual emphasis—it focuses on preaching as the act of a commissioned person—it's not just the preacher, and it's not just the thing preached—they are both in view. 2. By doing this, Paul changes the referent of "they." No longer are "they" unbelievers, "they" are now preachers. We are not now thinking of the hearers, but we are thinking of the preachers. We shift our eyes from the audience to the pulpit. Both are necessary for this activity, but Paul subtly slides from the one to the other.

How is a preacher to preach? He must be sent, Πῶς δὲ κηρύξωσιν ἐὰν μὴ ἀποσταλῶσιν. NIDNTT states

> The LXX, following the Heb. text uses *apostello* and its cognates to denote … the authorization … to fulfill a particular function or a task which is normally clearly defined. … If the sending is linked with a task in the use of *apostello*, it follows that attention is always focused on one who sends. In other words, the stress falls on the one who gives his authority to the one whom he sends and whom he takes into his service.[22]

The assumption here is that the ascended Lord is present and active in His church, commissioning men to speak His words as His representatives. This brings us back to our grand scale (*pactum/historia/ordo salutis*), Christ

[21] John Murray, *Commentary on the Epistle to the Romans* (Grand Rapids: Eerdmans, 1960), 2:58.

[22] *New International Dictionary of New Testament Theology* Grand Rapids: Zondervan, 1975), 1:127.

must send men to preach, and we must notice the emphasis on the present activity of Christ in preaching. They (unbelievers) call upon Him to find salvation. They believe on Him. They hear Him. A different "they" are sent by Him. And at all times, preaching is considered as an activity of Christ himself.

The Ambassador

Another text of real importance for our discussion is 2 Corinthians 5:20. It reads

> Ὑπὲρ Χριστοῦ οὖν πρεσβεύομεν ὡς τοῦ θεοῦ παρακαλοῦντος δι' ἡμῶν· δεόμεθα ὑπὲρ Χριστοῦ καταλλάγητε τῷ θεῷ.
>
> Therefore on behalf of Christ we are ambassadors since God speaks through us, we implore you on behalf of Christ be reconciled to God.

In order to open up this text, several comments may be made. Much of 2 Corinthians is about the ministry. Paul urges the Corinthians to think clearly, especially about his own ministry. Was he being rejected by them? Probably he sensed that he was being supplanted by pseudo-apostles and wrote to counter this problem. In our passage, he places his ministry in the context of the great works of Christ—*historia salutis* (verse 14–15) and *ordo salutis* (v. 17). Notice especially verse 19. Here, the plan and activity of God in reconciliation comes into human history through God's ministers—He has committed to us the ministry of reconciliation. But how does this work? Verse 20 gives us the indication. Notice some exegetical points. In both the first and second part of the verse, the phrase ὑπὲρ Χριστοῦ is prominent. In each case, it is Christ who is the object of appeal.

In the former part of the verse, ministers are said to be ambassadors. English does not have an exact equivalent for this verb. Literally it says something such as "we embassy for Christ." This verb is a technical term describing a designated messenger sent from an official source. It is something of a political term not unlike our modern usage. The term implies authority in the sender, in the messenger and in the message, because of its source. Everything relies on the origin. Notice then how the ambassador speaks: ὡς τοῦ θεοῦ παρακαλοῦντος δι' ἡμῶν. We must look at this phrase in some detail. In the first place, τοῦ θεοῦ παρακαλοῦντος is a genitive absolute. In the second place, the genitive absolute when preceded by ὡς has a very specific sense.

Alfred Plummer makes the point well. He states

> the force of ὡς with a genitive absolute is not always the same. The ὡς always gives a subjective view of what is stated by the gen. abs., but that subjective view may be shown by the context to be either right or wrong. When it is given as right, as in 2 Pet. 1.3, ὡς is rendered 'seeing that,' which RV has in that place. Where the subjective view is given as wrong, ὡς = 'as though,' which RV correctly has in 1 Cor iv.18; 1 Pet. iv:12, Acts xxvii:30 .... Here it is manifest that God's entreating is given as a fact, yet AV and RV have 'as though' .... The fact that 'God is entreating by us' is a momentous one, and the declaration of it is analogous to the formula of the Hebrew Prophet, 'Thus saith the Lord.'[23]

We should thus translate the phrase, "we are Christ's ambassadors, seeing that God is pleading through us." There is a very real sense in which the ambassador is viewed as endowed with God's authority. But it is more than that. It is not simply that there is a representative authority in the preacher. God does plead through him as he is an ambassador of Christ. And it doesn't stop here. Consider the latter part of the text. Paul the preacher, speaking in the plural as a representative of all preachers, states "we implore you for Christ's sake—be reconciled to God." What is this if not the actual pleading of the Savior through the preacher to the audience, to be saved? John Stott says

> it is by preaching that God makes past history a present reality. The cross was, and always will remain, a unique historical event of the past. And there it will remain, in the past, in the books, unless God Himself makes it real and relevant to men today. It is by preaching, in which he makes His appeal to men through men, that God accomplishes this miracle. He opens their eyes to see its true meaning, its eternal value and its abiding merit. 'Preaching' writes Dr. Mounce, 'is that timeless link between God's great redemptive Act and man's apprehension of it. It is the medium through which God contemporizes His historic Self-disclosure and offers man the opportunity to respond in faith." But it is more even than this. God not only confronts men through the preacher's proclamation; He actually saves men through it as well. This St. Paul states categorically: 'Since, in the wisdom of God, the world did not know God through wisdom, it pleased God through the folly of the kerygma to save those

[23] Alfred Plummer, *A Critical and Exegetical Commentary on the Epistle of St. Paul to the Corinthians* ICC (Edinburgh: T&T Clark, 1915), 185. Philip Hughes makes a similar point. See Philip Hughes, *Paul's Second Epistle to the Corinthians* NICNT (Grand Rapids: Eerdmans, 1962), 210.

> who believe' (1 Cor. 1:21). Similarly, the gospel is itself 'the power of God unto salvation to every one that believeth' (Rom. 1:16, A.V.).[24]

This is tremendous. When Christ's ambassadors preach, He speaks through them. While men may think it foolish, those who understand properly see the wisdom. And we recognize the importance of an utter dependence on the Spirit in preaching. Richard Baxter had it right when he said,

> I marvel how I can preach … slightly and coldly, how I can let men alone in their sins and that I do not go to them and beseech them for the Lord's sake to repent, however they take it and whatever pains or trouble it should cost me. I seldom come out of the pulpit but my conscience smiteth me that I have been no more serious and fervent. It accuseth me not so much for want of human ornaments or elegance, nor for letting fall an uncomely word; but it asketh me: 'How could'st thou speak of life and death with such a heart? Should'st thou not weep over such a people, and should not thou cry aloud and shew them their transgressions and entreat and beseech them as for life and death?"[25]

This points up the importance of the ministry, and places a great weight on the shoulders of those who exercise it. Why else would Paul say "Woe is me if I do not preach the Gospel!" 1 Corinthians 9:16.

At this point, we need to consider the herald/ambassador language.

We may make several points about this language. In the first place, there is probably little formal difference between a herald and an ambassador. We should think of these terms as essentially synonymous, and certainly complementary.

In their noun forms, the two words are relatively rare in the NT. Κῆρυξ is used of Noah in 2 Peter 2:5 and self-descriptively by Paul in 1 Timothy 2:7 and 2 Timothy 1:11. In 2 Peter, the Apostle calls Noah a herald of righteousness. This is in the context of a comparison between the judgment of the "ancient world" and the great judgment on the last day. God called him to prepare to pass through the judgment. But how was he a herald of righteousness? Moses doesn't tell us anything about Noah's actions except that "he did according to all that God commanded him" (Genesis 6:22). So, we are left to take Peter's word for it: Noah heralded righteousness.

[24] John R.W. Stott, *The Preacher's Portrait* (Grand Rapids: Eerdmans, 1961), 53.

[25] Cited in Stott, *Preacher's Portrait*, 58.

Paul twice uses the term to refer to himself. In 1 Timothy 2:7, it is the first in a series that describe his office and role. In 2 Timothy 1:11, the identical sequence is used. What is the point? Christ has sent him to be a herald—his chief work, proclaiming the message of another; an apostle—charged with the settlement of that which is central to the plan of God, the church; and a teacher—to instruct in everything Jesus Christ has commanded.

More common is the term κήρυγμα found in Matthew 12:41, Luke 11:32, Romans 16:25, 1 Corinthians 1:21, 2:4, 15:14, 2 Timothy 4:17 and Titus 1:3. BDAG define it as "an official announcement, proclamation, the content of a herald's proclamation … sent by God."[26] The term has some ambiguity inherent. It may refer to the message and the act of delivering the message. One might argue that these are inseparable from each other. The verb κηρύσσω is even more common. John the Baptist preaches, the gospel is preached, Moses can be preached (Acts 15:21), as also circumcision (Galatians 5:11), the word, faith, repentance and Christ. But the sense is the same as we have already seen—public declaration.

The related term πρεσβεία is found at Luke 14:32, 19:14. The verbal form is used in 2 Corinthians 5:20 and Ephesians 6:20. In the Lukan occurrences the word comes in parables and help us to understand the concept. The ambassador is the man charged with speaking the word of his master. The herald is sent by another: he does not send himself. The herald delivers the message of another; he does not alter it according to his own wisdom. But, we must ask, who speaks when the Christian preacher stands to deliver his message? Is it the human voice, or the divine? It is really both. Not that the human preacher is in any way inspired and delivers a message like unto that of a prophet, no not at all. But when he truly preaches the gospel, Jesus Christ is present to speak to the hearer and to save him or her. Preaching is an instrumental means in the life and death of the sinner.

What happens when we preach? First, the pre-conditions must be met. According to His eternal purpose, God must send men. These appointed individuals must faithfully declare the truth of Scripture, namely Christ as the One who brings salvation so that the hearers may call upon the name of the Lord. Secondly, when these things are present, Jesus Christ Himself speaks through the preacher. This is not inspiration nor mysticism, rather it is a recognition that as Lord, exalted to the highest place in heaven, claiming that "all authority in heaven and earth has been given" to Him, knowing that He is God-man, He sovereignly comes to bless His word as it is proclaimed, assuring that it will accomplish His eternal purpose.

[26] BDAG, s.v. κήρυγμα.

The preacher and the hearers may always expect that Christ the great Prophet will be present and address the church through the preached word. This implies at least two things. For preachers, it means that we must ensure that we speak the truth of Scripture. There is no promise to bless the preacher's own words or opinions. For hearers, it means that we must remember the words of Psalm 95:7b–8 and Hebrews 4:7 "Today if you will hear his words, do not harden your hearts." We must receive the preached word, as if Jesus Christ Himself was speaking to each of us. We must come with expectation, pay careful attention and listen with faith.

To put all of this together, we must state that preaching is, like living the Christian life, a complex interaction of the divine and the human. On the one hand, we assert the present activity of Christ in true preaching. He comes and speaks through the preacher. But on the other hand, the preacher must speak. He is the herald, sent to proclaim the message of his Sovereign. This is why the scriptural doctrine of appointed preachers is so important. No one can send himself—he must be sent by Christ. And the only approved instrument to send a preacher today is the church. But when the preacher is recognized by the church, we need to receive him as such.

Conclusion

As we serve Christ, our service must be saturated with this theological perspective. Why do we labor for the souls of men? Why do we strive to perfect them in holiness? Why do we reprove and rebuke and admonish and encourage? Why do we point out sin, or instruct in the ways of grace? It is because fundamentally all things in life have a theological reference—they have to do with God. Whether we think of the rehabilitation of a ruined creation, or the renovation of the heart of a bruised sinner, we must see our task in this light. If we serve as ministers, we distribute truth—not philosophical notions, but truth—truth that requires appropriate behavior. With our eyes turned to heaven, our minds full of these things, and the genuine needs of humanity before us, we will honor God in our service. But anything less will be miserable failure.

So let us strive to think of the ministry in these terms. We have only scratched the surface here. Every aspect of our service must be theological, rooted and grounded in God's revelation. Let us seek for a thoroughly integrative theology—one that stretches deeply into our ministries. In this way, we will have a truly pastoral theology, a theology of ministry drawn from Scripture. "Ultimately, everything is disciplined by theology." This must especially be true of our approach to the Gospel ministry. Our brother Dr. Malone has modeled this for us. May the Lord of the church raise up many to follow in his footsteps. *Soli Deo Gloria.*

7

Exalting Christ by Seeing Him As Supreme

The Centrality of Christ in the Ministry of Jonathan Edwards

Tom Nettles

Preaching Theory

Jonathan Edwards' concentrated on preaching as the premiere human activity and Christ as the sum of all the parts of preaching. In preaching, Edwards proclaimed and applied the many doctrines which compose the revelation of Scripture. He searched for appropriate words, analogies, and images, and engaged in as much precision and elaboration as a particular text required in light of the whole of revelation. His aim was to strike home to the conscience the necessity of the soul's relish for the beauty of God. This beauty shines preeminently in Christ.

The introduction to A Jonathan Edwards Reader describes Edwards' commitment to the task of preaching.

> The central vehicle for revivalism was pulpit oratory, and for virtually his entire life Edwards was first and foremost a preacher. The efflorescence of scientific, philosophical, and later, psychological rumination took place within a context of weekly preaching on the Word…[T]hese sermons…undergirded almost all of his philosophical work and lent that work much of its urgency. Ultimately, Edwards' ideas, vision, and insights

> were applied to the central task of converting hardened sinners in the pews from love of self-righteousness to disinterested love of God and divine righteousness.[1]

Edwards developed his sermons in accordance with an idea that included both experiential and theoretical components. At the experiential level, he did not share his grandfather Solomon Stoddard's idiosyncratic defense of the usefulness of unregenerate ministers. Though God might sovereignly use such through the power of the gospel itself, the minister's self-consciousness must rest on a deep experience of the grace of God in Christ. This undergirded an understanding of the true nature of saving faith. He must not be a "blind leader of the blind" but be fully acquainted with "experimental religion, and not ignorant of the inward operations of the Spirit of God."[2]

At the theoretical level he called into service all the intellectual powers with which he so abundantly was endowed, for the minister must be "pure clear and full in his doctrine." He must "not lead his people into errors, but teach them the truth only" and show himself "well acquainted with the written Word of God, mighty in the Scriptures, and able to instruct and convince gainsayers."[3]

In all of this Edwards reflects most worthily his Puritan heritage. Self-examination concerning an experience of saving grace, precise analysis of biblical components of the objective work of God outside of us, the full sufficiency of Christ for us, and a morphology of the work of the Spirit within us constituted the constant task of the Puritan minister. All of these were necessary if he were to be a curer of souls. Edwards was in dead earnest in this calling.

Experiential Preparation

Edwards' own spiritual encounter served as a background for the intensity of his sermonic application. He recorded, in May or June of 1721, his first memory of "that sort of inward, sweet delight in God and divine things that I have lived much in since." It came to him on reading the words "Now unto the King eternal, immortal,invisible, the only wise God,

[1] John E. Smith, Harry S. Stout, and Kenneth Minkema, eds. *A Jonathan Edwards Reader* (New Haven: Yale University Press, 1995), xvii.

[2] Jonathan Edwards, "The True Excellence of a Gospel Minister" in *The Works of Jonathan Edwards*, 2 vols. (Edinburgh: The Banner of Truth Trust, 1974), 2:957. This edition will be noted as *Works*.

[3] Ibid.

be honour and glory for ever and ever, Amen." These became a path for his soul to "a sense of the glory of the Divine Being; a new sense, quite different from any thing" ever experienced before. His whole experience became concentrated in a desire to "enjoy that God, and be rapt up in him in heaven, and be as it were swallowed up in him for ever!" His prayers now were engaged "with a new sort of affection." He pointed to an identifiable experience in which the union of affection and doctrine became a necessary element in his thought.

> From about that time, I began to have a new kind of apprehensions and ideas of Christ, and the work of redemption, and the glorious way of salvation by him. An inward, sweet sense of these things, at times, came into my heart; and my soul was led away in pleasant views and contemplations on them. And my mind was greatly engaged to spend my time in reading and meditating on Christ, on the beauty and excellency of his person, and the lovely way of salvation by free grace in him.... The sense I had of divine things, would often of a sudden kindle up, as it were, a sweet burning in my heart; an ardor of soul, that I know not how to express."[4]

These impressions, ever enlarging and intensifying, formed the basis of his life's work. His analyses of revival, religious affections, the will, original sin, true virtue, and the end for which God created the world showed the same grand assumption-that human purpose is fully constituted in a new sense and relish for the excellence and holy beauty of the divine being.[5]

Precisely this quality fascinated Edwards when he first heard of Sarah Pierrepont. In a famous description of his then-future bride, Edwards remarked how the young lady from New Haven was "beloved of that almighty Being, who made and rules the world," in such palpable experiences that "she expects after a while to be received up where he is... to be ravished with his love and delight forever." This consciousness filled her with "a strange sweetness in her mind, and singular purity in her affections" so that "you could not persuade her to do anything wrong or sinful, if you would give her all the world."[6]

[4] *Reader*, 284.

[5] In the very first section of his "Observations on the facts and evidences of Christianity, and the objections of infidels" he says, "It is easily proved that the highest end and happiness of man is to view God's excellency, to love him, and receive expressions of his love. This love, including all those other affections which depend upon, and are necessarily connected with it, are expressed in worship." [*Works*, 2:460]

[6] *Reader*, 281.

That a gospel minister should experience these graces was axiomatic to Edwards. In a sermon on John 5:35, "He was a burning and shining light," Edwards illustrated the necessity of both heat and light in a true gospel minister. A burning light has a heart filled with ardor; his ministrations are done in fervency and zeal.

> His fervent zeal, which has its foundation and spring in that holy and powerful flame of love to God and man, that is in his heart appears in the fervency of his prayers to God... and in the earnestness and power with which he preaches the word of God, declares to sinners their misery, and warns them to fly from the wrath to come, and reproves and testifies against all ungodliness; and the unfeigned earnestness and compassion with which he invites the weary and heavy laden to their Saviour; and the fervent love with which he counsels and comforts the saints; and the holy zeal, courage, and stedfastness, with which he maintains the exercise of discipline in the house of God, notwithstanding all the opposition he meets with in that difficult part of the ministerial work.[7]

Genuine and lasting heat, however, always is the product of light. Zeal, no matter how high it is pitched, abstracted from the spiritual understanding of truth, will produce bluster, but not either love or holiness. "Holy affections are not heat without light," Edwards taught, "but evermore arise from some information of the understanding, some spiritual instruction that the mind receives, some light or actual knowledge." Any affection not arising from "light in the understanding" most certainly is not spiritual. This light in the understanding, however, is not mere information, or only a notional understanding of true doctrine, Spiritual understanding of Scripture involves having "the eyes of the mind opened to behold the wonderful, spiritual excellency of the glorious things contained in the true meaning of it."[8] These truths always were in the Scripture but the eyes were blind to their excellency. A heightening of affections by the increase of spiritual understanding may arise from seeing "the amiable and bright manifestations of the divine perfections, the excellency and sufficiency of Christ, the suitableness of the way of salvation by him and the spiritual glory of the precepts and promises of the Scripture." The sight of the glory of these gospel elements gives an intuitive certainty of their truthfulness. This Spirit-taught certainty Paul invokes when he labors in proclamation for the Gentiles that "their hearts may be encouraged, having been knit together in love, and attaining to all the wealth that comes from the full assurance of understanding, resulting in a true knowledge of God's mystery,

[7] Edwards, *Works*, 2:957.

[8] Edwards, *A Treatise Concerning Religious Affections* in *Works*, 1:285.

that is, Christ Himself." Edwards argued that this assurance of knowledge was not irrational or opposed to reason, but could only arise from the work of the Spirit changing the heart and opening the spiritual eyes to see the "fitness and suitableness of this way, the admirable wisdom of the contrivance, and the perfect answerableness to our necessitites of the provision that the gospel exhibits."[9] When this true sense of divine beauty is given, "the soul discerns the beauty of every part of the gospel scheme." Such assurance is essential experiential preparation for preaching.

Theoretical Preparation

Edwards would teach us that effective preaching involves substantial theoretical commitments prior to engagement in the practice. Among these would be an understanding of the character of the canon, an integrated grasp of orthodox doctrine, a cogent understanding of the relation between reason and affections, and the appropriate use of words and arguments in light of that relationship.

His view of the progress and coherence of biblical revelation clearly penetrates every aspect of his preaching. Though the quantity of revelation increased throughout the history of the Bible, its quality was of one piece and its purpose was always single. The same qualitative or essential content was present in the gospel in every biblical epoch; thus the gospel never altered from age to age and evangelical faith always exhibited the same character. Man's duty has always been to love God with a complacent love because of God's infinite loveliness and perfection; never was or is there a time, therefore, when man did is without obligation under the covenant of works.[10] Since the fall, it has always been necessary to find favor with this God only through the mediatorial sacrifice of the seed of the woman, the Son of God, forced on the conscience by implication earlier in revelation history and made infallibly clear under the new covenant.

The fullness, however, or quantity of the revelation has not always been the same but gradually has increased until the fulfillment of all in the incarnation, passion, and exaltation of Christ. An even greater display of it all remains to be revealed at the appearance of Christ; but it will still be of the same quality as that given in Eden. This mode of interpretation and development struck Edwards as "most beautiful and entertaining."

[9] Ibid., 291.

[10] Jonathan Edwards, *The Works of Jonathan Edwards: The "Miscellanies"* edited by Thomas A. Schafer (New Haven: Yale University Press, 1994), 362, 363 [#250]. This series will be denominated Yale *Works*.

The use of reason was not seen as antithetical to biblical exegesis but as demanded by it and harmonious with it. Even in his most extended discussions from reason, his guiding premises are derived from biblical texts. Edwards' "A Dissertation Concerning the End for which God Created the World" is an example of conscious and extended application of reason parallel to scriptural exegesis. Reason thus informed and sanctified must be pressed to demonstrate the reasonableness of Christian doctrine and that the God of the Bible is the only possible God.[11]

Given this, we must not miss Edwards' undiminished pessimism about unaided reason making any progress at all in deciding matters of infinite importance. Inherent tensions within reality would strictly forbid the possibility of reason moving toward unity and resolution. "The best reasoner in the world," Edwards asserts, "endeavouring to find out the causes of things, by the things themselves, might be led into the grossest errors and contradictions, and find himself, at the end, in extreme want of an instructor." Reason, uninstructed by revelation, affords not a single historical example of any person or people that "emerged from atheism or idolatry, into the knowledge or adoration of the one true God."[12]

Like his Puritan progenitors, all of his doctrine was application and all of his application was doctrine. Beyond mere cognition or a simple exchange of words of theology for words of morality, Edwards sought godly affections and true piety. This involved the kind of exposition of doctrine in which the hearer senses that his eternal well-being is bound up with the accurate and deeply felt appropriation of the truth.

A sermon must seek to overcome the "prejudices of nature." In a sermon on Genesis 19:14 Edwards remarks, "The reason why men no more regard warnings of future punishment, is because it don't seem real to them." And again from the same sermon, "This opposition of nature to divine truth causes that the being of God and another world don't seem real to them." The preacher must seek to combine rational conviction with sensory awakening to the truth, that is, the commitment and subjection of one's affections to the idea.[13]

In speaking of "God Glorified in Man's Dependence" Edwards urged his fellow ministers not only to "ascribe to him all the glory of redemption" but to "increase in a sensibleness of our great dependence on God" and to mortify "a self-dependent and self-righteous disposition."[14] Sin not

[11] Edwards, *Works*, 1:94-121.

[12] Edwards, *Works*, 2:476.

[13] Edwards, "Warnings of Future Punishment Don't Seem Real to the Wicked," Yale *Works*, 14, 198-212.

[14] Edwards *Works*, 2:7.

only has made us God's enemies but has made us insensible that we are such. This particular insensibility may be the most egregious of all, Man are "naturally God's enemies" but "few of them are sensible that they are so called; for they are not sensible that they wish God any hurt, or endeavor to do him any."[15]

Though the preacher must try in word and passion to reach the heart, only the Spirit of God does this finally. The truths that are revealed in the Word of God convey the content of the notion or the proposition, but "seeing the excellency of the doctrine" only comes "immediately from the Spirit of God." Saving faith always involves "such a conviction of the truths of religion" as comes "from a sense of their divine excellency."[16]

In his preaching, therefore, one observes close biblical exegesis, instruction in doctrine, extended analogies and images drawn from nature (for "there is an analogy between the divine constitution and disposition of things in the natural and in the spiritual world"), a firm commitment to Scriptural typology, and confident attempts both at the rational demonstration of divine truth and urgent appeals to believe divine truth.[17] Not only in content, but in verbal impression, Edwards sought to do all that was consistent with the infinite importance and infinite loveliness of the subject matter to establish a platform for "sensibility" in the heart of the unbeliever. "And that all natural or unregenerate men are indeed such," he proposed in 'Men Naturally God's Enemies,' "is what I shall endeavour now particularly to show."[18]

How Edwards Preached Doctrine

None would doubt that Edwards was full of doctrine and apt instruction and that from a literary standpoint his appeals to the conscience and heart were incomparably compelling. Some doubt exists, however, concerning how effective Edwards was in delivery. With contemporaries so naturally gifted as Whitefield, Tennent, and Davenport, Edwards probably would not be considered among the first rank of dramatic preachers. Granting that, I would still argue that Edwards was committed in theory to a delivery style commensurate with the importance and urgency of his subject.

[15] Edwards, "Men Naturally are God's enemies," *Works*, 2:130.
[16] Edwards *Works*, 2:14, 15.
[17] Edwards, *Works*, 2:957.
[18] Edwards, *Works*, 2:130.

Stomping and Shouting

In his Life of Jonathan Edwards, Samuel Hopkins observes,

> Tho' … he was want to read so considerable a part of what he delivered; yet he was far from thinking this the best way of preaching in general; and look'd upon his using his notes … [as] a Deficiency and Infirmity. And in the latter part of his Life was inclined to think it had been better, if he had never accustomed himself to use his Notes at all.[19]

In his profoundly provocative introduction to Edwards' New York sermons, Wilson Kimnach provides manuscript evidence that Edwards worked diligently to secure a style of preaching suitable for oratorical presentation. The manuscript prepared for the publication of his first printed sermon , "God Glorified in Man's Dependence," shows differences from the manuscript used in its delivery. This is even more strikingly true in comparing the different rescensions of "Sinners in the Hands of an Angry God." Sometimes these changes for publication indicate Edwards' awareness that he is much bettter in print than in person and that his peculiar field of influence was to be the printed page.[20] An argument could also be made that these differences indicate a style of delivery designed to arrest the attention of the auditory and enhance the power of vocal delivery. In

[19] Samuel Hopkins, *The Life and Character of the Late Reverend Mr. Jonathan Edwards, President of the College at New Jersey* (Boston, 1765) p. 48, cited in Wilson H. Kimnach, ed, *The Works of Jonathan Edwards: Sermons and Discourses, 1720-1723* (New Haven: Yale University Press, 1992), 10:122.

[20] Kimnach indulges in some creative surmising concerning Edwards's self-consciousness about the effectiveness of his written compared to his oral style. He writes:

> Unlike Whitefield, Edwards had always lived with a pen in hand, and he was more apt to be at his best when he had a paper, rather than a room, to fill with words. Perhaps it occurred to Edwards that if Whitefield had been called to lead the battle in the field, he himself was best suited to carrying it on in the closet-both in the present and in future times, both at home and throughout the world. Knowing what doctrine most needed to be asserted, and feeling that he had proved his mastery of the revival sermon as well as his understanding of the process of religious experience in a revival, Edwards set about the composition of the ideal revival sermon, one so immediate and powerful as to be a model for the present and future, and memorial to, and justification of, his own work and that of his cohorts in the neighborting town during that momentous season. Certainly, the sermon was not delivered as it stands in print, nor is it probable that Edwards would have wanted to deliver such a sermon if he could have; rather Edwards attempted a literary coup that uti-

addition, they show sensitivity to the demands of his immediate pastoral charge. The earlier sermons include marks in the manuscripts to remind Edwards of the necessity of liveliness and to create the opportunity for extemporaneity. Kimnach argues that the marks can only be explained "in terms of pulpit delivery."

> Apparently, Edwards desired to make his delivery more dynamic and flexible, and the "pick up line" was his compromise, for the time between reading and memoriter delivery. Placed before each sentence or phrase containing a major thought or illustration, the lines enabled Edwards to do at least two things. First, he could look up from the manuscript more easily without losing his place, or without as much careful review of the sermon just before preaching. Second, the lines would make his delivery more flexible in a formal sense. If he desired to speak extemporaneously within the context of the written sermon, or if he desired to leave out certain sections for some reason, the lines would provide so many "handles" subdividing the text of the written sermon by which he could adust the relationship between the sermon as written and the sermon as spoken.[21]

These observations about literary style serve only to underscore what Edwards himself argued about the manner of preaching. Edwards' mythical mildness and detachment in delivery was entered as a polemical device in the early nineteenth century in an effort to shame the perpetrators of the wildness of the camp meeting revival on the frontier. In his *Complete History of Connecticut, Civil and Ecclesiastical*, Benjamin Trumbull devoted well over one hundred pages to the New England awakening of the 18th century. He reports that Edwards calmly read the sermon and responded to his listeners' spiritual distress with a request that they be silent so that he could be heard. Such an example should shock the shameless Methodists into greater order and decorum.

Edwards' own testimony makes the construction of a different scenario possible. After delivering "Sinners in the Hands of an Angry God" in Enfield, Connecticut, in July 1741, Edwards heard of rising complaints about the supposed sensationalism of Awakening preaching. Supposedly, preachers raised the affections of the congregations too high. It was probably not only in defense of his friends Whitefield and Tennent and others that Edwards argued for the necessity of lively preaching. An insipid, dry kind of delivery utterly betrayed the magnitude of the issues at stake.

lized techniques and rested upon precedents already established in preparing for the press *God Glorified*, *A Divine and Supernatural Light*, and *Discourses on Various Important Subjects*. The product of his efforts is undoubtedly the most "literary" performance of his career. Ibid., 115.

[21] Kimnach, Yale *Works*, 10:107.

To those who complained, Edwards asked if the affections were raised by the truth and if the height of raising was justified by the importance of the subject. "If the subject by in its own nature worthy of very great affection," Edwards observed, "then speaking of it with very great affection is most agreeable to the nature of that subject, or is the truest representation of it, and therefore has most of a tendency to beget true ideas of it in the minds of those to whom the representation is made." For his own part, Edwards expressed the desire to "raise the affections of my hearers as high as possibly I can, provided that they are affected with nothing but truth, and with affections that are not disagreeable to the nature of the subject." To those under a sense of misery Edwards would offer no false comfort. "I am not afraid to tell sinners who are most sensible of their misery, that their case is indeed as miserable as they think it to be, and a thousand times more so; for this is the truth."[22]

Too many in his day focused narrowly on "extent of learning, strength of reason, and correctness of method and language," but for the most proportionate correctness of perception the people needed something else. "Men may abound in this sort of light, and have no heat," Edwards judged. "Our people do not so much need to have their heads stored, as to have their hearts touched."[23]

He argued that Scripture presents a different mode of preaching from that highly touted by the established clergy of his day. "Cry aloud, … lift up thy voice like a trumpet," the Lord told Ezekiel. "Smite with the hand, and stamp with thy foot," were further instructions, all with the intent of enforcing the infinite importance of the message. A large number of other scriptures command, exhort, and predict a crying out in gospel proclamation giving the clear impression that "a most affectionate and earnest manner of delivery, in many cases, becomes a preacher of God's word."[24]

Enforcing the Truth

Benjamin Breckenridge Warfield in his article, "Edwards and the New England Theology," contended that the "richest fruit" of studying Edwards came from his sermons.[25] A single Edwards sermon is a marvel of doctrinal instruction. Each is a study in incisive, elaborate, and detailed statements

[22] Edwards, *Works*, 1:391, 392.

[23] Ibid., 391.

[24] Ibid.

[25] Benjamin Breckenbridge Warfield, "Edwards and the New England Theology" in *The Works of Benjamin B. Warfield*, 10 vols. (Grand Rapids: Baker Book House, 1981), 9:523.

of doctrinal truth replete with all the necessary distinctions and historical allusions. Though much of the precision and fullness of argument was fashioned and inserted for publication, the manuscripts show that in his sermons he endeavored "clearly and distinctly to explain the doctrines of religion, and unravel the difficulties that attend them, and to confirm them with strength of reason and argumentation, and also to observe some easy and clear method … for the help of the understanding and memory."[26]

Doctrine, however, never stands abstracted from the claims of God and His truth on the human soul. He was, in Warfield's words, as "arresting and awakening as he was instructive." Edwards sermon instruction in doctrine always came with a view to grip the heart with conviction, confession, repentance, adoration or other responses implicit within the doctrine. Because he was himself filled with "the profoundest sense of the heinousness of sin," Edwards "set himself to arouse his hearers to some realization of the horror of their condition as objects of the divine displeasure, and of the incredible goodness of God in intervening for their salvation."

> Side by side with the most moving portrayal of God's love in Christ, and of the blessedness of communion with Him, he therefore set, with the most startling effect, equally vivid pictures of the dangers of unforgiven sin and the terrors of the lost estate, The effect of such preaching, delivered with the force of the sincerest conviction, was overwhelming.[27]

Illustrations of the methodology abound in Edwards' sermons on the full spectrum of systematic theology. The remainder of this article will illustrate Edwards' skill and power in this manner of preaching by isolating his focus on Christ in his preaching. Edwards' applicatory scheme in Christology, both the incarnation and the atonement, was to convince his hearers of the wisdom and the inviolability of the character of God while demonstrating the infinite approvedness, suitability, beauty, and perfection of Christ. These discussions, as pointed out by Warfield, have the frightful reality of human depravity as their foil.

The intensity of Edwards' focus on Christ is a result of his view of the eternal relation between the Father and the Son. The "infinite love" between Father and Son is the "highest excellency and peculiar glory of the Deity."[28] The incarnation and death of the Son clearly manifests the distinction between the persons of the Trinity and the infinite love that naturally, eternally, and immutably constitutes the divine being. This inter-

[26] Edwards, *Works*, 1:391.

[27] Warfield, 9:523f.

[28] Jonathan Edwards, Yale *Works*, 406 [#327a].

nal ontology is expressed in the covenant of redemption in which "the infinite love of the Father to the Son" is manifested "in that he would forgive an infinite debt, would be reconciled with and receive into his favor and to his enjoyment those that had rebelled against him and injured his infinite majesty, and in exalting of him to that high mediatorial glory." In the same events, "Christ showed his infinite love to the Father in his infinitely abasing himself for the vindicating of his authority and the honor of his majesty." To attain the divine intention to save men, "Christ infinitely laid out himself that the honor of God's majesty might be safe and that God's glory might be advanced."[29]

In accordance with this, Edwards called the incarnation "the most remarkable article of time that ever was or ever will be."[30] All the images of redemption prior to Christ, the millions of sacrifices and the endless acts of ritual worship availed nothing for redemption; nothing accomplished any of the purchase until the incarnation. "But as soon as Christ was incarnate, then the purchase began immediately without any delay." Just as nothing was done for the purchase prior to his incarnation, so nothing can be done after his resurrection, for Christ himself has made it complete. "Nor will there ever be anything more done to all eternity. But that very morn that the human nature of Christ ceased to remain under the power of death, the utmost farthing was paid of the price of the salvation of every one of the elect."[31]

Christ's capacity to save His people does not derive from His omnipotence but from His condescension. "For though Christ as God was infinitely sufficient for the work, yet viewed as to his being in an immediate capacity for it, it was needful that he should not only be God but man."[32] In order that he be both conceived and born without sin, the supernatural insemination of Mary's egg was a creative act of the Holy Spirit. Christ was formed "in the womb of the virgin, of the substance of her body" so that Jesus was "the immediate son of the woman, but not the immediate son of any male whatsoever." Having been so conceived, "his human nature was gradually perfected in the womb of the virgin in a way of natural progress, and so his birth was in the way of nature."[33]

[29] Ibid. Edwards described the Spirit's ontology within this same framework. Cf. #'s 330, 331, 334, 336, 341.

[30] Jonathan Edwards, *A History of the Work of Redemption*, transcribed and edited by John F. Wilson, Yale *Works* (New Haven: Yale University Press, 1989), 9:294.

[31] Ibid., 295.

[32] Ibid.

[33] Ibid., 297.

Christ's human nature capacitated Him as our Redeemer in three ways. First, the requirement of the law was to be fulfilled by man-the creature made in his image bearing moral responsibility to his creator. Its righteousness could be fulfilled by none but man; for the justification of a man, therefore, the obedience must be that of a man. Second, the condemnation of death for disobedience to the law also must be paid by man. If a man does not die under the curse of the law, then its demands are not met. Third, this present world, fallen into ruin, "should also be the stage of his redemption." Within fallen human society, within the "world that was his proper habitation," the deed of redemption must be done. "It was needful that he should come into this sinful, miserable, and undone world to restore and save it."[34]

Such a work as the full redemption of fallen sinners, however, could not be done by one that was man only. The deity of Christ also is essential to His work as redeemer. Speaking about the phrase, "the church of God, which he hath purchased with his own blood" (Acts 20:28), Edwards considered "whose blood it was that was shed," and pointed out that "it was the blood of God."[35] The blood-shedder was "a divine person, being not only man but God." This was the blood of "him before whom all the kings of the earth are as grasshoppers, and the blood of one that was the great Creator and King of Angels." This was the one by whom all things were made and who presently holds all things together (Colossians 1:16, 17).[36]

In order to impress on his hearers the exceeding depth of humiliation voluntarily embraced by Christ, Edwards moved alternately between the infinite glory of the pre-incarnate consciousness of the Son of God and the consciousness of the Son of man. He had been "from all eternity infintely happy" but descended "into a state of affliction and torment." No self-denial can compare with that for "the self-denial in it is greater in proportion to the degree of happiness he descends from."[37] In a delicately woven comparison in which historically defended biblical orthodoxy determined the character of the language, Edwards wrote, "When Christ was on earth, his human soul had communicated to it a kind of memory or consciousness of the happiness which his person had with God the Father before the world was, as far as a human mind was capable of it." With such a communication of His previous happiness to His human mind, "he had that

[34] Ibid., 296.

[35] Jonathan Edwards, "The Work of the Ministry is Saving Sinners," in Richard Bailey and Greg Wills, *The Salvation of Souls* (Wheaton: Corssway Books, 2002), 161.

[36] Ibid., 162.

[37] Ibid.

happiness which he had with his Father from eternity to compare with the extreme sufferings that there were set before his eyes, which makes the self-denial infinitely greater than it otherwise would have been."[38] Christ's deity meant also that He was "infinitely above any need of us," or indeed "any need of any thing." As God He was "self-sufficient" having His being as "necessary and underived" including those essential attributes of "happiness and glory." He was in a state of absolutely and infinitely perfect social interaction in the "infinitely blessed union and society of the persons of the Trinity," eternally "happy in one another."[39] As one person within this eternally happy, self-existent, self-sufficient deity, it is impossible for any of those for whom He died to requite Him for His work for them; He cannot be profited by us for He is "one on whom we are universally and absolutely dependent."[40]

In His deity, He also was preeminently the one who was held as an enemy by those for whom He died. All of His attributes are manifestations of holiness, and it is holiness in particular that sinners hate; hatred and enmity, therefore, amounts to a direct contrariety, a peculiar "opposition to his perfections," that is, "to his life and essence and very being." As omniscient and knowing perfectly that those for whom He died were "altogether unworthy, filthy, odious, ill deserving," He knew also, even though they did not perceive that He was God, that every aspect of every malicious word was aimed directly at Him, the One who, in many cases, was shedding His blood particularly for them.[41] While He cannot properly suffer in His deity, it was peculiarly His deity that so greatly increased the suffering, the condescension, and the humiliation of His humanity, that provided it with so great a trial and increased the amazing purity of His patience and holy submission to the Father's glory.

Without the deity of the redeemer, no redemption would be possible. His infinite dignity as God was necessary for the suffering of the infinite gloom and despair of hell. "As the infinite dignity of Christ's person answered the eternity of punishment, so his dying with a sense of this his dignity, and infinite happiness he had before the world was, answered the sense of the eternity of punishment in the damned." In His undergoing the divine wrath, "he lost infinitely more than than the damned lose, because his blessedness in the love and communion with God was infinitely greater."[42] His deity served not only to overmatch the despair of the damned,

[38] Ibid., 163.

[39] Ibid.

[40] Ibid., 164.

[41] Ibid., 166.

[42] *"Miscellanies"*, 371 [#265].

but served to give fitting honor to the Father. As the creature had failed to give the honor due to the commandment of God when presented on such easy terms, even so had the Son (the co-creator), of equal honor with the Father, given the honor due to the commandment of God, but upon infinitely harder terms. He achieved a righteousness, not only of the law of nature and the "mediatorial law," but of all the provisions of the covenant of redemption, that is, positive commands not naturally obligatory to Him, for the manifestation of His Father's glory and pleasure. All of this, He did in his unique person as Messiah, His humanity making it fitting for the righteousness to be regarded as ours, His divinity defining its value.

> And it was of the highest value, for everything he did was under the influence of his divinity, and derived its value from thence. It was the action of one who was God as well as man; hence it was of the highest value in God's account, and infinitely pleasing to him; capable of making an atonement to God, and being a propitiation for sin. Nothing was so displeasing and injurious to God, as the righteousness of the Mediator was pleasing and honourable to him.[43]

In addition, the union of sinners with Christ by faith serves to give them acceptance for "Christ was one that God infinitely loved." If Christ would undertake for them and work on their behalf, they would be accepted for His sake, for "his infinite love to Christ counterbalanced his infinite hatred of sin."[44] God's love for the Son apart from the moral necessities involved does not redeem sinners, but God's acceptance of His Son's punishment for theirs is due to the love shown by the Son for them, as fully compliant with the Father's own love for them. "How would the punishment inflicted on him satisfy?" He and they are united as head to members, husband to wife, so that "he who suffers is one with them." Edwards contemplated that such love from Christ to men could exist "that it will be all one whether Christ or men suffer the punishment." His loving them so well "as to be willing to undergo the punishment that they have deserved, as to be willing to stand in their stead in misery and torment, is to love them so well as that they may be looked upon as one."[45]

Such an undertaking of redemption by such an excellent person gives depth to the reality of human sin and the justness of punishment for sin. In "Unbelievers condemn the Glory and Excellence of Christ," Christ's attributes emerge in a brilliance that makes human depravity despicable and repulsive. Sinners neither love nor have honor for the glory and excellence

[43] *"Miscellanies"*, 378 [#278].

[44] Ibid., 164 [b].

[45] Ibid., 165.

of Christ.[46] They have no desires to enjoy or be conformed to the glorious beauty of Christ. Not only do they have no value for His glory, they are "enemies to him on that very account." His glorious perfections are the very ground of that "enmity and opposition" which enflames their hearts against Him.

> By being such a holy and excellent Saviour, he is contrary to your lusts and corruptions. If there were a Saviour offered to you that was agreeable to your corrupt nature, such a saviour you would accept. But Christ being a saviour of such purity, holiness, and divine perfection, this is the cause why you have no inclination to him, but are offended in him.[47]

Christ's incarnation shows the superiority of divine wisdom to created wisdom. A consistent theme of Edwards, this idea carries the day in "The Wisdom of God Displayed in the Way of Salvation." If indeed, the Son of God be substituted in the sinner's stead, then He becomes obligated to suffer the punishment deserved by the sinner. But how could one "who is essentially, unchangeably, and infinitely happy, suffer pain and torment?" And how could the object of God's infinitely dear love, suffer His wrath? Created wisdom would never have superceded these difficulties. "But divine wisdom hath found out a way, viz. by the incarnation of the Son of God." Though a great mystery, yea impossible to us, "it was no mystery to divine wisdom"[48]

Christ is a glorious person perfectly fit as Saviour. He has sufficient power, wisdom, merit, and love fully to bring us to God. By His death He has "fully satisfied justice, and appeased God's wrath, for all that shall believe in him." The wisdom of God through the incarnation releases from hell and also procures perfectly satisfying and everlasting happiness. In Christ's work, we may "behold and contemplate … the glorious perfections" of the one who is "infinitely lovely, the fountain of all good," see God "face to face" and dwell with Him in "his own house in heaven." Our union with God, through Christ, makes us married, members of His body, and of one spirit with Him. Christ's work, as a manifestation of God's wisdom bestows on His beloved ones great wealth, unending pleasure, all that is needed for body and soul so that no want ever will be sensed. Every spiritual work in us necessary to dwell in His presence forever has been

[46] Edwards, "Unbelievers Contemn the Glory and Excellency of Christ," *Works*, 2:62.

[47] Ibid., 2:62, 63.

[48] Edwards, "The Wisdom of God Displayed in the Way of Salvation," *Works*, 2:143.

purchased by Christ: repentance, faith, perseverance, sanctification, perfect holiness.

> Christ has purchased all, both objective and inherent good: not only a portion to be enjoyed by us; but all those inherent qualifications necessary to our enjoyment of it. He has purshased not only justification, but sanctification and glorification; both holiness and happiness.[49]

In spite of such rich provision, sinners "remain in the same miserable state and condition… in a famishing, perishing state." "You remain dead in trespasses and sins," Edwards warned, "under the dominion of Satan; in a condemned state, having the wrath of God abiding on you, and being daily exposed to the dreadful effects of it in hell." In light of such extreme pleasure on the one hand and danger on the other, Edwards pleads with his hearers, to "turn to God through Jesus Christ, be numbered among the disciples and faithful followers, and so be entitled to their privileges."[50]

The glory of Christ, in Edwards' presentation of His saving work, is perceived in an expanded way when seen in the light of the hell from which His people have been delivered. The preaching of hell highlights the power and gratuity which actuates saving grace. Edwards loved to exalt the wisdom and grace of God and the glory of Christ in redeeming the elect from punishment. In themselves, the elect are "miserable captives of sin and Satan, and under oligations to suffer eternal burnings." But Christ is above all evil in "what he did to procure redemption for us." And when the devils and "all their instruments" are cast into the lake of fire to their consummate and everlasting misery, the saints shall be delivered everlastingly from it. "The work of redemption," Edwards said, "is the most glorious of all God's works that are made known to us."

> And this is one thing wherein its glory eminently appears, that therein Christ appears so gloriously above Satan and all his instruments; above all guilt, all corruption, all affliction, above death,and above all evil.[51]

[49] Ibid., 145-47.
[50] Edwards, *Works*, 2:155.
[51] Edwards, *Works*, 2:216.

8

Exalting Christ by Seeing Him As the Scope of Scripture[1]

Richard Barcellos

Terms such as Christ-centered and Christocentric are used often in our day. But what do they mean? The older way of describing the concept these terms point to, the target or end to which all of the Bible tends, is encapsulated by the Latin phrase *scopus Scripturae* (i.e., the scope of the Scriptures). This concept gained confessional status in the Westminster Confession of Faith, the Savoy Declaration and the Second London Baptist Confession of Faith in 1.5, which, speaking of Holy Scripture, says, "… the scope of the whole (which is to give all glory to God)…" Reformation and post-Reformation Reformed theologians understood scope in two senses. It had a narrow sense—i.e., the scope of a given text or passage, its basic thrust. But it also had a wider sense—i.e., the target or bull's eye to which all of Scripture tends.[2] It is with this second sense that we will give our attention. The goal of this study is to identify the Reformed concept of

[1] This chapter first appeared in *Journal of the Institute of Reformed Baptist Studies* 2015 and is used with permission. English Bible references are from the New American Standard Bible Updated Edition.

[2] See the discussion in Richard A. Muller, *Post-Reformation Reformed Dogmatics: The Rise and Development of Reformed Orthodoxy, ca. 1520 to ca. 1725, Volume Two — Holy Scripture* (Grand Rapids: Baker Academic, 2003 [Second Edition]), 206–23, where he discusses these distinctions.

Christ as *scopus Scripturae* and to attempt to show that it is firmly grounded in Holy Scripture itself.

We will give some space to the historical-theological background to the issue and then use John Owen and Nehemiah Coxe as examples of two within the Reformed orthodox theological tradition who articulated Christ as the scope of Scripture. Once the historical section is completed, a brief attempt will be made to illustrate the same concept assumed in and being applied by the words of our Lord Jesus Christ and some of his early disciples. The chapter will conclude with a challenge to utilize this hermeneutical principle in our interpretations of Holy Scripture.

Before embarking upon our study, it is appropriate for me to mention Fred Malone and his impact upon me. Those who know Fred know that the subject matter of this chapter is vintage Malone. Fred not only loves his Savior but he has taught others, including me, how to interpret the Scriptures in a way that not only honors our Lord but grounds interpretive method in the Scriptures themselves. Several years ago I sat under Fred while he was teaching a course on hermeneutics. Those lectures impacted me tremendously. Fred has impacted me in another way. When I think of Fred I think of God's grace to us in Christ Jesus. The reason I do so is because Fred exemplifies what a Christian man and pastor ought to be. Fred is a gracious, careful and loving man, pastor and friend. I am thankful for Fred's example of being like our Lord and consider him a highly esteemed brother, mentor and friend.

Some Historical-Theological Background on *Scopus Scripturae*

The post-Reformation Reformed orthodox theologians embraced a whole-Bible hermeneutic. This manifested itself in their understanding of the scope of Scripture.[3] Though *scopus* could refer to the immediate pericope, it also had a wider, redemptive-historical focus. *Scopus*, in this latter sense, referred to the center or target of the entirety of canonical revelation or that to which the entire Bible points. For the seventeenth-century Reformed orthodox and their Reformed predecessors, Christ was the scope of Scripture, being the primary means through which God gets glory for Himself.

[3] For a helpful historically and theologically aware introduction to this concept see Muller, *PRRD*, II:206–23. Cf. also Martin I. Klauber, "Hermeneutics and the Doctrine of Scripture in Post-Reformation Reformed Thought," *Premise*, Volume II, Number 9 (October 19, 1995): 8ff. and James M. Renihan, "Theology on Target: The Scope of the Whole," *Reformed Baptist Theological Review*, II:2 (July 2005): 36–53.

The First Helvetic Confession of 1536 gave early Reformed expression to this concept in Article V, entitled the Scope of Scripture.[4] The first sentence of that article reads as follows:

> The position of this entire canonical scripture [or of the entire actual canonical scripture] is this, that God is kindhearted [or shows kindness] to the race of men, and that he has proclaimed [or demonstrated] this kindness [or goodwill] through Christ his Son.[5]

The title of Article V indicates that the concept of the scope of Scripture goes back to at least 1536 (among the Reformed) and that Christ was seen as the revelation of God's kindness to man. This is the position of the "entire canonical scripture."

In 1629, William Ames said, "The Old and New Testaments are reducible to these two primary heads. The Old promises Christ to come and the New testifies that He has come."[6] The concept of Christ as the scope of Scripture is clear in Ames.

Isaac Ambrose gives eloquent expression to the concept of Christ as the scope of Scripture in later Reformed thought:

> Keep still Jesus Christ in your eye, in the perusal of the Scriptures, as the end, scope and substance thereof: what are the whole Scriptures, but as it were the spiritual swaddling clothes of the holy child Jesus? 1. Christ is the truth and substance of all the types and shadows. 2. Christ is the substance and matter of the Covenant of Grace, and all administrations thereof; under the Old Testament Christ is veiled, under the New Covenant revealed. 3. Christ is the centre and meeting place of all the promises; for in him the promises of God are yea and Amen. 4. Christ is the thing signified, sealed and exhibited in the Sacraments of the Old and New Testament. 5. Scripture genealogies use to lead us on to the true line of Christ. 6. Scripture chronologies are to discover to us the times and seasons of Christ. 7. Scripture—laws are our schoolmasters to bring us to Christ, the moral by correcting, the ceremonial by directing. 8. Scripture—gospel is Christ's light, whereby we hear and follow him; Christ's cords of love, whereby we are drawn into sweet union and communion with him; yea it is the very power of God unto salvation unto all them

[4] Cf. Philip Schaff, *The Creeds of Christendom, Volume III: The Evangelical Protestant Creeds* (Grand Rapids: Baker Books, Reprinted 1996), 212.

[5] This English translation of the original Latin was provided by Amy Chifici, MA. Cf. Schaff, *Creeds, III*, 212–13, for the German and Latin originals.

[6] William Ames, *The Marrow of Theology* (Durham, NC: The Labyrinth Press, 1983), 202 (XXXVIII:5).

> that believe in Christ Jesus; and therefore think of Christ as the very substance, marrow, soul and scope of the whole Scriptures.[7]

Richard A. Muller, commenting on *scopus* in seventeenth-century Reformed thought, says:

> Christ...is the *fundamentum* and *scopus* of Scripture inasmuch as he is the redemptive center on which the entire *principium cognoscendi* or cognitive foundation rests and in whom it find [*sic*] its unity.[8]
>
> ...the theologies of the Reformers and of their orthodox successors consistently place Christ at the center of their discussions of redemption, consistently understand Christ as the center and fulfillment of divine revelation, and equally consistently understand the causality of salvation as grounded in the divine purpose. Christ, as Mediator, must be subordinate to the divine purpose, even as Christ, considered as God, is the one who with the Father and the Spirit decrees salvation before the foundation of the world: Causal theocentricity guarantees redemptive Christocentricity. Neither the doctrine of God nor the doctrine of Christ, however, serves as the basis of a neatly deduced system: The *loci* themselves arise out of the interpretation of Scripture.[9]

According to seventeenth-century Reformed orthodoxy, then, Christ is the target to which the whole of Scripture tends. This view of the scope of Scripture was closely related to their view of the relation between the testaments. The relationship between the testaments was seen in terms of a promise/fulfillment, figure/reality, type/anti-type motif.[10] Hence, "the New Testament may be understood as the interpreter of the Old."[11] Revelation was progressive, self-interpreting and consummated in the coming of Christ.

Here we must be careful not to infuse later, neo-orthodox concepts of Christocentricity into the historical data. The Christocentricity of the Reformed and Reformed orthodox was redemptive-historical and revela-

[7] Isaac Ambrose, *Works* (1701), 201, as quoted in J. I. Packer, *A Quest for Godliness: The Puritan Vision of the Christian Life* (Wheaton, IL: Crossway Books, 1990), 103.

[8] Richard A. Muller, "Calvin and the "Calvinists": Assessing Continuities and Discontinuities Between the Reformation and Orthodoxy," *Calvin Theological Journal* 30 (1995): 156.

[9] Muller, "Calvin and the "Calvinists"," 155.

[10] Muller, *PRRD*, II:492.

[11] Ibid.

tional, not principial, as Muller points out.[12] In other words, it came as a result of Scripture functioning as the *principium cognoscendi* (i.e., principle of knowing) or cognitive foundation of our knowledge of God. Scripture, and not Christ the Mediator, is a fundamental principle or foundation of theology in Reformed orthodoxy.[13] They started with Scripture and concluded Christocentricity in terms of the *historia salutis* (i.e., the history of salvation). Their Christocentricity is revelational and connected to redemption. As Muller says, such "Christocentrism consistently places Christ at the historical and at the soteriological center of the work of redemption."[14] But we must still be careful with the term Christocentricity. Christology must not be viewed as the central dogma of the Reformed orthodox. As Muller says:

> Such doctrines as God, predestination, Christ, and covenant provide not alternative but coordinate *foci* — and the presence of each and every one of these topics in theology rests not on a rational, deductive process but on their presence as *loci* in the exegetical or interpretive tradition of the church.[15]

The method of Reformed orthodoxy, then, started with the text of Scripture and its exegesis. Christ as the scope of Scripture was a conclusion from Scripture not a presupposition brought to Scripture. The Reformed orthodox Christocentric interpretation of the Bible was an attempt at applying a principle derived from the Bible and an application of *sola Scriptura* to the issue of hermeneutics. In other words, they recognized the authority of Scripture in the interpretation of Scripture. Christ as the scope of Scripture conditioned all subsequent interpretation, to varying degrees depending upon the interpreter.

John Owen on Christ as *Scopus Scripturae*

Christ as the scope of Scripture can be seen in Owen's writings in many places. In his work on the person of Christ, Owen says, "The *end* of the Word itself, is to instruct us in the knowledge of God in Christ."[16] A few pages later he goes on to say:

[12] Muller, "Calvin and the "Calvinists"," 157.

[13] Richard A. Muller, *Dictionary of Latin and Greek Theological Terms* (Grand Rapids: Baker Book House, 1985, Second printing, September 1986), 245–46.

[14] Muller, "Calvin and the "Calvinists"," 157.

[15] Ibid.

[16] John Owen, *The Works of John Owen*, 23 vols., ed. William H. Goold (Edinburgh: The Banner of Truth Trust, 1987 edition), 1:65. Emphasis added.

> Christ is the image of the invisible God, the express image of the person of the Father; and *the principal end* of the whole Scripture, especially of the Gospel, is to declare him so to be, and how he is so.[17]

In these two instances Owen uses the term 'end' in a technical sense. In other words, Christ is the scope of Scripture.

Christ as *scopus Scripturae* can be seen from an exegetical standpoint in Owen as well. Commenting on Genesis 3:15 as the first promise of the only means of delivery from the effects of sin—Christ, Owen says:

> This is the very foundation of the faith of the church; and if it be denied, nothing of the economy or dispensation of God towards it from the beginning can be understood. The whole doctrine and story of the Old Testament must be rejected as useless, and no foundation be left in the truth of God for the introduction of the New.[18]

Without a soteriological/Messianic interpretation of Genesis 3:15, in the mind of Owen, subsequent Scripture makes no sense. A Christocentric hermeneutic is foundational for proper biblical interpretation.

In his "Exercitations on the Epistle to the Hebrews," Owen says:

> The great design, whose lines are drawn in the face, and whose substance lies in the bowels of the Old Testament, and which is the spirit that enlivens the whole doctrine and story of it, the bond of union wherein all the parts do centre, without which they would be loose, scattered, and deformed heaps, is the bringing forth of the Messiah, the Saviour of the world. Without an apprehension of this design, and faith therein, neither can a letter of it be understood, nor can a rational man discover any important excellency in it. *Him* it promiseth, *him* it typifieth, *him* it teacheth and prophesieth about, him it calls all men to desire and expect.[19]

Owen, writing on the "Oneness of the Church" throughout redemptive history, argues that the object of saving faith throughout that history is "the *Seed* that was in the promise…"[20] In this brief exercitation, Owen argues that God first gave the promise of salvation to Adam based on Genesis 3:15. In fact, God's Church is founded "in the promise of the Messiah given to Adam."[21] Owen argues that all subsequent revelation serves to

[17] Owen, *Works*, 1:74. Emphasis added.

[18] Owen, *Works*, 1:120. Cf. Richard Daniels, *The Christology of John Owen* (Grand Rapids: Reformation Heritage Books, 2004), 230–61.

[19] Owen, *Works*, 17:370.

[20] Owen, *Works*, 17:121, 142.

[21] Owen, *Works*, 17:120.

unfold the first promise of the gospel to Adam. This promise is the first revelation of the covenant of grace.[22] Subsequent revelation unfolds the promise of the Redeemer and, in fact, depends upon it.

Returning to Owen's treatise on the person of Christ, he says:

> This principle is always to be retained in our minds in reading of the Scripture,—namely, that the revelation and doctrine of the person of Christ and his office, is the foundation whereon all other instructions of the prophets and apostles for the edification of the church are built, and whereinto they are resolved; as is declared, Eph. ii. 20–22. So our Lord Jesus Christ himself at large makes it manifest, Luke xxiv. 26, 27, 45, 46. Lay aside the consideration hereof, and the Scriptures are no such thing as they pretend unto,—namely, a revelation of the glory of God in the salvation of the church; nor are those of the Old Testament so at this day unto the Jews, who own not this principle, 2 Cor. iii. 13–16. There are, therefore, such revelations of the person and glory of Christ treasured up in the Scripture, from the beginning unto the end of it, as may exercise the faith and contemplation of believers in this world, and shall never, during this life, be fully discovered or understood; and in divine meditations of these revelations doth much of the life of faith consist.[23]

For Owen, "the revelation and doctrine of the person of Christ and his office" is the hermeneutical key providing interpretive cohesiveness for all of Scripture.

Owen's Christocentricity has been identified by several recent studies. In an article on John Owen dealing with his *Dissertation on Divine Justice* and subtitled "An Exercise in Christocentric Scholasticism," Carl Trueman says, "...his theology is, at heart, thoroughly christocentric."[24] Trueman entitles his conclusion "Owen's Christocentrism" and says:

> In asserting the necessity of Christ's sacrifice, Owen is presenting a Reformed theology that cannot displace the historical person of the mediator from the center of the drama of redemption. There can be no eternal justification based purely on the decree: Salvation is as surely linked to history as it is to eternity. It is those who predicate the necessity of incarnation and atonement solely on the decretive will of God who run the risk of marginalizing the historical person of Christ and undermining the importance of salvation history. In this context, Owen's scholasticism serves not to eclipse Christ but to place him at the center. Indeed, as is clear from his argument, if it was not for his Thomist understand-

[22] Owen, *Works*, 17:120.

[23] Owen, *Works*, 1:314–15.

[24] Carl R. Trueman, "John Owen's *Dissertation on Divine Justice*: An Exercise in Christocentric Scholasticism," *Calvin Theological Journal* 33 (1998): 97.

> ing of God's causal relationship to creation and his acceptance of the validity of the analogy of being, Owen would have no way of attacking his opponents' position. While it is true that his use of such arguments depends on assumptions that he does not justify, it is also true that any rejection of their validity renders his christocentrism epistemologically unsustainable. In the context of this dispute, at least, it is the rejection of natural theology, not its acceptance, that is the enemy of Christ-centered theology.[25]

In fact, Trueman goes so far as to say that on the issue of divine justice and the incarnation, Owen "is arguably not less christocentric than [his] opponents, including Calvin himself, but actually more so."[26]

Kelly M. Kapic says of John Owen:

> For Owen, all Scripture points to Christ, for "the revelation of the person of Christ and his office, is the foundation whereon all other instructions of the prophets and apostles for the edification of the church are built and whereinto they are resolved" (*Works*, 1:314–15). Owen attempts to avoid allowing the original context and meaning of any Old Testament passage to be lost; yet, he also maintains that a Christian exegete must ultimately find the passage's Christological meaning.[27]

Kapic argues that Owen's anthropology is formulated "in a christocentric pattern, pointing to Jesus Christ as the incarnate and true image of God."[28] Even the Sabbath is Christologically transformed by Christ, thus further displaying the Christocentricity of Owen's thought.[29]

Sebastian Rehnman says of Owen, "His theology has, for all its adherence to scholasticism and contrary to the argument of much modern scholarship on Reformed orthodoxy, a Christocentric and practical character."[30]

Richard W. Daniels shows that not only redemption, but creation and providence are Christocentric for Owen.[31] Commenting on the doctrines of creation and providence in Owen's thought, Daniels says, "It is difficult

[25] Trueman, "John Owen's *Dissertation on Divine Justice*," 103.

[26] Ibid.

[27] Kelly M. Kapic, "Owen, John (1616–1683)" in Donald K. McKim, editor, *Dictionary of Major Biblical Interpreters*, 797–98.

[28] Kelly M. Kapic, *Communion with God: The Divine and the Human in the Theology of John Owen* (Grand Rapids: Baker Academic, 2007), 65.

[29] Kapic, *Communion with God*, 212–14. Cf. Owen, *Works*, 18:263–460 for Owen's masterful treatment of a day of sacred rest.

[30] Sebastian Rehnman, *Divine Discourse: The Theological Methodology of John Owen* (Grand Rapids: Baker Academic, 2002), 181.

[31] Daniels, *Christology of Owen*, 178–93.

to conceive of a more Christocentric view of the purpose of God in creation than this, which subjects the creation and history of the universe to the manifestation of the glory of God in its renovation by the Son."[32] After acknowledging that Owen's Christocentricity was not unique among the English Puritans, he then says:

> In the development of this Christocentric theological system, however, Owen was unsurpassed. The lines which he traces from the doctrine of the person of Christ are bold, and long enough to reach every subject of doctrinal inquiry, showing that "by him, all things" [including all doctrinal truths] consist" (Col. 1:17).[33]

In Daniels' concluding words to his study on Owen's Christology, he gives this tribute to him:

> It is one thing to say Christian theology ought to be Christocentric, it is quite another to actually understand the entire spectrum of theological *loci* Christocentrically, or to articulate one's theology in a way that manifests this Christocentricity. Owen does this, as we have observed with regard to the knowledge of God, creation, providence, the redemption of man, the mediatorial kingdom, the church, and the Christian life.[34]

According to John Owen, Christ is the scope of Scripture.

Nehemiah Coxe on Christ as *Scopus Scripturae*

Nehemiah Coxe was a Particular Baptist.[35] He is important in our brief survey for at least two reasons: 1) Coxe was the co-editor (and most likely the "senior" editor) of the Particular Baptist Second London Confession of Faith (2LCF) and 2)[36] he authored *A Discourse of the Covenants*

[32] Daniels, *Christology of Owen*, 180.

[33] Daniels, *Christology of Owen*, 517.

[34] Daniels, *Christology of Owen*, 519.

[35] For a brief biography cf. James M. Renihan, "An Excellent and Judicious Divine: Nehemiah Coxe" in Nehemiah Coxe and John Owen, edited by Ronald D. Miller, James M. Renihan, and Francisco Orozco, *Covenant Theology From Adam to Christ* (Owensboro, KY: Reformed Baptist Academic Press, 2005), 7–24; James M. Renihan, "Confessing the Faith in 1644 and 1689" in *Reformed Baptist Theological Review*, III:1 (July 2006): 33ff.; and Michael A. G. Haykin, *Kiffin, Knollys and Keach* (Leeds, England: Reformation Today Trust, 1996) for an introduction to three key Particular Baptists of the seventeenth century.

[36] Cf. Renihan, "An Excellent and Judicious Divine: Nehemiah Coxe," 19–21 and Renihan, "Confessing the Faith in 1644 and 1689," 33ff.

that God made with men before the Law..., which is structured after the federal model, utilizes Reformed orthodox theological nomenclature, concepts, and sources and is semantically Reformed orthodox, except portions of his exposition of the Abrahamic covenant(s).[37]

In his *Discourse of the Covenants*, he says:

> 11. It was from this design of love and mercy that when the Lord God came to fallen man in the garden in the cool of the day, and found him filled with horror and shame in the consciousness of his own guilt, he did not execute the rigor of the law on him. Instead he held a treaty with him which issued in a discovery of grace. By this a door of hope was opened to him in the laying of a new foundation for his acceptance with God and walking well pleasing before him.
> 1. For in the sentence passed on the serpent (which principally involved the Devil whose instrument he had been in tempting man, and who probably was made to abide in his possession of the serpent until he had received this doom, Genesis 3:15) there was couched a blessed promise of redemption and salvation to man. This was to be worked out by the Son of God made of a woman, and so her seed, and man was to receive the promised salvation by faith and to hope in it. In this implied promise was laid the first foundation of the church after the fall of man which was to be raised up out of the ruins of the Devil's kingdom by the destruction of his work by Jesus Christ (1 John 3:8).[38]

Coxe adds later:

> From the first dawning of the blessed light of God's grace to poor sinners faintly displayed in the promise intimated in Genesis 3:15, the redeemed of the Lord were brought into a new relation to God, in and by Christ the promised seed, through faith in him as revealed in that promise.[39]

This understanding of Genesis 3:15 gives Coxe's work a Christocentric flavor from the beginning. In the first paragraph of his work, he says:

> The great interest of man's present peace and eternal happiness is most closely concerned in religion. And all true religion since the fall of man must be taught by divine revelation which God by diverse parts and after a diverse manner[40] has given out to his church. He caused this light

[37] Cf. Coxe and Owen, *Covenant Theology*, 71–140.

[38] Coxe and Owen, *Covenant Theology*, 55.

[39] Coxe and Owen, *Covenant Theology*, 59.

[40] Here he is dependent upon Beza. Cf. Coxe and Owen, *Covenant Theology*, 33, n. 1.

> gradually to increase until the whole mystery of his grace was perfectly revealed in and by Jesus Christ in whom are hid all the treasures of wisdom and knowledge. God, whose works were all known by him from the beginning, has in all ages disposed and ordered the revelation of his will to men, his transactions with them, and all the works of his holy providence toward them, with reference to the fullness of time and the gathering of all things to a head in Christ Jesus. So in all our search after the mind of God in the Holy Scriptures we are to manage our inquiries with reference to Christ. Therefore the best interpreter of the Old Testament is the Holy Spirit speaking to us in the new. There we have the clearest light of the knowledge of the glory of God shining on us in the face of Jesus Christ, by unveiling those counsels of love and grace that were hidden from former ages and generations.[41]

Not only is this statement programmatic for a Christocentric understanding of Scripture, it also reflects the fact that Coxe viewed special revelation as progressive. The 2LCF, 7.2 says, "This covenant is revealed in the Gospel; first of all to Adam in the promise of Salvation by the seed of the woman, and afterwards by farther steps, until the full discovery thereof was completed in the new Testament." Coxe saw Christ as the hermeneutical center and focal-point of the whole Bible (i.e., its *scopus*). Coxe understood redemptive revelation as progressive and Christocentric.

Christ, according to Nehemiah Coxe, is the scope of Scripture.

Our Lord Jesus on Christ as *Scopus Scripturae*

Commenting on the New Testament's view of the Old Testament as a witness to Christ, Richard Gaffin says:

> For Jesus and the New Testament writers the Old Testament is one large prophetic and promissory witness to Christ, a diverse but unified witness that centers in his sufferings and consequent glorification. The Old Testament has its overall integrity, its various parts cohere, in terms of this death-and-resurrection focus.
>
> Put negatively, the Old Testament does not have multiple and discordant trajectories of meaning, but only one. That is the unidirectional path that leads to Christ, however obscure and difficult it may be for us to follow that path at points along the way.[42]

[41] Coxe and Owen, *Covenant Theology*, 33.

[42] Richard B. Gaffin Jr., ""For Our Sakes Also": Christ in the Old Testament in the New Testament" in Robert L. Penny ed., *The Hope Fulfilled: Essays in Honor of O. Palmer Robertson* (Phillipsburg, NJ: P&R Publishing, 2008), 79.

Probably the most often cited words of our Lord to illustrate His view of Himself in terms of Scripture occur at the end of Luke's Gospel (Luke 24:25–27 and 44–47). But John's Gospel contains a severe rebuke by Jesus of some Jewish leaders which may illustrate Gaffin's point above even better than Luke 24. Listen to these words by Jesus:

> Do not think that I will accuse you before the Father; the one who accuses you is Moses, in whom you have set your hope. For if you believed Moses, you would believe Me, for he wrote about Me. But if you do not believe his writings, how will you believe My words? (John 5:45–47)

These words were spoken after Jesus had said, "You search the Scriptures because you think that in them you have eternal life; it is these that testify about Me" (John 5:39). The more inclusive statement (5:39) is followed by a specific statement concentrating on the writings of Moses (5:45–47). These texts indicate not only that Jesus viewed the Old Testament as a witness to Himself but that it functioned this way apart from His own self-witness. In other words, the Old Testament was a Messianic document on its own. Commenting on these texts, Gaffin says:

> Here Jesus affirms the relative overall clarity and independence of Moses (the Old Testament), as a witness to himself, distinct from his own teaching (and so, by implication, of the New Testament). So much is the case that this Old Testament witness to Christ serves as an adequate basis for the just condemnation of those rejecting him (verse 45), in itself and independent of his own self-witness.[43]

These words of Jesus illustrate that He viewed the Old Testament as a perspicuous witness to Himself. Read in conjunction with Luke 24:25–27 and 44–47, it seems clear that Jesus viewed the Old Testament as a whole finding its goal in Him.

I will assume that my readers agree that Jesus viewed Himself as the scope of Scripture and follow this brief discussion about our Lord with a look at some of His early disciples.

Some Early Disciples on Christ as *Scopus Scripturae*

The discussion in this section is very limited in scope. I will not attempt to look at the New Testament use of the Old Testament as proof of Christ as *scopus Scripturae*, though I think that could be done with much

[43] Gaffin, "For Our Sakes Also," 75.

profit and support my thesis. Instead, I want to look briefly at John 2. In this passage, we will note that some early disciples give evidence of the concept of Christ as the scope of Scripture. Here is John 2:13–22.

> [13] The Passover of the Jews was near, and Jesus went up to Jerusalem. [14] And He found in the temple those who were selling oxen and sheep and doves, and the money changers seated *at their tables*. [15] And He made a scourge of cords, and drove *them* all out of the temple, with the sheep and the oxen; and He poured out the coins of the money changers and overturned their tables; [16] and to those who were selling the doves He said, "Take these things away; stop making My Father's house a place of business." [17] His disciples remembered that it was written, "ZEAL FOR YOUR HOUSE WILL CONSUME ME." [18] The Jews then said to Him, "What sign do You show us as your authority for doing these things?" [19] Jesus answered them, "Destroy this temple, and in three days I will raise it up." [20] The Jews then said, "It took forty-six years to build this temple, and will You raise it up in three days?" [21] But He was speaking of the temple of His body. [22] So when He was raised from the dead, His disciples remembered that He said this; and they believed the Scripture and the word which Jesus had spoken.

We often think of hermeneutics, interpreting the Bible, as something we do. That is true. However, notice verses 17 and 22 of John 2. John 2:17 begins by saying, "His disciples remembered that it was written…" This is John's commentary on the thought process of some of Christ's disciples in the first century prior to the writing of the New Testament. The words "it was written" refer to what was already written at that time. John tells us what "was written" and what Old Testament text these disciples were thinking about by quoting Psalm 69:9, "ZEAL FOR YOUR HOUSE WILL CONSUME ME" (Cf. John 15:25 and 19:28 where Jesus applies this Psalm to Himself.). The disciples were interpreting the Old Testament (independent of the New Testament) during the life of our Lord. John's comment informs us that they started connecting the dots from the Psalms to Jesus while our Lord was on the earth. In other words, their minds were making hermeneutical moves while Christ's zeal for God's temple, His Father's house, was being manifested. As the Word who became flesh manifested Himself among men, those who believed in Him began to interpret Scripture in light of Him (or Him in light of Scripture!).

John 2:22 says, "So when He was raised from the dead, His disciples remembered that He said this; and they believed the Scripture and the word which Jesus had spoken." Note first the time when "His disciples remembered that He said this," that is, "when He was raised from the dead…" The resurrection, among other things, triggered the memories of these disciples. Note second to what "this" of "He said this" refers. It refers to what Jesus said as recorded in verse 19, where we read, "Destroy this temple, and in three days I will raise it up." Note third John's comment about what Jesus said. "But He was speaking of the temple of His body" (John 2:21). Note fourth that "they believed the Scripture and the word which Jesus had spoken" (John 2:22). The "Scripture and the word which Jesus had spoken" are not the same thing. The "word which Jesus had spoken" is recorded in John 2:19. The Scripture must refer to the Old Testament. The disciples were interpreting the Old Testament, not only during the ministry of our Lord, but also after His resurrection and prior to the writing of the New Testament (and surely during and after its writing). The resurrection became an interpretive event through which the early disciples "believed the Scripture and the word which Jesus had spoken." Just as they began connecting the dots during our Lord's life-unto-death sufferings (John 2:17), so they continued to connect the dots when he entered into His glory, His resurrection (John 2:22; Cf. John 12:16 for the same phenomenon with reference to connecting the dots between our Lord and the book of Zechariah.).

Though it is true that we interpret the Bible in our day, it is also true that the early Christians interpreted the Bible of their day—i.e., the Old Testament. Some of their interpretations made it into the New Testament, as illustrated above. Though this does not mean that all of their personal interpretations of the Old Testament reflected the divine intent of the ancient text, it does mean that their interpretations recorded in the New Testament and affirmed by the authors of the New Testament (e.g., John) are infallible interpretations,[44] reflecting the intention of God who first gave the text. This is so because "All Scripture [i.e., Old and New Testament] is inspired by God" (2 Timothy 3:16) and inspiration implies infallibility.

It is obvious that interpreters of Scripture today have an advantage over the first-century interpreters mentioned above. We have God's own interpretation of the historical sufferings and glory of Christ—our New Testaments. But I think there is a good lesson for us to learn from the discussion above. When our Lord Jesus was on this earth, the Spirit of God was causing the disciples of Christ to recall texts of Scripture due to the presence and ministry of Christ. What their musings on the Old Testament contained in the New Testament show us is that the Old Testament points to Christ. The early disciples saw this more and more as they contemplated our Lord and the Old Testament. The inspired documents of the New Testament confirm that they were right. Not only was

[44] This is not the same as claiming they were infallible interpreters.

Jesus Christ the promised One, He was that to which the Old Testament pointed. The early disciples did not reinterpret the Old Testament in light of Christ; they interpreted it as pointing to Christ. And our New Testament is God's confirmation that they were right to do so. If it was right for them to do so, then it is right for us to do the same. The Old Testament is not about Christ simply because the New Testament says so. It is about Christ because that was God's intention from the beginning. This is how the early Christians (and our Lord) read the Old Testament. This is how we ought to read it as well.

Concluding Thoughts on Christ as *Scopus Scripturae*

An attempt has been made to display that Christ as *scopus Scripturae* is a concept attested in the Reformed tradition. It is present in Reformation and post-Reformation Reformed literature. It is clearly illustrated in John Owen and Nehemiah Coxe. Christ as *scopus Scripturae*, according to the Reformed, is a result of the exegesis of Scripture and the resultant identity of the target of all its parts.

We have also sought to display that this concept predates the Reformed confessions and theologians. Indeed, what has been argued is that it was the view of our Lord Himself. Our Lord Jesus Christ understood His identity and vocation in light of our Old Testament and He saw it as a collective arrow pointing to Him in His sufferings and glory (Luke 24:25–27, 44–47). It is clear from the writings of the New Testament that the Apostles utilized the same hermeneutical principles used by our Lord (cf. Luke 24:25–27, 44–47 and John 5:39, 45–47 with Matthew 2:13–15; Acts 2:14–36; 3:17–26; 9:1–19;[45] 15:12–19; 26:22–23; Romans 5:14; 1 Peter 1:10–12). It is also clear that the principles which led to the interpretive conclusion that Christ is the scope of the Old Testament predate our Lord. The principles that He utilized were not invented in the first century. They were applied in the first century though predating it.

What is more interesting, maybe even perplexing to some, is that Jesus and the authors of the New Testament give ample testimony that the authors of the Old Testament possessed a Messianic consciousness reflected in their writings (e.g., Luke 24:25–27, 44–47; John 5:39, 45–47; Acts 2:30–31; 3:21–26; 26:22–23; 1 Peter 1:10–12). In other words, the New Testament sees the Old Testament as a Messianic document on its own terms. This is the divine commentary on the scope of the Old Testa-

[45] Cf. Seyoon Kim, *The Origin of Paul's Gospel* (1981; reprint, Eugene, OR: Wipf and Stock Publishers, 2007), where Kim argues that Paul's hermeneutic was permanently altered on the Damascus road.

ment. James Hamilton claims, "... from start to finish, the OT is a messianic document, written from a messianic perspective, to sustain a messianic hope."[46] I think he is right. He goes on to offer two caveats to this claim.

> First, I wish to make plain the inductive steps that led to this hypothesis. We inductively observe that there is much messianic speculation in second temple Judaism (both in the NT and the intertestamental literature). We add to this the observation that this speculation is anchored in the OT. We then set aside the possibility that ancient people were stupid, which seems to be an implicit assumption of a good deal of modern scholarship, and we seek a hypothesis that explains the data. Since the authors of these texts are presumably seeking to be persuasive to their contemporaries (see, e.g., John 20:31), it seems to me unlikely that their contemporaries would grant the imposition of new meanings onto these texts. One hypothesis that explains the fact that "Early Christians, rabbinic sources, and the sectarians at Qumran cite the same biblical texts in their portrayals of the royal messiah" (J. J. M. Roberts, "The Old Testament's Contribution to Messianic Expectations," in *The Messiah* [ed. J. H. Charlesworth; Minneapolis: Fortress, 1992], 41 n. 2) is that the OT is a messianic document, written from a messianic perspective, to sustain a messianic hope. This would mean that these disparate groups are not *imposing* a messianic interpretation on these texts but rightly interpreting them. This is not the only available hypothesis, but it seems to me to be the most convincing. I agree with John Sailhamer, who writes, "I believe the messianic thrust of the OT was the *whole* reason the books of the Hebrew Bible were written. In other words, the Hebrew Bible was not written as the national literature of Israel. It probably also was not written to the nation of Israel as such. It was rather written, in my opinion, as the expression of the deep-seated messianic hope of a small group of faithful prophets and their followers" ("The Messiah and the Hebrew Bible," *Journal of the Evangelical Theological Society* 44 [2001]: 23). The variations in messianic expectation show that the developing portrait of the coming Messiah was not crystal clear, but the pervasive expectation supports the hypothesis.
>
> My second caveat is that though I am calling this "messianic," I do recognize that this term seems not to receive a technical meaning until the second temple period. But as Rose has written, "It is a matter of confusing language and thought . . . to conclude on this basis that one can speak of messianic expectations properly only after a particular word was used to refer to the person at the center of these expectations" (W. H. Rose, "Messiah," in *Dictionary of the Old Testament: Pentateuch* [Downers

[46] James Hamilton, "The Skull Crushing Seed of the Woman: Inner-Biblical Interpretation of Genesis 3:15," *The Southern Baptist Journal of Theology* 10.2 (2006): 30.

Grove: InterVarsity, 2003], 566). Cf. also John J. Collins, *The Scepter and the Star: The Messiahs of the Dead Sea Scrolls and Other Ancient Literature* (New York: Doubleday, 1995), 11–12.[47]

What Hamilton says of the Old Testament is agreed upon by all evangelicals concerning the New Testament. No one denies that the New Testament's scope is the coming, ministry, sufferings and glory of Christ, along with the implications of these events drawn out and applied to the life of the early church. But our study presents a challenge to view the entirety of Scripture as finding its target or scope as our Lord Jesus Christ. Though it is true that neither Testament was intended by God to stand on its own, it is also true that the Old Testament, while it was on its own, witnessed to Christ, contained the saving knowledge of Christ, and produced believers in Christ. The same could be said of the New Testament, except that it never stood on its own. Since the documents that contained the promise of Christ had as its scope the person and office of the Messiah, then certainly the documents that contain the fulfillment in Christ do the same. Christ, then, is the target, the goal, the scope of the Scriptures, which give all glory to God.

[47] Hamilton, "The Skull Crushing Seed of the Woman," 44, n.5.

Part Three

Exalting Christ in the Church

9

Exalting Christ by Shepherding the Flock

Tom Ascol

The renewed call for Christ-centered preaching in recent years is a welcome return to the emphasis of the New Testament. Both in their sermons and in their letters the apostles demonstrate the importance of preaching Christ. As Luke puts it, "Every day, in the temple and from house to house, they kept right on teaching and preaching Jesus as the Christ" (Acts 5:42, NASB).

In addition to preaching Christ the apostles also oriented their lives and ministries around Him. Paul's famous declaration, "For to me, to live is Christ and to die is gain" (Philippians 1:21), reveals his sense of self-identity that shaped everything he did. When defending his ministry against the attacks of supposed "super-apostles" he reminds the Corinthians of the centrality of Christ not only for his preaching but for the way that he served them. "For what we proclaim is not ourselves, but Jesus Christ as Lord, with ourselves as your servants for Jesus' sake" (2 Corinthians 4:5).

That is what a pastor is—a servant of God's people for Jesus' sake. Understanding and embracing that role enables a man to exalt Christ through pastoral ministry. Fred Malone exemplifies this ideal as well as any pastor I know. He was my first and has been my best teacher of Christ-centered ministry.

St. Patrick was born in the late fourth century in Britain. At the age of sixteen he was captured by Irish pirates and enslaved for six years. When he finally escaped and made it back home he felt the Lord calling him into the priesthood and, ultimately, at age forty-five, back to Ireland as a missionary. Once, when the High King was demanding that all Ireland join in the worship of the sun god, Patrick openly and intentionally refused to comply. The king summoned him to appear in the royal court to answer for his crime. As Patrick made that journey he began to chant a hymn along the way. It has been handed down to us by the name, "St. Patrick's breastplate," and it includes these lines:

> Christ beside me
> Christ before me
> Christ behind me
> Christ within me
> Christ beneath me
> Christ above me
> Christ to the right of me
> Christ to the left of me
> Christ in my lying, my sitting, my rising
> Christ in heart of all who know me
> Christ on tongue of all who meet me;
> Christ in eye of all who see me;
> Christ in ear of all who hear me.

Legend has it that when Patrick marched by the king chanting this song, the king was blinded to him and reported that all he saw was a herd of deer walking by.[1] Laying aside the legend, the song has much to commend it.

Patrick and those traveling with him knew they were walking through dangerous territory. In fact, he had been warned that an ambush awaited them on the way. So he sang. And he taught others to sing, calling on God for protection; calling to mind particularly the all sufficiency, all encompassing provision and protection of Jesus Christ for his people.

Such big thoughts about Jesus Christ are exactly what believers need to sustain us day by day. This is true for every Christian, and especially so for those of us who are called to serve our Lord as leaders in His church.

In the last letter Paul wrote to his young colleague Timothy, who was pastoring the church in Ephesus, the elderly apostle said this in chapter 2, verse 8: "Remember Jesus Christ, risen from the dead, offspring of David, as preached in my gospel" (NASB). That simple admonition, if heeded, will shape our lives and ministries.

[1] Don Schwager, "Deer's Cry or St. Patrick's Breastplate." www.rc.net/wcc/ireland. 2001. Accessed May 27, 2016.

We need to remember Jesus Christ—to think regularly and deeply about who He is, what He has done and what difference that makes in our lives. We tend to forget, and when we forget, we go astray spiritually. When we forget Christ, we easily give into sin. When we forget Christ, we do not resist temptation. When we forget Christ, we become focused on ourselves. When we forget Christ, we believe things that are not true, like: "Nobody cares about me; no one understands my situation; I deserve better than this; if only he/she would change, my life would be complete; if I just had more money, all would be well; if I could just get married, I would be happy; if I hadn't messed up so badly back then, I wouldn't be so miserable now, etc. etc."

The one, overarching reason that we live such self-absorbed, self-centered lives is because we forget Jesus Christ. We need larger visions, bigger thoughts of Jesus. We need to see our lives in light of who He is for us. We need to recognize in fresh ways what it means to be a disciple of Jesus.

If this is true of all Christians in general, it is true of every pastor in particular. Paul understands this and so he does not hesitate to admonish his experienced, young colleague in the ministry to "remember Jesus Christ." When a pastor heeds this admonition then Christ will shape the character of his ministry. As that happens then Christ will inevitably be exalted through pastoral ministry.

Jesus affects everything about us—not only what we believe and consequently what we proclaim to others so that they will believe—but also how we live, how we relate and how we minister in his Name. The Apostle Paul understood this and exemplified it. James Stalker aptly notes, "After his conversion the whole life of St. Paul was comprehended in one word; and this word was Christ."[2]

New Testament scholar, Stewart, also described Paul as a "Christ-apprehended, Christ-filled man."[3] This is made apparent in the letters we have from him in the New Testament. "What meets us in the epistles," Stewart says, "is not a man creating a new religion, or even giving a new direction to one already existing: it is simply the Gospel of Jesus in action, the original, authentic Gospel first changing a man's life, and thereafter moulding all his thought."[4]

"The Gospel of Jesus Christ in action." Jesus Christ changed Paul. He changed his thinking, changed the way he understood the world and the

[2] James Stalker, *The Preacher and His Morals* (New York: Hunt & Eaton, 1891; reprint ed., Charleston, SC: Nabu Press, 2010), 191.

[3] James Stewart, *A Man in Christ* (New York: Harper & Row, 1935), 24.

[4] Ibid., 19.

way he related to people. So when Paul gave himself to the work of gospel ministry both his message and his manner of communicating it were shaped by Jesus Christ. Consequently, not only his work as an apostle but also his whole identity reflected his love for and esteem of Jesus.

In this Paul is a model for all pastors to emulate. Christ is not only the content of what we proclaim. His life, death and resurrection also shape the manner of our ministry. There is a necessary connection between what we profess and how we live. We believe and preach Christ and we are to live according to Christ.

The church at Corinth was filled with misunderstanding about this. They had learned the gospel of Jesus Christ and could no doubt recite the important facts about his life, death and resurrection. But there were huge disconnects between their belief in Christ and their living according to Christ. So when Paul writes to instruct and correct them he says in 1 Corinthians 4:17, "That is why I sent you Timothy, my beloved and faithful child in the Lord, to remind you of my ways in Christ, as I teach them everywhere in every church."

"My ways in Christ." Paul is not referring to his doctrine, but about his ministry. He wants Timothy to remind them about the character of his life, the manner of his ministry, which he describes as "my ways in Christ." These are the very ways of living that he taught "everywhere in every church."

Paul and the other apostles viewed life in terms of who Jesus Christ is and what He has done for us and they conducted their ministries accordingly. By doing so, they point the way forward for all pastoral ministry to exalt Christ. There are at least four ways that we see this operating in his New Testament letters.

Lordship

The lordship of Christ establishes the nature of pastoral ministry. The New Testament is filled with affirmations of Christ's lordship. Some of these are clear ascriptions of his deity, as we find in Romans 10:13, "For everyone who calls on the name of the Lord will be saved." In this verse Paul is quoting Joel 2:32 where Yahweh, the true God, is in mind. Other passages, such as Philippians 2:10–11, highlight Jesus' sovereign authority as Lord. "So that at the name of Jesus every knee should bow, in heaven and on earth and under the earth, and every tongue confess that Jesus Christ is Lord, to the glory of God the Father."

Pastor as Slave

How should a pastor view himself in response to the lordship of Christ? As a slave. At least, that is the way the Apostle Paul saw himself in relationship to the Lord. *Doulos* (servant, bondservant, slave) is one of Paul's most graphic and frequently used self-designations for himself and his apostolic team (see Philippians 1:1; Titus 1:1; Romans 1:1; Galatians 1:10; Colossians 4:12).

In a culture where pastors often aspire to (and sometimes attain) the status of celebrities the idea of being a *doulos* sounds foreign. As Lenski rightly notes, however, "many who today love to be called 'church workers' should learn what Paul means by 'slaves', namely, men who in all their work have no will of their own but only their Owner's will and Word."[5]

Submitting to Jesus Christ as Lord means seeing yourself as a slave who looks to Him as your master. This means that His desire is your duty. Your life is not your own, but you see yourself having been purchased by Christ and now you belong to Him to live and carry out your responsibilities according to His will.

Paul makes this connection in his encouragement to those first century Christians who actually were slaves of other men. In Ephesians 6:5–6, he writes, "Bondservants, obey your earthly masters with fear and trembling, with a sincere heart, as you would Christ, not by the way of eye-service, as people-pleasers, but as bondservants of Christ, doing the will of God from the heart, …"

This admonition forbids me from justifying a sinful attitude toward my job or my employer because I do not like the way I have been treated. Such attitudes can easily become the default response of employees toward employers.

Yet, if we remember that Christ is our Lord and we are His slaves, we will be reminded to honor Him in the way we serve our employers. Paul employs the master-slave relationship when he admonishes pastors about the way they are to deal with difficult, cantankerous people. He writes to Timothy in 2 Timothy 2:24–26, "And the Lord's servant must not be quarrelsome but kind to everyone, able to teach, patiently enduring evil, correcting his opponents with gentleness. God may perhaps grant them repentance leading to a knowledge of the truth, and they may come to their senses and escape from the snare of the devil, after being captured by him to do his will."

[5] Cited in Geoffrey B. Wilson, *Philippians* (Edinburgh: Banner of Truth Trust, 1983), 16.

How inappropriate for a slave to be harsh, impatient and arrogant when dealing with other people! As a pastor remembers this about his relationship to Christ, he will be strengthened to deal humbly with people and thereby display the greatness of Christ through his personal ministry.

Pastor as Ambassador

The lordship of Jesus Christ not only calls a pastor to see himself as a slave, but also to acknowledge that his ministry is that of an ambassador. An ambassador is someone who represents the interests of another. When Paul wrote letters to churches while being imprisoned he described himself as an "ambassador in chains" for the gospel of Jesus. Similarly, as he considered his stewardship by virtue of being entrusted with the message of reconciliation he wrote, "Therefore, we are ambassadors for Christ, God making his appeal through us. We implore you on behalf of Christ, be reconciled to God" (2 Corinthians 5:20).

All Christians, but especially ministers of the gospel, represent Jesus Christ to the world. A pastor does not minister in his own name or for his own sake, but in the name and for the sake of Jesus Christ. It is not just our message but also our very lives that should display His honor. People judge Him by the way pastors conduct themselves—and rightly so, because pastors are His ambassadors.

Because Christ is Lord, every aspect of our lives must be brought under the scrutiny of His revealed will. We live both for Him and before Him. One day we will give an account to Him as His servants and ambassadors. Paul invokes this weighty accountability in the charge he gives to Timothy in 2 Timothy 4:1–2, "I charge you in the presence of God and of Christ Jesus, who is to judge the living and the dead, and by his appearing and his kingdom: preach the word; be ready in season and out of season; reprove, rebuke and exhort, with complete patience and teaching."

This is how a pastor must carry out his ministry day by day-always aware that he is under the watchful eye of Jesus Christ who is our Lord and Judge. As His ambassadors, we represent Him in this world. As His slaves, we are responsible to carry out His will on earth. When this self-understanding is embraced and these identities characterize our ministries, then Christ will be exalted in our work as pastors.

Sufficiency

Not only does the lordship of Christ establish the nature of pastoral ministry, the sufficiency of Christ liberates us from self-consciousness in ministry.

When Paul corrects the disunity in the church at Corinth he reminds them in 1 Corinthians 3:21 that "all things are yours." Because they have Christ, they have everything. In Ephesians 1:3 we read that God "has blessed us in Christ with every spiritual blessing in the heavenly places." Those who belong to Christ lack nothing. This is why Paul could so confidently say to the Philippians in 4:19, "And my God will supply every need of yours according to his riches in glory by Christ Jesus." Everything we need is found in Jesus Christ. Paul makes the point again in 1 Corinthians 1:30–31, "And because of Him you are in Christ Jesus, who became to us wisdom from God, righteousness and sanctification and redemption, so that, as it is written, 'Let the one who boasts, boast in the Lord.'"

To see this, believe it and remember it is to be delivered from the pride of self-sufficiency and the despair of inadequacy. Consider what D. Martyn Lloyd-Jones has to say about this:

> In the gospel, I find satisfaction to my mind that I find nowhere else. It is here alone I feel I am in direct contact with ultimate realities and absolute truth. There is no problem of my life but that the gospel deals with it and answers it. I find intellectual rest and answer to all my questions.
>
> And thank God, my heart and my desires are also satisfied. I find complete satisfaction in Christ. There is no desire, there is nothing that my heart can crave for but He can more than satisfy. All the restlessness of desire is quelled by Him as He breathes his peace into my troubles and problems and restlessness....[6]

Finding our sufficiency in Jesus Christ liberates us from self-sufficiency that tempts us to manipulate others. This danger seems always to be lurking at the door of those who are trying to serve the Lord in this world. There are two sources from which this temptation arises. First, it can stem from coveting that which is not yours. Paul attaches this sin to those false teachers who supposed that "godliness is a means of great gain" (1 Timothy 6:5). He makes sure to distance himself from such desires both to the elders of Ephesus and the church at Corinth. "I coveted no one's silver or gold or apparel" (Acts 20:33). "I seek not what is yours but you" (2 Corinthians 12:14).

A second source of the temptation to self-sufficiency is found in the mistaken notion that the kingdom of God can be advanced through carnal means. When Jews demanded a sign and Gentiles were seeking worldly wisdom, Paul resisted giving into their felt needs knowing that to do so

[6] D. Martyn Lloyd-Jones, *The Heart of the Gospel* (Wheaton, IL: Crossway, 1991), 165.

would be to compromise the gospel. Christ sent him, he said, "to preach the gospel, not with words of eloquent wisdom, lest the cross of Christ be emptied of its power" (1 Corinthians 1:17).

In fact, when his apostolic authority and integrity was challenged by the so-called "super-apostles" who had infiltrated Corinth he clearly distanced himself and his ministry from those who employed carnal methods to advance God's Word. "But thanks be to God, who in Christ always leads us in triumphal procession, and through us spreads the fragrance of the knowledge of him everywhere. For we are the aroma of Christ to God among those who are being saved and among those who are perishing. To one a fragrance from death to death, to the other a fragrance from life to life. Who is sufficient for these things? For we are not, like so many, peddlers of God's word, but as men of sincerity, as commissioned by God, in the sight of God we speak in Christ" (2 Corinthians 2:14–17). Paul knew he was not sufficient in himself and he knew that being in Christ was enough for him to be "always" led in triumph as he ministered the gospel.

Seeing the complete adequacy of Jesus Christ delivers us from having to manipulate others in order to get what we want—no matter how noble or ignoble our goals. He is enough for the soul that has learned to be satisfied by him. And when I am living in such satisfaction, I do not have to maneuver and plot in order to get other people to do what I want. Why? Because I have Jesus! And having him, I have all my soul could desire.

Furthermore, as I grasp the sufficiency of Christ in the gospel I am increasingly set free from having to pressure anyone to do God's will. I do not have to use trickery or craftiness to see His kingdom expand. I simply have to preach Jesus Christ crucified, in the power of His Spirit, confident that as the Lord blesses that message, knees will bow and wills will bend and lives will be transformed by His grace and power alone. All praise will rightly go to Him because all of the work will be His.

Not only does the sufficiency of Christ set us free from self-sufficiency that tempts us to manipulate, it also liberates us from self-preservation that tempts us to fear. Self-preservation is a natural instinct. Paul makes this point when he comments that "no one ever hated his own flesh" (Ephesians 5:29). God has wired us with a sense of inherent self-preservation. But that sense can easily morph into a crippling fear that always looks for the safe and easy path even at the expense of what is good and right. A deep confidence in the sufficiency of Christ delivers from this.

We see this confidence in Christ working in Paul's life. In his last conversation with elders from Ephesus he said: "And now, behold, I am going to Jerusalem, constrained by the Spirit, not knowing what will happen to me there, except that the Holy Spirit testifies to me in every city that imprisonment and afflictions await me. But I do not account my life of any value nor as precious to myself, if only I may finish my course and the ministry that I received from the Lord Jesus, to testify to the gospel of the grace of God" (Acts 20:22–24). This same attitude is displayed a little later as he was on his way to Jerusalem. When the prophet, Agabus, prophesied that Paul would be arrested and persecuted by Jewish leaders, Luke and others began to beg him not to continue on his journey. How did he respond? Not out of fear. "Then Paul answered, 'What are you doing, weeping and breaking my heart? For I am ready not only to be imprisoned but even to die in Jerusalem for the name of the Lord Jesus'" (Acts 21:13).

What did Paul see that enabled him to live and minister this way? I believe that 1 Corinthians 15 holds the key that answers that question. In that chapter he persuasively argues that the resurrected Christ is all we need. By his life, death and resurrection Jesus will conquer all our enemies—including the last one, death. Confidence in that victorious work of Christ is what enabled Paul to "die every day" (v. 31) and to risk his life standing against those who were like "wild beasts" (v. 32). He had Christ, and that was enough.

This explains the point he makes in Philippians 1:21 that "to die is gain." If Christ is your life, then death simply means more of Christ. To see this, believe it and remember it sets us free from the debilitating fear that prevents us from risking our lives and doing something daring for the sake of the gospel.

This is how missionaries are made. When the sufficiency of Christ captivates a believer's heart and mind then no challenge is too daunting and no cost is too high when it comes to spreading His gospel throughout the world. This is also the way that children's teachers and youth workers are made and how moms and dads and young adults and students become evangelists. Resting in, delighting in, finding satisfaction in Jesus Christ sets us free to risk rejection, ridicule and popularity for the sake of making Him known to others. We are free to live this way because we know that our lives are secure and protected as they are hidden in Jesus Christ.

This explains how Paul could write these incomparable words at the end of Romans 8:

> What then shall we say to these things? If God is for us, who can be against us? He who did not spare his own Son, but gave Him up for us all, how will He not also with Him graciously give us all things? Who shall bring any charge against God's elect? It is God who justifies. Who is to condemn? Christ Jesus is the one who died—more than that, who was raised—who is at the right hand of God, who indeed is interceding for us. Who shall separate us from the love of Christ? Shall tribulation, or distress, or persecution, or famine, or nakedness, or danger, or sword? As it is written, "For Your sake we are being killed all the day long; We are

> regarded as sheep to be slaughtered." No, in all these things we are more than conquerors through Him who loved us. For I am sure that neither death nor life, nor angels nor rulers, nor things present nor things to come, nor powers, nor height nor depth, nor anything else in all creation, will be able to separate us from the love of God in Christ Jesus our Lord (vv. 31–39).

The security that we have in Jesus Christ is eternal and unshakeable. We do not have to be paralyzed by slavish fears nor do we have to let safety be the deciding factor in whether or not we attempt to do something significant in spreading his gospel. What God has done for us in Jesus Christ is so awesome, so powerful, so complete that in having him we truly have everything.

The sufficiency of Christ liberates us from that self-sufficiency that tempts us to manipulate others, and from that self-preservation that tempts us to fear. It also sets us free from self-doubt that tempts us to quit.

Closely related to the fears that sometimes assault us in our efforts to live boldly for Jesus Christ are the self-doubts and discouragements that flood our minds with thoughts that we are not up to the challenge. Paul knew what this was like. Even though he was as bold as a lion and as confident in his Lord as any man ever has been, he also experienced seasons of doubts and discouragements, what he describes as being "afflicted at every turn-fighting without and fear within" (2 Corinthians 7:5).

Acts 17–18 tells us that he first went to Corinth after preaching in Athens where he had been mocked and largely dismissed by the philosophical elites of that city. As he looks back on his early ministry in Corinth he reminds the believers there that he came to them "in weakness and in fear and much trembling" (1 Corinthians 2:3). Though we do not know all of the details, Paul admits to be being discouraged in his work there. In fact, the Lord came to him in a vision and spoke words of specific encouragement him. "Do not be afraid, but go on speaking and do not be silent, for I am with you, and no one will attack you to harm you, for I have many in this city who are my people" (Acts 18:9–10).

How did Paul cope? What kept him going? It was not his own courage. He did not draw from deep wells of self-sufficiency. Rather, he cast himself back on Jesus Christ. The Lord admonished him then promised him: "Do not keep silent [in other words, "Don't quit!], for I am with you." The promise of Christ's presence provoked his perseverance.

When Paul stood in the synagogue of Corinth to preach and he was trembling and perhaps feeling faint, he may well have been tempted to give up and go back to making tents with Aquila and Priscilla. Yet, he resisted the temptations that come with fear and trembling. What did he do instead of quitting? He tells us: "I decided to know nothing among you except Jesus Christ and Him crucified" (1 Corinthians 2:2). Confident in Christ, he preached Christ. When Paul was afflicted with a "thorn in the flesh" (2 Corinthians 12:7–10), God delivered him through it (not from it) by convincing him again of the sufficiency of the grace and power that is found in Jesus Christ. This lesson was so important for Paul to learn that God intentionally did not grant the repeated (three times!) apostolic prayer to take the problem away. Instead, the Lord told Paul, "My grace is sufficient for you, for My power is made perfect in weakness" (v. 9). And how did Paul respond? "Therefore I will boast all the more gladly of my weaknesses, so that the power of Christ may rest upon me. For the sake of Christ, then, I am content with weaknesses, insults, hardships, persecutions, and calamities. For when I am weak, then I am strong" (v. 10).

Refreshed with the assurance of the grace and power of Christ, Paul embraced his weakness as a platform on which his Savior might be exalted rather than give in to it as a reason to quit.

In Hebrews 12 Christ is set before Jewish Christians to encourage their perseverance in the face of persecution and hardship. Like Paul in Corinth, many of these believers were being tempted to give up on the way of Christ and return to their old ways. How does the author encourage them to stay the course? By setting Christ before them so that in considering him they will find all that they need to keep running the race of faith.

> Therefore, since we are surrounded by so great a cloud of witnesses, let us also lay aside every weight, and sin which clings so closely, and let us run with endurance the race that is set before us, looking to Jesus, the founder and perfecter of our faith, who for the joy that was set before Him endured the cross, despising the shame, and is seated at the right hand of the throne of God. Consider Him who endured from sinners such hostility against Himself, so that you may not grow weary or fainthearted (Hebrews 12:1–3).

What they needed was not more personal resolve or new revelation. What they needed was a fresh reminder of all that Christ is for His people. As the one who establishes our faith, will perfect our faith and has walked the road of suffering before us, Christ is all that we need.

The sufficiency of Christ delivers us from self-sufficiency, self-preservation and self-doubt. It also delivers us from self-importance that tempts us to expect, or even demand, esteem, respect, approval or appreciation. Are you familiar with this tendency? It often is framed like this (whether the actual words ever cross our lips): "After all I have done for you the least I should get in return in a little respect!" Pastors who are sincerely motivated to minister for the sake of Christ are not immune from the temptation to harbor that attitude.

If any servants of the Lord deserved to be respected and appreciated certainly it was the apostles. They were given the responsibility of writing Scripture, planting the first Christian churches and seeing to it that the gospel spread to the nations. As the foundation of the New Testament church they were vested with the authority of Christ Himself (Ephesians 2:20).

Despite their significance in the establishment of the work of the gospel on earth, the apostles were some of the most mistreated, misunderstood ministers in history. They were often abused, unappreciated, second-guessed and rejected by the very people whom they served. Paul expresses his sense of this in 1 Corinthians 4:9–13, "For I think that God has exhibited us apostles as last of all, like men sentenced to death, because we have become a spectacle to the world, to angels and to men.... To the present hour we hunger and thirst, we are poorly dressed and buffeted and homeless, and we labor, working with our own hands. When reviled, we bless; when persecuted, we endure; when slandered, we entreat. We have become, and are still, like the scum of the world, the refuse of all things."

How did they respond to this kind of mistreatment? Paul explains his response very straightforwardly. He refused to allow the opinions of others about him and his ministry distract him. As he puts it, "But with me it is a very small thing that I should be judged by you or by any human court. In fact, I do not even judge myself. For I am not aware of anything against myself, but I am not thereby acquitted. It is the Lord who judges me" (1 Corinthians 4:1–4). In other words, he is completely satisfied to have his work left unappreciated by others. In fact, he does not even try to measure the success of his ministry himself. Why? Because, as he says in verse 1 of 1 Corinthians 4, he is a "servant of Christ and steward of the mysteries of God." One day his stewardship will be judged in the only court that matters—the court of the Lord. He is performing for an audience of One, the One who gave His life for him.

The only opinion that matters is Christ's. His honor and glory are our goal. If He chooses to magnify Himself through the mistreatment of those whom He has appointed stewards in the gospel ministry, then so be it. Remembering this will set us free from demanding that others applaud our lives and labors.

His Example

We have seen that the Lordship of Christ establish the nature of our ministry and the sufficiency of Christ liberates us from self-consciousness in ministry. A third way that pastors can exalt Christ through their work is by recognizing that His example calls us to self-denying consecration in ministry. Because Jesus Christ is so much more than an example for us, sometimes I fear that we do not fully appreciate the power that His example can be for us. Listen to what Octavius Winslow says about this:

> There is no single practical truth in the Word of God on which the Spirit is more emphatic than the example which Christ has set for his followers to imitate. The church needed a perfect pattern, a flawless model. It wanted a living embodiment of those precepts of the gospel so strictly enjoined upon every believer, and God has graciously set before us our true model. "Whom he did foreknow, he also did predestinate to be conformed to the image of His Son" (Romans 8:29).[7]

What higher aspiration can a pastor (or any Christian) have than to be like Jesus Christ? Because of the nature of the incarnation and atonement, such aspiration must necessarily include self-denial. If the eternal Son of God humbled Himself to become a man and die on a cross, how can anyone claim to follow His pattern without cultivating a self-sacrificing spirit?

Paul follows this line of thinking when he calls believers to live sacrificially for the sake of the gospel. He tells the Corinthian church, "Be imitators of me, as I am of Christ" (1 Corinthians 11:1). Just before this he admonishes to do everything for the glory of God (10:31) which includes living blamelessly (v. 32) and, as Paul describes himself, trying "to please everyone in everything I do, not seeking my own advantage, but that of many, that they may be saved" (v. 33).

Paul's chosen lifestyle can be explained in terms of following the example of Christ. Rather than insisting that others provide for his needs, he worked so as not to be a burden to anyone. Rather than seek an easy life, he endured hardships and trials of every kind. Rather than "take along a believing wife," he lived as a single man (1 Corinthians 9:5). He lived this way so as not to "put an obstacle in the way of the gospel of Christ" (1 Corinthians 9:12). Just as Jesus "did not come to be served but to serve and give his life as a ransom for many" (Mark 10:45) so Paul lived his life as a servant in order to make the person and work of Jesus known to others.

This self-denying demeanor of Christ exemplifies the kind of loving relationships that Christians are to have with each other. In fact, those who are stronger believers—more Christ-like—are obligated to deny themselves for the welfare of weaker brethren. "We then who are strong have an obligation to bear with the failings of the weak, and not to please ourselves. Let each of us please his neighbor for his good, to build him up. For Christ did not please himself, but as it is written, 'The reproaches of

[7] Octavius Winslow, *Morning Thoughts* (Grand Rapids, MI: Reformation Heritage Books, 2003), 543.

those who reproached you fell on Me'" (Romans 15:1–3). If our Master did not live to please Himself then those who seek to follow His example must do so, either.

When Paul wants to encourage believers to cultivate that humility and deferential spirit which are the fruit of self-denial, how does he do it? He appeals to the example of Jesus Christ. To the Philippian church he writes,

> Do nothing from selfish ambition or conceit, but in humility count others more significant than yourselves. Let each of you look not only to his own interests, but also to the interests of others. Have this mind among yourselves, which is yours in Christ Jesus, who, though he was in the form of God, did not count equality with God a thing to be grasped, but emptied Himself, by taking the form of a servant, being born in the likeness of men. And being found in human form, He humbled Himself by becoming obedient to the point of death, even death of a cross (2:3–8).

Though "very God of very God," as the Nicene Creed puts it, Christ willingly denied Himself the blessings and benefits of deity in order to fulfill God's mission by becoming a man. Then, as a man and even though He was the giver of life itself, He laid down his life on the cross for sinners. As we relate to other people He is our example. As we try to emulate His mentality how can we not regard others as more important than ourselves? The mentality of our humble, self-denying Savior calls pastors to consecrate themselves in ministry, like Him, in service to others.

The Apostles John and Peter also appeal to the example of Christ when encouraging Christians to live faithfully in the world. Their instructions for all believers also apply to the way that pastors carry out their ministries. Jesus indicates that Christians inevitably will emulate him as a part of their life of faith. He said, "My sheep hear My voice, and I know them, and they follow Me" (John 10:27). To hear the voice of Christ and follow Him cannot mean less than to adopt the values, judgments and perspectives of Jesus as revealed in Scripture. John later uses this as a test for being a true disciple. He writes, "Whoever says he abides in Him ought to walk in the same way in which He walked" (1 John 2:6). A pastor ought to shepherd God's people the way that Great Shepherd cares and provides for His people.

Peter's instructions about suffering also have practical application for pastors. After all, a servant is not greater than his master, as Jesus said, and if they persecuted Him they will persecute those who stand with Him (John 15:20). So, how are the Lord's servants to respond when mistreated? What is a pastor to do when the very people he serves speak maliciously against him and deal him grief unjustly? Peter tells us we are to endure such treatment with patience. "For to this you have been called, because

Christ also suffered for you, leaving you an example, so that you might follow in his steps. "He committed no sin, neither was deceit found in His mouth" (Isaiah 53:9). "When He was reviled, He did not revile in return; when He suffered, He did not threaten, but continued entrusting Himself to Him who judges justly. He Himself bore our sins in His body on the tree, that we might die to sin and live to righteousness. By his wounds you have been healed" (1 Peter 2:21–24). Suffering is part of our calling as disciples of Jesus and He Himself has taught us how to suffer by suffering for our salvation.

There is far too much posturing and preening among those who labor in gospel ministry. Too often emphasis is placed on appearances. Too often ministry leadership paradigms are taken from the corporate world with the result that the pastor fancies himself something like a CEO. "Never let them see you sweat!" "Be so impressive that they will naturally want to be on your side!" "Make a good impression!" These are the mottos that have often crept into modern thinking about pastoral ministry.

John Stott shows how foolish this approach is by citing a scene from Mark Twain's, *The Adventures of Huckleberry Finn*. "Huck gets into a conversation one day with Joanna, the youngest daughter of Peter Wilks, who has died. He tells her that in the church of the Rev. Henry Wilks (her uncle from Shefield) there are 'no less than seventeen clergy,' although, he adds,

> 'They don't *all* of 'em preach the same day—only one of 'em.'
>
> 'Well, then what does the rest of 'em do?'
>
> 'Oh, nothing much. Loll around, pass the plate—and one thing or another. But mainly they don't do nothing.'
>
> 'Well, then' asks Joanna in wide-eyed astonishment, 'what are they for?'
>
> 'Why, they're for style,' Huck responds. 'Don't you know nothing?'[8]

It is a sad reality that much of the attitude and effort in ministry is dictated by what we think will impress others. We like to be impressive, don't we! But our Lord and Master, Jesus Christ has left us an example, to encourage us to deny ourselves, take up our cross and follow Him as we give ourselves to minister to others. As the Puritan John Flavel put it so well, "A crucified stile best suits the preachers of a crucified Christ."[9]

[8] Cited in John Stott, *Basic Christian Leadership* (Downers Grove, IL: Intervarsity Press, 2002), 99–100

[9] John Flavel, "The Character of a True Evangelical Pastor," in *The Works* (Edinburgh: Banner of Truth Trust, 1968), 6:572.

Remembering that our Master chose to suffer and die for our salvation will help those of us who pastor in His name to practice self-denial as we engage in gospel ministry.

Glory

Just as the lordship of Christ establishes the nature of our ministry, the sufficiency of Christ liberates us from self-consciousness in ministry and the example of Christ calls us to self-denying consecration in ministry, so also the glory of Christ delivers us from settling for superficial successes in ministry.

The pressure to be successful in ministry is at times almost overwhelming. Any pastor worthy of his calling wants to be successful in his labors. Understood properly, that is a right and proper desire. What sincere pastor does not want to see people converted and the church built up under his ministry? Consider the way that Spurgeon urges pastors to think about their work. "Even when we are most successful, we must long for more success. If God has given us many souls, we must pine for a thousand times as many. Satisfaction with results will be the knell of progress. No man is good who thinks that he cannot be better. He has no holiness who thinks that he is useful enough."[10] This kind of God-honoring burden causes faithful pastors to grieve when little fruit is evident from their labors.

There are, however, great dangers that attend such desires. One is to compromise the message that we have been entrusted to proclaim. When the rough edges of the gospel are obviously offensive to those we seek to win the temptation is to alter the message in order to make it more palatable to people. Yet, changing the message was exactly the danger that the Galatian churches faced when false teachers infiltrated their ranks. Paul minced no words in addressing their failure. "I am astonished that you are so quickly deserting Him who called you in the grace of Christ and are turning to a different gospel, not that there is another one, but there are some who trouble you and want to distort the gospel of Christ" (Galatians 1:6–7). Then he pronounces an apostolic curse on anyone who would dare to preach an altered message as the gospel. "But even if we or an angel from heaven should preach to you a gospel contrary to the one we preached to you, let him be accursed. As we have said before, so now I say again: If anyone preaching to you a gospel contrary to the one you received, let him be accursed" (1:8–9).

[10] C. H. Spurgeon, *An All Around Ministry* (Edinburgh: Banner of Truth Trust, 1981), 352.

Why did Paul respond this way? What motivated his strong language? He tells us: "For am I now seeking the approval of man, or God? Or am I trying to please man? If I were still trying to please man, I would not be a servant of Christ" (Galatians 1:10). His eye is on God. Paul understands that "the Gospel is the brightest manifestation of the Divine character, and those who corrupt the Gospel do what in them lies to tarnish and obscure the glory of God."[11] Commitment to the glory of God in Christ kept Paul from allowing any compromise to the message of the gospel.

Along with pressures to change the message that God has revealed, pastors and churches also face temptations to compromise the methods whereby they minister and apply that message. This is what happened to the church at Corinth. Though they began well with the gospel, in the face of pressure to be regarded as loving and accepting, they did not maintain the witness of the gospel as they should have. Paul warns against this precisely in 1 Corinthians 3:10–17.

> According to the grace of God given to me, like a skilled master builder I laid a foundation, and someone else is building upon it. Let each one take care how he builds upon it. For no one can lay a foundation other than that which is laid, which is Jesus Christ. Now if anyone builds on the foundation with gold, silver, precious stones, wood, hay, straw—each one's work will become manifest, for the Day will disclose it, because it will be revealed by fire, and the fire will test what sort of work each one has done. If the work that anyone has built on the foundation survives, he will receive a reward. If anyone's work is burned up, he will suffer loss, though he himself will be saved, but only as through fire. Do you not know that you are God's temple and that God's Spirit dwells in you? If anyone destroys God's temple, God will destroy him. For God's temple is holy, and you are that temple.

In his excellent exposition of this passage, R.L. Dabney shows that Paul's concern is to warn pastors against compromising the way that they carry out their gospel ministries.[12] The "master builder" represents Paul and his fellow apostles. "Someone else" is the pastor (or pastors) who follow after the apostolic foundation has been laid. The manner of their ministry is characterized either by "gold, silver, precious stones" or by "wood, hay, straw." The former is costly and results from careful, perhaps painful ministry and it lasts. The latter is cheap, easy and quickly assembled. The

[11] James Haldane, *Exposition of the Epistle to the Galatians*, (Springfield, MO: Particular Baptist Press, 2002 reprint), 42.

[12] R. L. Dabney, *Discussions*, Volume 1 (London: Billings and Sons, Ltd., 1890), 551–574.

point Paul makes is important. True gospel ministry may not be immediately impressive and the good that it accomplishes may not be obvious. But such ministry will last. Methods that do not correspond to the gospel can be employed for more rapid and apparent growth, but the results are superficial. The day of judgment will make plain the character of each kind of ministry.

Along with this impending future revelation is the awareness that the church is God's temple indwelt by God's Spirit (v. 16). That temple is holy (v. 17) and therefore the ministry that is carried out in it must likewise by holy—in keeping with the revealed will of God. The manifested glory of Christ is at stake. His gospel builds His church in His way. Compromising that gospel or ministering in ways that are out of step with that gospel will detract from His glory.

This is what happened in the church at Sardis. Jesus said to that body, "I know your works. You have the reputation of being alive, but you are dead" (Revelation 3:1). They were engaged in many impressive activities but spiritually had lost the source of life, which at least means that they had forsaken the gospel. If they had been more concerned with the judgment of Christ, they would not have settled for having a great reputation with people. In other words, if Christ and his glory had been their ultimate concern they would not have settled for superficial success.

Conclusion

Jesus is Lord. He is enough. He has gone before us. He is all-glorious. When a pastor is governed by these truths in his ministry then Christ will be exalted. In his letter to the Philippians Paul gives a high commendation to his young colleague in the ministry, Timothy. He says, "I hope in the Lord Jesus to send Timothy to you soon, so that I too may be cheered by news of you" (Philippians 2:19). Timothy was his trusted co-worker, someone Paul knew he could depend on. He then goes on to describe him with these words: "For I have no one like him, who will be genuinely concerned for your welfare. For they all seek their own interests, not those of Jesus Christ. But you know Timothy's proven worth, how as a son with a father he has served with me in the gospel" (2:20–22).

Timothy could be counted on to care for the Philippian church because he ministered not out of a concern for himself or even primarily out of a concern for them, but out of a concern for Christ Jesus. Christ was not only his message, he was Timothy's life. Christ was exalted in his ministry.

May the Lord give his church an army of such pastors in every generation.

10

Exalting Christ by Preparing His Church for Missionary Service

Allen Beadmore

Not another sermon! For an unconverted not quite ten-year-old-boy whose parents made him attend church twice on Sundays and every Wednesday night, the thought of listening to more preaching in the middle of the week was less than thrilling. But Grace Baptist Church in Carlisle, Pennsylvania, had decided to host the annual RBMS conference and the fourth grade teacher of the Christian school associated with the church had decided that her entire class would be present for one of the sessions. So it was that on March 5, 1992 I found myself trudging up the steps leading to the balcony complaining all the way because I wouldn't get my full recess time.[1] I heard the speaker introduced as Dr. Fred Malone. His topic was the life of John G. Paton, the famous missionary to the New Hebrides Islands.

Pastor Fred had not realized it yet, but by the end of the year he would move to the small town of Clinton, LA in order to continue a work of church reformation at First Baptist Church. Something else he didn't know was that his future associate minister at First Baptist was grumpily settling into his balcony pew and resigning himself to another long-winded sermon. However, immediately upon hearing Fred's opening remarks, I began to take an interest in the speaker. Having grown up under the pulpit ministry of Walt Chantry and having heard many well-known and gifted

[1] I am indebted to Vickie Bookamer's research on this date.

preachers at the annual family conferences, I was used to good preaching but this was different. What kind of accent was that? Upon further inquiry, I was informed by my teacher that Pastor Fred sounded funny because "he's from the South."[2] While it was the accent that held my attention initially, it was the life of Paton that held my interest the rest of the way. I was so fascinated by the story that I asked my mother to purchase the tape of Fred's message. On my own time at home I re-listened to the account of Paton's trials and successes. What I didn't know at the time was that almost exactly 24 years later on April 10, 2016 I would kneel down and have Fred Malone and the rest of the church officers place their hands on me and pray for me as First Baptist Church sent out their first missionary in the 180 year history of the church.

A Missionary's Preparation for the Field

How does one prepare to be an overseas missionary? In one sense the best analogy might be that of a car when it hits a slippery patch of winter ice and goes skidding off the road. At that point, the best of drivers can only manage to aim their vehicle in the general direction of the softest bush rather than the huge oak tree trunk just off the shoulder of the road. When a man commits himself, and his family if he has one, to becoming an overseas church planter, it is impossible to adequately account for every variable. Many aspects of the planning are completely out of the man's control. Will he receive full funding prior to leaving? When will he receive the funding? How much more time will he have to spend away from home visiting churches in the hopes they will support him? And all of the above questions deal only with part of the complex financial aspects of missions and assume the presence of an association of churches eager to have him visit them and explain the new work.[3]

Cross-cultural training is also a necessity as well as perhaps visiting the intended sphere of future ministry to get an initial feel for how many individuals or families might be interested in a reformed Baptist church. It may be necessary to have language training and survival training de-

[2] This information cemented an early desire to travel to the South and see if everyone spoke this way. However, after many years spent living in South Carolina, Mississippi and Louisiana I can attest that Fred's accent remains unique.

[3] With regard to raising support, the Preacher probably wasn't thinking about missions when he wrote Ecclesiastes 1:15b but when trying to reach 100% support the truth certainly applies. Fortunately in God's providence many churches and individuals generously gave so that my family and I could be fully supported.

pending on the host country. Sifting through all of the latest literature on church planting may also be helpful. Deciding on an exit plan from the sending church is also important since it is more than likely that the future missionary has been functioning as an elder in his home church. The work involved will take years not months. Where does a man start?

Fixing Our Eyes on Jesus in Personal Sanctification

A man intending to go overseas and begin a new life's work must first keep his eyes firmly fixed on his Savior for his own personal sanctification. But isn't it obvious that someone as spiritually mature as a future missionary need hardly bother remembering this while he takes care of so many essential details for his overseas work? After all, his sending church needs him to preach and shepherd the people on a regular basis; any members of the future core group require regular communication and certainly his family cannot be ignored during such a stressful transition period. Shouldn't the elders and deacons of the sending congregation be busy forming a missions committee and urging the people to pray and fast and to be excited as their newly commissioned missionary departs?

While it is true that the work listed above is usually necessary for any successful missionary endeavor, Paul's words in I Thessalonians 3:1–3a are also true.

> Finally then brothers, we ask and urge you in the Lord Jesus, that as you received from us how you ought to walk and to please God, just as you are doing, that you do so more and more. For you know what instructions we gave you through the Lord Jesus. For this is the will of God, your sanctification.

God's will for the believer doesn't change simply because he grows in his responsibilities to others. Each unexpected variable thrown at the man preparing to go overseas is a God-given opportunity for faith to be at work clearing away anything that would hinder his view of Christ. Each fresh separation from his wife and children is a chance for him to entrust his family to the Lord in his absence. Each time he feels frustrated that the members of his home church don't appreciate the sacrifice he is making for those in a foreign country with limited gospel access, he must realize the patience with which Christ constantly ministers to him. Each time the people of the future church don't appreciate that he still bears the burden of shepherding his brothers and sisters at home while building his relationship with them, the man must be freshly amazed that Jesus Christ bore his own sins at Calvary. Every new obstacle, whether it is lack of funding, government red tape concerning a visa or ill health and fatigue must be redeemed by remembering Jesus Christ "the same yesterday and today and forever."

Practically speaking how does this work during the man's time of preparation? From what direction does he receive the constant counsel to keep his eyes fixed on Christ in personal sanctification? Very simply, the man must be shepherded by a faithful gospel minister whose preaching ministry and personal life are devoted to Jesus Christ. The best place to maintain one's dedication to personal sanctification is in the local church. And the best local churches are those cared for by men who have learned to look to Jesus Christ the author and perfecter of their own faith. It is not enough for a man heading to the mission field to complete cross-cultural training or read books on church-planting or even study the doctrine of sanctification. He must see a mature man putting faith in Christ into practice on a regular basis. He must have a man who can absorb all the obstacles and trials of trying to get out the door to go build Christ's kingdom elsewhere without being thrown into a panic. He must have a man who delights in the fact that Christ is the steward of the Father's wise and eternal purpose in his life and who knows that Christ will never break a bruised reed or quench a smoldering wick. After all, what happens when all the variables are finally figured out? What happens once the man is actually on the field and doing the work he had planned to do? Has life now become easier? Are all of his problems solved? Was lack of funding really the problem? Was separation from his family? Wasn't it always his own sinful heart? Wasn't it always his own lack of trust in the Savior? Only a mature man who has gone through his own trials with his eyes on Christ and experienced the joy of putting to death the sin in his own heart will grasp these truths. And while a man prepares for his work overseas, it is a *necessity* that he have such a man standing beside him.

Fixing Our Eyes on Jesus in Worship

Oftentimes the most stressful part of the week for the church planter is the Sunday worship service. Knowing this, the man carefully prepares his messages each week so that the people will be well fed with exactly the right amount of truth and that in proper proportion. During the week, strategic outreach plans afford contact with the lost or nominally Christian and those contacts are faithfully followed up. Diligently the man communicates with members of the core group to make sure everyone knows their assignment in order for worship to run smoothly so that what is presented looks like it has been well-thought out rather than slapped together at the last minute. And then the big day arrives. Where is everyone? My lost neighbor said they would come! Why isn't that person greeting people who enter like I asked them to do? I don't want a reputation as an unfriendly church! Why does the sound system keep giving me embarrassing feedback? Surely my sermon notes were right here a minute ago? And then, even after the conclusion of a successful worship service, there is the growing realization that in the middle of making sure everything ran smoothly, the whole reason why we gathered together in the first place was lost. Even if the people worshipped God, the man in the pulpit certainly did not because he was too distracted.

Knowing that these types of distractions will be multiplied, and a business-like attitude can pervade his ministry, how ought a man to prepare for a solo pastorate in a foreign country? Once again the answer is very simple. He must worship in a local church where the senior pastor focuses the worship service on the glory of Jesus Christ. The preparing missionary must see a man leading worship who genuinely wants to be in the pulpit and does not rush through the "preliminaries" such as the call to worship and the pastoral prayer in order to get to the sermon. He must get the feeling that the man in the pulpit would rather be with Christ's people than anywhere else because they are Christ's people and the Father has called them out of the world to his Son. He must hear the minister tell the congregation that Sunday is the Lord's Day because on this day Jesus Christ rose from the dead. He must hear forgiveness preached in Christ's name, as Jesus commanded his disciples to do. He must hear that repentance is a gift from Jesus not an activity only to be associated with the law. The man preparing to speak to the lost must hear his own pastor persuade self-righteous young people in the congregation to come to Christ for salvation because Jesus died for sinners. When a man thinking about those in a foreign land who have never heard the gospel sees his senior pastor weep over the truths he so ardently preaches, he will rejoice in a Savior who wept over Jerusalem and cares for the lost far more than he does.[4] Men who go to other countries and call the ungodly to glorify Christ do not arise in a vacuum. Humanly speaking they must be developed in a context where they themselves have been properly shepherded in worship. A man intending to serve God on the mission field *must* first worship under a pastor who directs him to Christ in the entire worship service.

[4] As Walt Chantry memorably once said, "I can preach and I can cry but I can't do both at the same time. Fred Malone can."

Conclusion

The details of my own path to the mission field do not provide a model for all whom the Lord our God will call to do His work. It is Jesus Christ who will build His church and He does so by sending His Holy Spirit upon men according to His own purposes. However, the man who is best prepared to serve his Savior is the one whom the Spirit has taught by the Christ appointed means of a local church, led by a pastor whose faith is fixed on Jesus Christ. If you are a pastor, how can you raise up young men to go as missionaries to foreign lands? You must look to Christ yourself in personal sanctification and public worship and be an example in these areas to your flock. If you are a man on fire for the Lord where ought you to prepare for work overseas? The New Testament's answer would be in a local church under the ministry of a man who directs you to Jesus Christ, who was born of the virgin Mary, lived a perfectly righteous life, died a perfectly righteous death and rose again from the dead three days later. We live in an age of gurus and experts. In the United States we have access to a great deal of educational material on how to be a missionary. However, it ought to come as a comfort that there remains no replacement for the faithful local pastor in the preparatory work of a foreign church planter. Pastor Fred has been that pastor to me. Often when I would speak to him in glowing terms of how God had spiritually blessed First Baptist or how frustrated I was with something that wasn't going as well as I thought it should he would say, "Well, it may all fall apart tomorrow but Jesus Christ is risen from the dead." What a rebuke! What an encouragement! I think somewhere somebody named Paul told that to his own son in the faith.[5]

[5] 2 Timothy 2:8a.

11

Exalting Christ by Emphasizing The Great Commission

Jerry Slate, Jr.

> "And Jesus came and spoke to them, saying, 'All authority has been given to Me in heaven and on earth. Go therefore and make disciples of all the nations, baptizing them in the name of the Father and of the Son and of the Holy Spirit, teaching them to observe all things that I have commanded you; and lo, I am with you always, even to the end of the age'" (Matthew 28:18–20).[1]

Very early in the morning on Thursday, May 5, 2016, a godly couple named Allen & Katie Beardmore landed at the airport in Perth, Australia along with their four young children Ethan, Thomas, Abigail, and Logan. Their arrival in "the land down under" was the culmination of countless hours of praying, planning, and preparing, for they had been commissioned and sent by the First Baptist Church of Clinton, LA to labor as missionaries of Jesus Christ among the Australian people. First Baptist of Clinton was founded in 1836, and as far as anyone has been able to discern this is the first time in the church's 180 year history that a missionary has been sent out from their congregation. It has pleased the Lord of the Nations to use the life and ministry of Pastor Fred Malone as an instrument in His hands to nourish, equip, and send out these laborers into His harvest field.

[1] Unless otherwise noted all Bible quotations in this chapter are taken from *The New King James Version* (Thomas Nelson, Inc.: 1982).

But what is it, exactly, that First Baptist of Clinton and the Beardmores hope to achieve in Western Australia? What is their task? What, specifically, has the Head of the Church commanded them to do? And what is their ultimate goal? The verses quoted above from Matthew 28 are doubtless familiar to us all. We frequently refer to this command of our Lord as "the Great Commission." But how often do we actually hear these precious words expounded phrase by phrase, line upon line? Truth be told, we rarely get past the word "Go," as if this is the central and sole emphasis of the text. But there are so many priceless riches to be mined from these all-encompassing words. So, let us consider the premise, the precepts, the promise, and the purpose of the Great Commission.

The Premise of the Great Commission

"All authority has been given to Me in heaven and on earth" (Matthew 28:18b) is the foundation upon which Jesus' command to reach the nations is built. Because Jesus rules over the universe as an absolute Sovereign, the King over all kings and the Lord over all lords, we are to make followers of Him from citizens of every nation over which He rules. Allen Beardmore has said that his family is not traveling overseas to tell the Australian people to make Jesus their King, but to declare to them that He is already their King and that they must repent and bow the knee to His rule over their lives.

But this declaration of our Lord is not something hastily tacked on to the end of Matthew's gospel as some kind of afterthought. It is the fulfillment of God's eternal purposes as revealed in Old Testament prophecy. In Isaiah 49:5–6 the Holy Spirit invites us as it were to put our ears to the keyhole of heaven's door and listen in as God the Father and God the Son enter into the great intra-Trinitarian covenant of redemption. We listen as the Son of God tells us what His Father has said to Him:

> And now the Lord says, who formed Me from the womb to be His Servant, to bring Jacob back to Him, so that Israel is gathered to Him (for I shall be glorious in the eyes of the Lord, and My God shall be My strength), indeed He says, 'It is too small a thing that You should be My Servant to raise up the tribes of Jacob, and to restore the preserved ones of Israel; I will also give You as a light to the Gentiles, that You should be My salvation to the ends of the earth.'

The glory of Jesus' Name is of such weightiness and infinite worth that the Father decreed that He would not only be the exalted by Jewish people who believe in His name, but also by men, women, boys, and girls from every tribe, tongue, people, and nation. In Psalm 2 we read similar language yet again as the only begotten Son of God tells us:

> I will declare the decree: The Lord has said to Me, 'You are My Son, today I have begotten You. Ask of Me, and I will give You the nations for Your inheritance, and the ends of the earth for Your possession.' (Psalm 2:7–8)

The Father was offering His beloved Son a throne, a crown, and a scepter. He was giving Him authority to rule over every nation.

But the Father also set a condition with His offer; there was a price the Son of God would have to pay as the Son of Man if He was to inherit the nations. He would obtain the crown only if He would first endure the cross. He must lay down His life as a vicarious sacrifice for sinners. He must be punished for all the sins of all God's elect, fully satisfying God's justice and wrath for them. Only then would He receive authority as the Son of Man to be both the Savior of God's elect and the Judge of the whole earth. To this condition the Lord Jesus joyfully and willingly submitted. "No one takes [My life] from Me," He said, "but I lay it down of Myself" (John 10:18a).

So when we come to the end of Matthew 28, the crucified and risen Christ is standing before His Apostles with the scars in His hands and feet plainly visible, the purchase price of our redemption. Having endured the cross, He now declares that He has obtained the crown. The Father has given Him all authority in both the spiritual and material realms. As Isaiah says, "He shall see the labor of His soul, and be satisfied. By His knowledge My righteous Servant shall justify many, for He shall bear their iniquities" (Isaiah 53:11).

It is often claimed that belief in the absolute sovereignty of God is the destroyer of all evangelistic and missionary zeal. But our Lord says, in essence, "*Because* I am Sovereign, evangelize the nations!" The particular redemption accomplished by Jesus has made the salvation of His elect from every nation an infallible certainty. What confidence this should give us as we engage in the awkward labor of evangelism and world missions!

The Precepts of the Great Commission

The word "Go" is actually not the central emphasis of our Lord's commandment. In fact, verse 19 might be better translated "As you are going." The principle weight of His words is upon disciple making and all the things that this involves. But these followers of Jesus are to be developed from the citizens of all nations, and this can never happen if preachers are not sent to other lands and people groups to proclaim the good news concerning Jesus Christ and Him crucified (Romans 10:13–15). In our Lord's words we can easily discern three specific commands: make disciples, baptize disciples, and teach disciples.

Make Disciples

In many ways, this is the central command of all three precepts. Baptizing and teaching disciples are subordinate commands to the imperative of "making disciples." Obedience to the Great Commission begins with evangelism. But the goal of evangelism is not to get sinners to "make a decision for Jesus" nor to "pray the sinner's prayer" with sincerity. When a lost sinner is truly enabled by God's grace to enter into His kingdom through the narrow gate of conversion for the rest of his life, he will be found walking on the difficult path of discipleship until he enters into heaven (Matthew 7:13–14). In Biblical evangelism, sinners hear the good news about Jesus Christ, repent of their sins and believe the gospel, are baptized, and are added to the membership of a local church where "they continue steadfastly in the apostles' doctrine and fellowship, in the breaking of bread, and in prayers" (Acts 2:42). The word "disciple" means "follower" or "student." A truly converted man or woman is someone who has bowed their knees to the Lordship, the authority, of the risen Christ and who perseveringly follows Him the rest of their days. The Great Commission by its very nature excludes the cheap grace and easy believe-ism that is so rampant in our own evangelical culture. We must call sinners to repent of their lawless rebellion against their Creator, and the fruit of that repentance is imperfect but obedient followers of Jesus Christ who love the things He loves and hate the things He hates.

But where are these disciples to come from? "Of all nations" (Matthew 28:19a). In Luke's version of the Great Commission we are given greater insight into how each local church is to accomplish this:

> But you shall receive power when the Holy Spirit has come upon you; and you shall be witnesses to Me in Jerusalem, and in all Judea and Samaria, and to the end of the earth (Acts 1:8).

As we study the Acts of the Apostles it becomes obvious that Luke uses these words as the natural framework and outline of his book. The Apostles were standing on the Mount of Olives next to Jerusalem when they heard these words from the lips of Jesus and He was telling them to start by evangelizing their own city. But the city of Jerusalem was situated in the region of Judea, an area populated by Jews. So, Judea was both geographically and culturally near to the Apostles. As the gospel spread throughout

Jerusalem it was then to spill over the banks of the city limits into the surrounding region. The church I pastor is located in the city of Hiram, GA and the analogous application for our congregation is to spread the gospel throughout the city of Hiram and then to move on to reaching all of Paulding County, the region in which the city of Hiram is located.

But Jesus did not stop there. As God's people proclaimed the gospel throughout the region of Judea they were to reach out to Samaria as well. Samaria was geographically near but culturally far, far away. The Samaritans were Jewish half-breeds who were despised by the Hebrews. The hostility between these two cultures was enormous. Yet our Lord commanded His kosher Jewish Apostles to let the love of Christ overcome their prejudices against the Samaritan people so that they could hear the gospel and be reconciled to God. Who are the despised minority groups in the area where you live? To again use the church I pastor as an example, we are surrounded by a large Hispanic population. Many of them migrated to Georgia from Mexico to obtain work in residential and commercial construction and their presence permeates that industry. They are geographically close to us but culturally and linguistically diverse. They are a part of our Samaria. So, obedience to the Great Commission starts where you live and where your local church meets. It begins with evangelizing your own children and the neighborhood where your congregation assembles. But from that central point the gospel is to radiate out in ever expanding concentric circles, penetrating the surrounding regions and entering into the wonderful diversity of cultures that God in His providence has placed near to you.

But Jesus is still not finished. Each local church must be involved in taking the gospel "to the end of the earth" (Acts 1:8c). Our concern must not end with the borders of our own nation. Jesus' name is far too glorious to be worshiped only in the land of our birth! As Solomon cries out concerning Him:

> Yes, all kings shall fall down before Him; all nations shall serve Him…. His name shall endure forever; His name shall continue as long as the sun. And *men* shall be blessed in Him; all nations shall call Him blessed. Blessed *be* the Lord God, the God of Israel, who only does wondrous things! And blessed *be* His glorious name forever! And let the whole earth be filled *with* His glory. Amen and Amen (Psalm 72:11; 17–19).

Here is the drive behind all evangelism and world missions! Here is the ultimate goal of the Great Commission! As John Piper has famously said "Missions exists because worship doesn't."[2]

[2] John Piper, *Let the Nations Be Glad! The Supremacy of God in Missions*, 2nd ed. (Grand Rapids, MI: Baker Academic, 2004), 17.

Now, certainly, most of us are not called to leave our homeland to make disciples from other nations, but some of us are. And we who stay behind are to (to borrow the phrase of William Carey's friend, Andrew Fuller) "hold the ropes"[3] for those who are sent out. Each local church has the responsibility to send those who are called by God to go to the mission field, to pray for them continually, and to support them financially as we are able. Missiology is not just for missionaries. It is for every Christian, goers and senders alike!

Baptize Disciples

But once a sinner is converted to Christ what is the church to do with them? "Baptizing them in the name of the Father and of the Son and of the Holy Spirit" (Matthew 28:19b). Baptism is the first act of obedience to be observed by the newly converted as they take their first steps on the difficult path of discipleship. But what does baptism mean? Baptism is all about identification. Have you ever asked yourself why Jesus was baptized by John the Baptist? John himself was certainly astonished by His request (Matthew 3:14)! After all, John's baptism was a baptism of repentance for sinners, but the innocent Jesus was not a sinner and needed no repentance. But it was fitting that at the beginning of His earthly ministry Jesus should undergo a sinner's baptism, for by it He was making it clear from the start that He had come to be *identified* with sinners, to be "numbered with the transgressors" (Isaiah 53:12b). Jesus the Righteous One was numbered among the transgressors so that we transgressors could be numbered among the righteous! And so, believer's baptism is a sign of our union with Christ, the singular name of the Triune God is placed upon us and we are forever after marked out as the disciples of Jesus.

We owe a debt of gratitude to Fred Malone for the clarity of teaching he has bequeathed to us on the subject of baptism in his wonderful book *The Baptism of Disciples Alone: A Covenantal Argument for Credobaptism Versus Paedobaptism.*[4] In this work Dr. Malone skillfully demonstrates that the unique blessings of the New Covenant and the Regulative Principle of Worship demand that we baptize only those men, women, boys, and girls who demonstrate that they have a credible profession of faith, for each local church is to be composed of a regenerate church membership. The preaching of the gospel, exclusive believer's baptism, the fencing of the Lord's Supper, and the exercise of restorative church discipline are gracious

[3] S. Pearce Carey, *Samuel Pearce: The Baptist Brainerd*,3rd ed. (London: The Carey Press, n.d.), 171.

[4] Fred Malone, *The Baptism of Disciples Alone: A Covenantal Argument for Credobaptism Versus Paedobaptism* (Cape Coral, FL: Founders Press, 2003).

safe guards to warn professing Christians against the dangers of false conversion, to guard the purity of the local church, and to protect the honor of Christ's name.

And the practice of exclusive believer's baptism is necessary if we are to give full orbed obedience to Christ's Great Commission, for those whom Jesus has commanded the church to baptize are only those who have been made disciples through the preaching of the gospel. There is a sweet simplicity to be found in questions 98 and 99 of The Baptist Catechism:

> *Q. 98: To whom is baptism to be administered?*
> A. Baptism is to be administered to all those who actually profess repentance toward God, faith in and obedience to our Lord Jesus Christ, and to none other.
>
> *Q. 99: Are the infants of such as are professing believers to be baptized?*
> A. The infants of such as are professing believers are not to be baptized, because there is neither command or example in the Holy Scriptures, or certain consequence from them to baptize such.[5]

Teach Disciples

To be marked out as a believing disciple of Christ in the waters of baptism is to also be identified with God's people, the church, "for by one Spirit we were all baptized into one body" (1 Corinthians 12:13a). As we read how the Apostles themselves obeyed the Great Commission in the book of Acts we continually read statements like this:

> Then those who gladly received his word were baptized; and that day about three thousand souls were added *to them* ... and the Lord added to the church daily those who were being saved" (Acts 2:41; 47b).

If regeneration & conversion is the entrance way into the invisible church, believer's baptism is the gateway of admission into the membership of the visible church. To again quote from The Baptist Catechism:

> *Q. 101: What is the duty of such who are rightly baptized?*
> A. It is the duty of such who are rightly baptized to give up themselves to some particular and orderly church of Jesus Christ, that they may walk in all the commandments and ordinances of the Lord blameless.[6]

[5] *The Baptist Confession of Faith & The Baptist Catechism* (Vestavia Hills, AL: Solid Ground Christian Books, 2010), 117–118.

[6] *The Baptist Confession of Faith & The Baptist Catechism*, 118.

The third precept of the Great Commission is "teaching them to observe all things that I have commanded you" (Matthew 28:20a). If a disciple is a submissive follower of the Lord Jesus then he must know what his Master commands him to do and follow Him by obeying what He has said. And so we are commanded to instruct those who have been made and baptized as disciples what their Lord and Savior requires of them. To put it another way, we are responsible to teach them the whole counsel of God's Holy written Word (Acts 20:27). Although obedience to the Great Commission begins with evangelism, it does not end there; its requirements are not fulfilled *exclusively* by evangelism. We must labor diligently for the conversion of the lost, but we must also work for the sanctification of the converted. And this brings us to a very important and oft-neglected point: *Obedience to the Great Commission requires us to plant local churches that are self-governing, self-supporting, and self-propagating!*

All throughout the pages of the New Testament we see this apostolic pattern repeated. The gospel is preached to people groups who have never heard these things before (Romans 10:13–15; 15:20–21). And while some scoff at the message, others are regenerated by the Holy Spirit and baptized as disciples of Christ by ministers of the gospel (Acts 2:41; 10:47–48; 16:13–15). These new believers are then organized into churches where they are regularly taught the Word of God, pray, sing God's praises, observe the Lord's Supper, and fellowship with one another through the grace of hospitality (Acts 2:42; 20:7–12; Romans 12:13; Hebrews 13:2). From these local churches the gospel continues to spread to the surrounding communities and new converts are baptized and added to the membership of the church (1 Thessalonians 1:8–10). Whenever a professing Christian falls into soul destroying and scandalous sin they are called to account by the loving rebukes of God's people and, if necessary, placed under their discipline until they repent (Matthew 18:15–20; Acts 5:1–14; 8:18–24; 1 Corinthians 5:1–13; 2 Corinthians 2:3–11). And as the Lord grows faithful men in the congregation to greater depths of spiritual maturity they are mentored and groomed for spiritual leadership by the Apostles and their traveling companions (Acts 15:36–41; 16:1–3; 2 Timothy 2:2) until a plurality of elders is installed in each local church (Acts 14:21–23; Titus 1:5). These pastors then continue the Apostles' work by laboring in preaching, prayer, evangelism, discipleship, and spiritual mentoring (2 Timothy 4:1–5). And thus, the kingdom of God and the glory of His name continue to advance throughout the entire earth! Making disciples, baptizing disciples, and teaching disciples are the three precepts Jesus has given to us in His Great Commission. These are His marching orders through which He receives the inheritance of nations His Father has promised to Him.

The Promise of the Great Commission

But who is sufficient for these things? We live in a world that is either indifferent or openly hostile to the message we proclaim. We are tasked with telling others to be reconciled to a God whom they hate and with whom they do not desire peace. We call upon lost men and women to repent of sins that they love and cherish and do not want to part with, even if it means the damnation of their own souls. We proclaim a message of deliverance to people who have no natural desire to be delivered! No wonder Jesus warns us, "Behold, I send you out as sheep in the midst of wolves" (Matthew 10:16), which usually does not turn out too well for the sheep. And this is of course the very point Jesus is making! The bloody history of Christian martyrs over the past two millennia is a living testament to the truth of Jesus' words.

Coupled with the hardness of our culture is the near universal sense of awkwardness and inadequacy that most every Christian feels within his or her breast when it comes to sharing the gospel with the lost, not to mention the insecurities every pastor, church planter, and missionary secretly harbors concerning our own very limited gifts and skill sets. And add to these things the hostility and spiritual oppression of the devil who will not give up his sons without a fight and the temptations to grow weary and discouraged in our souls seem virtually insurmountable! We simply do not have the goods to fulfill Jesus' Great Commission with our own intelligence, strength, skill sets, and will power.

But it is just at this point that Jesus Himself gives us an exceedingly great and precious promise: "and lo, I am with you always, *even* to the end of the age" (Matthew 28:20b). It is important to recognize that while Jesus gave His Apostles a command to "Go," He also gave them a command to "Wait!" He says in Luke 24:49, "Behold, I send the Promise of My Father upon you; but tarry in the city of Jerusalem until you are endued with power from on high." In Acts 1:4 He reiterated this same commandment just before He ascended into heaven, for "He commanded them not to depart from Jerusalem, but to wait for the Promise of the Father…." And then He makes clear what this promise of the Father is: "But you shall receive power when the Holy Spirit has come upon you" (Acts 1:8a). C.H. Spurgeon summarized it well: "If we have not the Spirit which Jesus promised, we cannot perform the commission which Jesus gave."[7]

[7] Steven J. Lawson, *The Gospel Focus of Charles Spurgeon* (Sanford, FL: Reformation Trust Publishing, 2012), 107.

Jesus is not with us physically, but He is with us spiritually. For two thousand years there has never been so much as a nanosecond that has passed by where Jesus Christ has not been with His church. He who cannot lie has promised us that He will be with us spiritually through the Person and work of His Holy Spirit until He returns to us physically to take us home to glory. And in the context of the Great Commission this means that His presence and power will be with us as we seek to obey Him in evangelism, world missions, church planting, and ministerial training.

All throughout the narrative of Acts the Holy Spirit never lets us forget this. The book opens with "The former account I made, O Theophilus, of all that Jesus began both to do and teach…" (Acts 1:1). What we call "the Acts of the Apostles" is in truth "the Continuing Acts of Jesus Christ." In terms of *accomplishing* redemption Jesus has finished His work once for all and has sat down at the right hand of God, but in terms of *applying* His work of redemption our Prophet, Priest, and King was just getting started! We go on to read of Peter preaching at Pentecost, but "the Lord added to the church daily those were being saved" (Acts 2:47b). When Peter and John first experienced persecution for preaching the Word "they … prayed … and they were all filled with the Holy Spirit, and they spoke the word of God with boldness" (Acts 4:31). When evangelistic success came to the city of Antioch we are not left to wonder why it was so: "And the hand of the Lord was with them, and a great number believed and turned to the Lord" (Acts 11:21). And while Paul was faithful to evangelize the ladies gathered for prayer beside the river in Philippi, Lydia among them, we are told very specifically that "The Lord opened her heart to heed the things spoken by Paul" (Acts 16:14b). As Paul so eloquently says in 1 Corinthians 3:6, "I planted, Apollos watered, but God gave the increase." It is Christ who is the Great Architect and Builder of His church (Matthew 16:18). He was advancing His kingdom before we were born, and He will continue to do so once we are gone.

What hope this should give us all! We feel insufficient and inadequate for the task before us because we are. But His grace and His abiding presence are more than sufficient for us in all our weaknesses! Martin Luther had it exactly right when he said:

> Did we in our own strength confide, our striving would be losing;
> Were not the right man on our side, the man of God's own choosing.
> Dost ask who that may be? Christ Jesus, it is he!
> Lord Sabaoth his name, from age to age the same.
> And he must win the battle.
>
> And though this world, with devils filled, should threaten to undo us,
> We will not fear, for God has willed his truth to triumph through us.

The prince of darkness grim, we tremble not for him;
His rage we can endure, for lo! his doom is sure;
One little world shall fell him.

That Word above all earthly pow'rs, no thanks to them, abideth;
The Spirit and the gifts are ours through him who with us sideth.
Let goods and kindred go, this mortal life also;
The body they may kill; God's truth abideth still;
His kingdom is forever.[8]

The Purpose of the Great Commission

Certainly it is true that the goals of the Great Commission are the salvation of sinners, the planting of local churches, and the discipleship of the saints in every nation. But there is a far greater over-arching purpose that transcends even these noble and worthwhile ends: the glory of God. When we read the last book of the Bible we hear heaven itself resounding with the praises of God's elect people:

> And they sang a new song, saying "You are worthy to take the scroll, and to open its seals; for You were slain, and have redeemed us to God by Your blood out of every tribe and tongue and people and nation, and have made us kings and priests to our God; and we shall reign on the earth .... Worthy is the Lamb who was slain to receive power and riches and wisdom, and strength and honor and glory and blessing ... blessing and honor and glory and power be to Him who sits on the throne, and to the Lamb, forever and ever" (Revelation 5:9, 12, 13)!

Before time began, God the Father had both a chosen people and a chosen Lamb. He promised to give His only begotten Son the very nations of earth as His inheritance. If He endured the cross, He would obtain the promised crown. Jesus did endure the cross, and He has obtained the crown. And at the consummation of all things we will see clearly that all our sacrificial labors in evangelism and missions were not in vain, for a great multitude whom no man can number from every nation under heaven, from every people group, will be for all eternity extolling the praises of the One who redeemed them to God by His blood. The Lord Jesus will see the travail of His soul, and He will be satisfied.

[8] Martin Luther, "A Mighty Fortress is Our God" *Trinity Hymnal* (Suwanee, GA: Great Commission Publications, Inc.: 2004), Hymn 92.

12

Exalting Christ by Teaching His Church to Pray

Walt Chantry

The God who made us has always displayed a desire to fellowship with the creatures He made in His own image. There seems to have been a regular pattern of God communing with the first man and woman. After both of the first pair of humans had intentionally disobeyed God's command, "...they heard the sound of the Lord God walking in the garden (of Eden) in the cool of the day." This approach to them by God is represented as nothing unusual on His part. But for the first time Adam and Eve "hid themselves from the presence of the Lord God." A guilty conscience caused them to avoid usual companionship with their Lord and Maker (Genesis 3:8-24).[1] A very special relationship was degraded.

God did not cut off friendship with mankind due to Adam and Eve's partial withdrawal. For example, the Lord had a very long relationship with Enoch for 365 years. Of Enoch's long life on earth we read, "Enoch walked with God and he was not, for God took him" (Genesis 5:21-24). Enoch was obviously a friend of God. Luke tells us (Luke 3:37) that Enoch was an ancestor of Jesus. Hebrews 11:5 adds, "By faith Enoch was taken up so that he should not see death, and he was not found, because the Lord had taken him. Now before he was taken he was commended as having pleased God."

Of course you will remember that Abraham was a friend of God, and that God would not destroy the cities of Sodom and Gomorrah until He

[1] All Scripture quotations in this chapter are taken from the ESV.

had made a visit to Abraham's tent and discussed the matter of Sodom with His friend.

A similar friendship existed between the Lord and David. David too was an ancestor of Jesus. The New Testament opens with these words: "The book of the genealogy of Jesus Christ, the son of David, the son of Abraham" (Matthew 1:1).

When Saul, king of Israel, ignored the commandments given to him through the prophet Samuel, "The Lord sought him a man (out of Israel) "after God's own heart" (1 Samuel 13:14). Samuel was told that he must not be dejected about Saul's failures and sins. There *was* "a man after God's own heart." Samuel was sent to Jesse's home in Bethlehem to anoint this young man who walked closely with God-to be the next king of Israel.

In the historic context of this event, "a man after God's own heart" must be a man who obeys God's commands-in contrast to Saul. But additionally, David's being "a man after God's own heart" would extend far beyond his obedience to there being a bond of mutual love between him and the Lord.

Reading David's compositions, the psalms linked to his name, we discover that to lead others in worship requires that one actually be "a man after God's own heart." This means that, in addition to obeying God's commands, the leader must have a nurtured relationship with God, a seeking to be in God's presence, speaking with Him and rejoicing in His presence.

In our day we are blessed to have access to what it feels like to be a man after God's own heart or a woman after God's own heart. Although David's compositions of music are no longer available to us, the lyrics of many of his psalms *have been preserved* through the centuries. Thus we may meditate upon the very thoughts of this "man after God's own heart."

For instance, there is Psalm 63, "A Psalm of David when he was in the wilderness of Judah". This was the occasion when David and his most loyal friends and servants were chased into the wilderness by Absalom. Absalom had arranged a mutiny against his father to seize his throne and to kill his father-king.

Psalm 63 captures what David prayed in the most dangerous hours of flight from a rebel army. In crises a believer in God displays his heart, and in David's case it must be remembered that he was "a man after God's own heart". His opening words are profound and revealing:

> *O God*, you are *my God*; earnestly I seek *you*;
> my soul thirsts for *you*; my flesh faints for *you*,
> as in a dry and weary land where there is no water (Psalm 63:1)

We all can remember times when we lacked many things which distracted us from the Lord Himself as our chief longing, delight, and need. But our focus must be to draw near to *Him* and to be satisfied by our God's nearness.

David continues: "So I have looked upon you in the sanctuary" (the tent of meeting before Solomon built the temple). There David's eyes were fixed upon "beholding your power and glory" (v. 2). He did so because: *"your steadfast love is better than life"* (v. 3). ("Life is dear, but God's love is dearer," writes Spurgeon, and "to dwell with God is better than life at its best… life is but transient, mercy is everlasting.") Hence David writes, in verse 4: "I will bless *you* as long as I live." To express such words in times of trouble and danger is an expression of a human heart "after God's own heart."

So David speaks in prayer under duress in just the way he does when he has access to the tabernacle.

Yet he is not finished. When David is in the comfort and safety of his own bed, and he awakes, he reports:

> … I remember *you* upon my bed and meditate upon *you*
> in the watches of the night; for *you* have been my help,
> and in the shadow of *your* wings I will sing for joy.
> My soul clings to *you; your* right hand upholds me (Psalm 63:6-8)

Lastly, in circumstances when enemies seek to destroy his life:

> "But the king shall rejoice in *God*…" (Psalm 63:11)

Here is a man after God's own heart. Is the Lord so central to your life experiences? Should not our prayers, seeking to lead the flock before God, be filled with similar confidence in and desire for God's nearness? We *must* come near to God in our own devotions in order to lead a congregation into His presence.

For many generations of human life on earth it was promised that the Messiah (the Son of God) would appear on the earth. The earliest prophecy of Jesus' coming is in Genesis 3 when Satan, from within a serpent, spoke to the first woman. The promise was that the woman's seed would bruise the head of the tempter, and Satan would bruise Christ's heel. In other words, "…The reason the Son of God appeared was to destroy the works of the devil" (1 John 3:8).

In addition to Christ's appearing on earth there would come "a voice crying in the wilderness, 'prepare the way of the Lord; make straight in the desert a highway for our God'" (Isaiah 40:3).

"In those days (when Jesus had come) there was heard: 'The voice of one crying in the wilderness of Judea: Prepare the way of the Lord...'" (Matthew 3:3). This was John the Baptist.

Matthew 3:13-17 gives the account of Jesus being baptized by John. It is one of the most astounding events in Messiah's life on earth. Jesus presented Himself to be baptized by John the Baptist; as the Son of God was being baptized the heavens opened and the Spirit of God visibly descended in the form of a dove upon Christ. All of this occurred while the voice of God the Father audibly spoke, saying, "This is my beloved Son, with whom I am well pleased."

Apparently from that time onward there were occasions when Jesus' disciples interacted with John's followers. In this way Jesus' disciples discovered that John the Baptist had taught his own disciples to pray. That fact impressed Jesus' followers. They had also observed the Lord Jesus Himself in prayer. On one occasion, when Jesus had been praying in a certain place, one of Jesus' disciples, "...said to Jesus, 'Lord, teach us to pray, as John taught his disciples'" (Luke 11:1).

On that occasion Jesus used as an outline the same prayer which He taught in His Sermon on the Mount (Matthew 6:5-13, with Luke 11:2-4). Additionally, in Luke He emphasized the importance of persistence in prayer (Luke 11:5-13).

The history of our Lord Jesus and his disciples emphasizes the necessity of ministers teaching their sheep to pray. This must be done by *example*—as Christians hear their pastors pray, and by *precept*—as they teach biblical passages on prayer. This necessity for the wellbeing of our congregations must be ever on the consciousness of ministers.[2]

Teaching prayer by example presents a multitude of opportunities to ministers. There are parts of worship in which to lead all the congregation in prayer weekly: congregational prayers in stated times of worship, prayers in connection with baptisms, the Lord's Supper, the receiving of new members are some of these occasions.

Also the minister visits the homes of members, visits in hospitals, conducts weddings, funerals, and graveside services. Counseling sessions with the troubled must also be noticed as times requiring our prayers.

[2] A remarkable book to assist ministers in understanding this vast subject of prayer is *Theology of Prayer*, written by B. M. Palmer of New Orleans, LA, and most recently published by Sprinkle Publications. A large segment of this book outlines the Covenant of Grace. Then the author proceeds to explain how prayers to Father, Son and Holy Spirit are appropriate by the function of each Person in the Covenant of Grace.

Because a variety of needs require that we pray with our flocks, it would be advisable for every minister to form a notebook of biblical prayers for different occasions. He may find that additional suggestions from the Word of God cause him to add to his notebook as he continues in his own pilgrimage, including daily Bible reading.

Of course the psalms are rich with suggestions for prayers in times of sorrow and distress as well as moments of joy and gratitude to God. The prayers of our Lord Jesus Christ are also a rich garden of devotional instruction. And we must not ignore apostolic prayers. In summary, the Bible itself is a true prayer guide.

Additionally, we need to add to our instruction via ministerial example in prayer by teaching often on prayer, so that our members gain an understanding of the subject. Attention must be given to the various kinds of prayer which we must address to the Father, the Son, and the Holy Spirit.

Scripture gives examples of *adoration* of the Holy Trinity and each member thereof. Close to, but not necessarily identical to adoration is *praise*. Then allied to, but not precisely the same, is *thanksgiving*—offering thanks to God for being *our* God and definitely giving thanks for all the kind blessings heaped upon us.

Certainly the incident in Luke 17:12-19 smites our consciences. There Jesus miraculously healed ten lepers. Yet only one of them returned to Him to give glory to God for this heavenly blessing. What great things the Lord does for us! Yet how often we fail to give glory or thanksgiving in return to Him. It is a further rebuke that Jesus pointed out that the one who did give thanks was a stranger to Judaism, uninstructed in true religion.

It is not uncommon to attend church meetings where *supplications* are made on behalf of our beloved brothers and sisters in Christ who are in one sort of crisis or another. *Intercessions* are made for missionaries and their church plants. But there is an absence of *adoration* or even *thanks* being given to our Lord. Nor are *confessions of sin* and *neglect of God* addressed.

It would be inappropriate for an individual to confess his personal sins in a congregational prayer time. Yet national sins might be addressed. Church failures could be brought before God with repentance.

At this point let us take note that many kinds of prayer are offered up to God through our hymns. Perhaps we, as pastors, need to call attention to the kinds of prayer the congregation is about to sing to God through our hymnal. For instance we are confessing our sin as we sing:

> We have not *known* thee as we ought,
> Nor learned thy wisdom, grace and pow'r;
> The things of earth have filled our thought,
> And trifles of the passing hour.

Lord, give us light, thy truth to see,
And make us wise in knowing thee.

We have not *feared* thee as we ought,
Nor bowed beneath thine awful eye,
Nor guarded deed, and word, and thought,
Remembering that God was nigh.
Lord, give us faith to know thee near,
And grant the grace of holy fear.

We have not *loved* thee as we ought,
Nor cared that we are loved by thee;
Thy presence we have coldly sought,
And feebly longed thy face to see.
Lord, give a pure and loving heart
To feel and own the love thou art.

When shall we *know* thee as we ought,
And *fear*, and *love*, and *serve* aright!
When shall we, out of trial brought,
Be perfect in the land of light!
Lord, may we day by day prepare
To see thy face, and serve thee there.

—Thomas Benson Pollock

What a heart-moving confession is this hymn! There are others like it. The emphasis here is that God's people must understand that there are many aspects of our hearts involved in approaching God. All of them must be consciously engaged in by us all.

In the same way hymns give adoration, thanksgiving and praise to our God. One of the church's finest hymns of adoration was composed by Bernard of Clairvaux more than 800 years ago. It reads as follows:

Jesus, thou Joy of loving hearts,
Thou Fount of life, thou Light of men,
From the best bliss that earth imparts,
We turn unfilled to thee again.

Thy truth unchanged hath ever stood;
Thou savest those that on thee call;
To them that seek thee thou art good,
To them that find thee All in all.

We taste thee, O thou living bread,
And long to feast upon thee still;
We drink of thee, the Fountainhead,
And thirst our souls from thee to fill.

Our restless spirits yearn for thee,
Where'ere our changeful lot is cast;
Glad when thy gracious smile we see,
Blest when our faith can hold thee fast.

O Jesus, ever with us stay,
Make all our moments calm and bright;
Chase the dark night of sin away,
Shed o'er the world thy holy light.

How often are there prayers of this spiritual depth found in our congregational prayer times? I think the authors of the above hymns, Thomas B. Pollock and Bernard of Clairvaux, spent much time in preparation for these prayers. Spontaneity is not always the best source of worship.

More expressions of our affections for *God*, more of delight in *His* nearness and presence in our assemblies are called for. After all, our greatest need is that we be found in fellowship with the Father, Son and Holy Spirit.

13

Exalting Christ by Observing The Church's Ordinances

Conrad Mbewe

The Water That Divides is a book that was first written in 1997 and was revised and updated in 2008. It is about baptism. In a positive sense, baptism is truly the water that divides between a person's past life and new his life in Christ. However, that is not the division that the title is meant to convey. It speaks about the division that baptism has caused in the church between Baptists and Paedo-baptists. Its current updated edition goes to great length to show the two views side-by-side. Of course, in the end it still leaves us divided by water!

This is because we feel quite strongly about the ordinances of baptism and the Lord's Supper. Christ commanded that we observe them and their meaning is tied up with the way in which we observe them. We cannot claim to be honouring and exalting Christ when we are doing with His ordinances as we please. That is why the water that divides continues to divide us.

In any church, its membership comprises individuals who are either newly converted or are coming from other church denominations. It is important to bring them to an understanding of why we practice baptism and the Lord's Supper the way we do. It is vital that we show them that our practice is based on the clear teaching of Scripture so that any wrong views they have are corrected and they are encouraged to hold firmly to a practice rooted in Scripture.

Dr. Fred Malone's Journey

This book is being written and compiled in honor of the ministry of Dr. Fred Malone. The Lord has enabled His servant to sustain an excellent ministry over many years. During that period Dr. Malone has written a few books and perhaps his *magnum opus* is the book entitled *The Baptism of Disciples Alone*. This fact alone should convince us all that this man is concerned about exalting Christ through the church's ordinances as we all should be.

The book *The Baptism of Disciples Alone* was born out of the author's journey of faith. Dr. Malone started out as a Baptist. He was brought up in a Baptist church and got converted there. However, while training for the ministry he came to the conviction that to be consistent with his newly found Reformed Faith he needed to become a paedobaptist. So, he was ordained in the Presbyterian church. Yet each time he baptised a baby his conscience almost killed him. That was how in 1977, he came back to the Baptist fold. So, if there was ever a man who has taken a high view of the church's ordinances it must be Dr. Malone. That alone is what has caused him to cross fences twice. He still has a lot of respect for paedobaptists as fellow believers but he is convinced that on this point they have erred.

What precisely convicted Dr. Malone so that he would reverse his views, especially on baptism? The first was the regulative principle of worship. He was convinced that this is "an essential doctrine in both Baptist and Presbyterian churches."[1] Whereas baptism is not essential to salvation, Jesus commanded the baptism of those who believe (Matthew 28:18–20). We have no right to do anything else. The second was the way Scripture was being interpreted in order to make infant baptism acceptable.

One reason Dr. Malone has felt that the issue of the ordinances—baptism and the Lord Supper—is important is because there are many other issues that stand or fall with them. He states, "The issue of the sacraments (ordinances) is not minor by any stretch of the Reformed imagination. Along with infant baptism come issues regarding the nature of the church and church membership, the evangelism of "covenant children," church discipline, and so forth."[2]

Another reason Dr. Malone feels that ordinances are important is simply that every man must be true to his conscience. He states, "Whether a Baptist or paedobaptist pastor, to be unable to hold or defend one's practice of a sacrament from Scripture alone with sincere conviction is a viola-

[1] Fred A. Malone, *The Baptism of Disciples Alone*, (Cape Coral, FL: Founders Press, 2003), xiv.

[2] Malone, *The Baptism of Disciples Alone*, xxv.

tion of conscience, ones own confession, and ministerial ordination vows."[3] And whatever is not from faith is sin (Romans 14:23). This is what ultimately led to his resignation from the Presbyterian ministry.

Very well, then, let us search the Scriptures and see what they teach concerning both baptism and the Lord's Supper so that we may exalt Christ through the way in which we administer these ordinances. We will begin with baptism simply because it is the door through which we enter into the local church's life and part of that life is the regular partaking of the Lord's Supper. However, we need to begin by showing that Christ commanded the observance of both of these ordinances.

Commanded by Christ

In the Gospel of Matthew Jesus said to His disciples, "All authority in heaven and on earth has been given to me. Go therefore and make disciples of all nations, baptizing them in the name of the Father and of the Son and of the Holy Spirit, teaching them to observe all that I have commanded you. And behold, I am with you always, to the end of the age" (Matthew 28:19–20).[4] It is clear from these words of our Lord that He expected His disciples to baptize those who became His disciples as a result of their ministry.

People often ask the question, "Why should we be baptised? Is it not enough that we are interested in joining the church? Why get plunged into water in public in the twenty-first century?" The answer is quite simple: Christ commanded it! Jesus Christ is exalted as He is joyfully obeyed, and this obedience commences when a person becomes a Christian. Conversion comprises repentance towards God and faith in the Lord Jesus Christ (Acts 20:21). One of the ways in which the repentance and faith become visible is when a new believer participates in baptism and the Lord's Supper. Both of these were not initiated in the New Testament church through the cleverness of its first leaders. Rather they were initiated through the command of the Lord Jesus Christ. That is why they are called "ordinances." Jesus *ordained* that they should be carried out. Our role is to obey by doing them!

In 1 Corinthians the apostle Paul writes,

> For I received from the Lord what I also delivered to you, that the Lord Jesus on the night when he was betrayed took bread, and when he had

[3] Malone, *The Baptism of Disciples Alone*, xxx.

[4] Unless otherwise indicated all Scripture quotations in this chapter are taken from the ESV.

> given thanks, he broke it, and said, 'This is my body which is for you. Do this in remembrance of me.' In the same way also he took the cup, after supper, saying, 'This cup is the new covenant in my blood. Do this, as often as you drink it, in remembrance of me.' For as often as you eat this bread and drink the cup, you proclaim the Lord's death until he comes (1 Corinthians 11:23–26).

What Paul received from the Lord as a command, he also passed on to the Corinthian church as a command. The Lord's Supper is a command that the church must obey regularly.

Whatever view we may have of the finer details of both baptism and the Lord's Supper, we must at least agree on one thing; the Lord commanded that they should be observed in His church until He returns. They were the only two ordinances that Jesus commanded. This is important to note because those of our members coming from, say, a Roman Catholic background will join our churches with a truckload of other ordinances, which they normally call "sacraments". The Roman Catholic Church has added five other sacraments and so they have seven altogether. These are in three categories. There are the sacraments of initiation, which are Baptism, Confirmation, and the Lord's Supper (called the Eucharist); the sacraments of healing, which are Penance and the Anointing of the Sick; and finally the sacraments of service, which are Holy Orders and Matrimony.

But we must ask further, "Why did Jesus choose these two ordinances to be the only ones to be observed by His church until His return?" It is primarily because these two are good visible representations of vital spiritual truths that nourish our faith. Water baptism represents in a physical way the spiritual baptism you undergo when you become a Christian. The Holy Spirit immerses you into the body of Christ. You die and are buried to your past life, and you enter into a new life with Christ so that all that belongs to Christ begins to flow to you. This is what the apostle Paul says in Romans 6:3, "Do you not know that all of us who have been baptized into Christ Jesus were baptized into his death? We were buried therefore with him by baptism into death, in order that, just as Christ was raised from the dead by the glory of the Father, we too might walk in newness of life." Undergoing baptism and seeing others baptized is a great reminder of this glorious truth, which explains why our lives ought to be morally and spiritually different. We will look at this in more detail later.

Similarly, in the Lord's Supper you are regularly depicting your spiritual participation in the body and blood of Christ. Remember, the apostle Paul said to the Corinthians, "For as often as you eat this bread and drink the cup, you proclaim the Lord's death until he comes" (1 Corinthians 11:26). Nothing can be clearer than that. The Lord's Supper is an enactment that shows us again and again that our Saviour suffered and died for our sins. So, by doing this outwardly you are playing out spiritual truth in parable form to nourish your faith.

There is yet another reason why Jesus chose these two ordinances to be the only ones to be observed by His church until His return. It is the fact that Jesus wants every Christian to tell the world publicly what He has done for them. Have you repented from your sin and put your trust in Christ? Jesus wants you to "stand up and be counted" by coming forward to be baptised. Are you in fellowship with Christ and with His people? Jesus wants you to show it regularly (not just once, as is the case with baptism) by sharing with them in this meal called the Lord's Supper. So, these two ordinances help you to make a clean break with the world and be an ongoing part of a new humanity and community in Christ.

Let us now look at each of these two ordinances, one at a time.

Baptism

Water baptism—an outward expression of an inward experience

We have already touched on this, but let us now go into a little more detail. The inward experience is taught in Romans. The apostle Paul says, "What shall we say, then? Shall we go on sinning so that grace may increase? By no means! We died to sin; how can we live in it any longer? Or don't you know that all of us who were baptized into Christ Jesus were baptized into his death? We were therefore buried with him through baptism into death in order that, just as Christ was raised from the dead through the glory of the Father, we too may live a new life" (Romans 6:1–4). In other words, the reason why a true Christian cannot continue in sin is because he died to sin. How? By the spiritual baptism he underwent at conversion. Just as Jesus died to this world of sin, was buried and rose again to newness of life, so also every true Christian is identified with that experience. He dies to sin, is spiritually buried as far as that life is concerned, and commences a new life.

Let us listen to the apostle Paul as he puts it in his own apostolic way, "For if we have been united with him in a death like his, we shall certainly be united with him in a resurrection like his. We know that our old self was crucified with him in order that the body of sin might be brought to nothing, so that we would no longer be enslaved to sin. For one who has died has been set free from sin" (Romans 6:5–7). Christians are individuals who have been so united to Christ that His experience in dying and rising is bequeathed to them. The death was in order to crucify "the old self" so that the body of death is rendered ineffective and powerless. That is how we are freed from sin in actual experience. Every true Christian knows this.

The apostle Paul continues,

> "Now if we have died with Christ, we believe that we will also live with him. We know that Christ, being raised from the dead, will never die again; death no longer has dominion over him. For the death he died he died to sin, once for all, but the life he lives he lives to God. So you also must consider yourselves dead to sin and alive to God in Christ Jesus" (Romans 6:8–11).

This may sound like a repetition but it is not. The apostle Paul is making the point that sin in us has received a final blow that it can never recover from through Christ. Just as Jesus will never again be subjected to the power of death, and now "the life he lives he lives to God", so also we who are true Christians will never ever be enslaved to sin but instead will forever live for God.

Water baptism simply reflects that experience. When you go into the water you are telling the world that you have died to it and all its wickedness. The person you used to be has been buried. That person is no more! Then when you come out of the water you are telling the world that the person they are now seeing and relating to is a brand new person— a person whose only desire in life is to obey the Lord Jesus Christ and to live to the glory of God. That is what baptism symbolizes. It is important to be baptised because it is important for you to tell the world, in this God ordained way, what has happened to you. You are fundamentally and permanently transformed. This is glorious!

The only appropriate recipients of baptism

By implication, the major lesson we learn from this passage is who the appropriate recipients of baptism are. It must surely be those who are testifying of this glorious experience. It must be only those who have come to believe the good news of salvation in Jesus Christ. They alone are the ones who have had this fundament and permanent transformation. There are many examples of this in the Bible. For instance, look at the Philippian jailor. He wanted to be saved. The apostles shared the gospel with him and his whole household, and then they were baptised. Notice the same pattern in all references to baptism in Acts (2:41, 8:12, 36–38, 9:17–22, 10:47–48, 11:16, 16:14–15, 18:8, 19:4–5, and 22:15–16). See also the order in Matthew 28:19 and Mark 16:16. Despite such a overwhelming evidence, people still insist on paedobaptism. Clearly, baptism is only for those who repent and believe.

Despite the fact that there is no explicit instance of an infant being baptised in the whole of the New Testament, this practice has been taking place in the church for many centuries. Whereas churches like the Roman Catholic Church would consider the children being baptised as being cleansed from sin, most Protestant churches that practice paedobaptism simply see this as the New Testament form of the Old Testament circumcision, which was performed on infants. They also argue from the household baptisms in the Book of Acts (Acts 16:15, 33, and 18:8), assuming that there must have been infants in those households. Further arguments are built on the passages of Scripture where Jesus was telling his disciples to let the children go to him (Matthew 19:13–15, Mark 10:14, and Luke 10:21). Another reference used to justify infant baptism is the statement by Peter on the Day of Pentecost when he said, "…the promise is for you and your children…" (Acts 2:39).

This is clearly clutching at straw. The established pattern, as we have already observed, is that baptism followed repentance and faith in the Lord Jesus Christ. We do not need to repeat this. Besides, there is no evidence that the households referred to in the Book of Acts had any infants. Why should we argue from silence when there are so many passages teaching the opposite? Finally, the New Testament equivalent of circumcision is not baptism but circumcision of the heart (see Romans 2:29 and Colossians 2:11). And this spiritual circumcision only takes place upon a person's conversion.

The proper method of baptism

A little less obvious from this passage is another lesson, i.e. what the proper method of baptism is. The phrase "to baptise" in the Greek is simply "to immerse, dip, sink, drown, or bathe". Sprinkling is not one of the meanings. Baptism denotes someone or something going under a liquid and thus being totally covered over by it. Sadly, due to the fact that many churches had already been practicing infant baptism through sprinkling, it has proved very difficult to translate baptism as immersion. That it has been transliterated instead, causing us to lose its most basic meaning. (The same thing has been done with the word "deacon", which simply means "servant").

It is absurd for a person to say he was baptised by sprinkling. That is equivalent to saying, "I was immersed by sprinkling"! That is a contradiction in terms. You were either immersed or sprinkled. So, it only makes sense that you are immersed if you are to claim to be baptised. In the Bible we have a classic example that shows us that even in Bible times baptism had to be by immersion. It was when Philip the evangelist baptised the Ethiopian eunuch. The eunuch was on a journey in the desert reading the Bible. Philip preached to him the good news about Jesus as Saviour. He obviously also told him the importance of baptism because we read that, "… as they travelled along the road, they came to some water and the eunuch said, 'Look, here is water. Why shouldn't I be baptised?' And he gave orders to stop the chariot. Then both Philip and the eunuch went down into the water and Philip baptised him" (Acts 8:36–38). A traveller on a journey across the desert would have carried drinking water, which would have been used if sprinkling was the way baptism was conducted. However, it is clear from this passage that the Ethiopian eunuch was not pointing to a bottle of water but to large body of water like a stream or river because they later "went down into the water" and that was where Philip baptised him. There is no doubt that baptism was by immersion.

Baptism—the way in which you join the church of Jesus Christ on earth

This is where, again, pointing out the spiritual meaning of baptism is so important. Since you were joined to Christ's mystical body through spiritual baptism, it only makes sense that you should join the church (Christ's earthly body) through water baptism. The Bible says, referring to spiritual baptism, "The body is a unit, though it is made up of many parts; and though all its parts are many, they form one body. So it is with Christ. For we were all baptized by one Spirit into one body—whether Jews or Greeks, slave or free—and we were all given the one Spirit to drink" (1 Corinthians 12:12–13). This is the way in which we were joined to Christ. The Holy Spirit immersed us into the body of Christ. Water baptism is meant to show outwardly what has already happened inwardly through the work of the Holy Spirit. That is why it is the God-ordained way of joining the church of Jesus Christ, which is his body on earth. Even paedobaptists seem to see this when they equate it to circumcision, which was the means by which male Israelites came under God's covenant with Abraham and thus were considered part of Israel as a nation. Thus, they reason that believers *and their children* become members of the church through baptism.

The main reasons for baptism

We must again ask the question, "Why go through this hassle?" The first answer is simply that Jesus commanded it (we've just seen this in Matthew 28:19 and Mark 16:16). It is your first act of obedience to prove that you have truly repented from your rebellious ways. Remember also that it is an aid to your faith and a witness to the world. You make a statement when you get baptized because baptism is an outward expression of an inward experience. You are saying to yourself and to the world that you are one with Christ in what He went through to save you, i.e. his death, burial and resurrection.

The Lord's Supper

Let us also briefly look at the Lord's Supper. Although it is not one of the main areas where Mr. Valiant-for-Truth, whose life and ministry is being honoured through this book, fought for the faith. Yet because it is one of the two ordinances commanded by the Lord Jesus, we should also take a look at it.

In order for us to learn a few lessons about the Lord's Supper, let us go back to one of the accounts of its inauguration by the Gospel writers. Matthew writes,

> "Now on the first day of Unleavened Bread the disciples came to Jesus, saying, 'Where will you have us prepare for you to eat the Passover?' He said, 'Go into the city to a certain man and say to him, "The Teacher says, My time is at hand. I will keep the Passover at your house with my disciples."' And the disciples did as Jesus had directed them, and they prepared the Passover. When it was evening, he reclined at table with the twelve…Now as they were eating, Jesus took bread, and after blessing it broke it and gave it to the disciples, and said, 'Take, eat; this is my body.' And he took a cup, and when he had given thanks he gave it to them, saying, 'Drink of it, all of you, for this is my blood of the covenant, which is poured out for many for the forgiveness of sins. I tell you I will not drink again of this fruit of the vine until that day when I drink it new with you in my Father's kingdom'" (Matthew 26:17–29).

Transubstantiation or consubstantiation

Whereas people undergo baptism without thinking there is something spiritual in the water itself, many people see in the bread and wine of the Lord's Supper some magical powers, which are at the least superstitious and at the worst idolatrous. They handle the bread and the cup as if they were holding magic charms in their hands. It is important if they are going to exalt Christ through the church ordinances that they come to a proper understanding of its biblical nature.

Historically, there were arguments related to whether the bread and the wine literally converted in substance into the body and blood of Christ (this position is called "transubstantiation") or that the body and blood of Christ simply became part of or co-existed with the bread and the wine (this position is called "consubstantiation"). Martin Luther, the great 16th century protestant reformer championed consubstantiation as a way of reforming the doctrine of transubstantiation.

These arguments came to the fore because of Jesus' words quoted above when He was inaugurating the Lord's Supper. When Jesus gave his disciples the bread, He said, "Take, eat; this is my body" (Matthew 26:26). And when He gave them the cup He said, "Drink of it, all of you, for this is my blood…" (Matthew 26:27–28). It needs to be understood that Jesus was using figurative language. Hence, when He finished giving the bread and cup to His disciples He said, "I tell you I will not drink again of this fruit of the vine…" (Matthew 26:29). It had not changed into His blood. It was still the fruit of the vine! The bread and the wine simply represent the body and blood of Christ. What makes this meal unique is our understanding of what it symbolises even as we partake of it.

Metaphoric speech is a form of speech that refers to an item by the very item it symbolised. For instance, you can say, "This is my wife", when you are pointing at a photo of your wife. It does not mean that your wife is literally there. The image shows something of what your wife looks like. Also, often the significance lies in what that item symbolises. So, a man can get very upset when you tear a photo of his darling wife. It is not because the photo has become his wife. Rather, he has an attachment to that photo because it reminds him of the woman that he loves. That is also how we feel about the ring of gold around our fingers. It symbolises the covenant we are in, the covenant of marriage. So, the bread and the wine remain bread and wine.

The witness of the meal

We also learn from this account that the Lord's Supper is a New Testament version of the Passover of the Old Testament. Until verse 26, the disciples thought they were eating the Passover! All Jesus did was to change what this meal symbolised, from the salvation of Israel from Egyptian captivity to the salvation of sinners from sin's captivity. The Passover was a witness to the world of God's saving power (Exodus 12:21–36). The Lord's Supper serves the same purpose. The people who eat this meal are saying they were totally powerless to save themselves from sin, but the Lord delivered them through Christ!

The right recipients

It was the disciples of Jesus that He had the meal with in a secluded place (the upper room). In the book of Acts, we find that the believers shared this meal together. In 1 Corinthians 11:29, the apostle Paul warns that this meal should only be eaten by those who "discern the Lord's body" in order to avoid incurring God's wrath. If we are to exalt Christ through this ordinance we must take extra pains to ensure that only those who qualify partake of this meal.

Dr Malone only briefly deals with the Lord's Supper in his book *The Baptism of Disciples Alone*. He contends that it is inconsistent to baptize infants and then deny them the Lord's Supper. Surely, the recipients of one ordinance should also be the recipients of the other. Paedobaptists are divided over this issue. Men like John Murray argued that (1) there was no evidence that newly born babies would have partaken of the Passover meal in the Old Testament, which is the equivalent of the Lord's Supper in the New Testament, and (2) the very nature of the food being eaten militates against the inclusion of infants. Dr. Malone's answer would, however, be that infants should simply be excluded from both ordinances because those ordinances are only for Christ's disciples. It is Christ's disciples alone who are able to meaningfully participate in them because they alone can appropriate by faith the meaning of these ordinances.

Sadly, there is a woeful neglect of the Lord's Supper by many Christians and a readiness by the ungodly to lay their hands on this sacred meal. The Puritan preacher, Thomas Doolittle (1630–1707), wrote this in his wonderful treatise on the Lord's Supper:

> "The long absence of some believers from, and the careless hasting of all ungodly to, the Supper of the Lord is much to be lamented. The former, being explicitly charged by the Lord to do this in remembrance of Him, yet will not. The latter, threatened with damnation if they do, yet will … The former neglect this means of their spiritual growth, and slight the love and forget the words of their dying Lord, as though they could thrive in grace while they neglect their spiritual food. The other, neglecting the means of their spiritual birth, forget the words of the Apostle: 'Let a man examine himself, and so let him eat of the bread and drink of the cup … ' Such is the unthankfulness of some who should, but do not, and the wickedness of some who do, but should not come unto this gospel feast."

As I close this chapter, let me reiterate the need for us to take both baptism and the Lord's Supper seriously. We must take their biblical form seriously too because their meaning is tied up with the way in which we observe them. We cannot claim to be honouring Christ when we are doing with His ordinances as we please. Let us ensure that new converts who come into our churches are taught the biblical form of both baptism and the Lord's Supper. Our desire to ensure unity in the wider evangelical family should not cause us to be silent on this matter. We must exalt Christ through church ordinances.

Let me end with an appeal from Dr. Malone's book, *The Baptism of Disciples Alone*. He pleads with us Baptists not to fear persecution to the point where we are willing to serve in any denomination. Truth matters! He says, "Oh, that we had more Baptist "pioneers" willing to endure hardship to build new churches or to reform our established Baptist churches! Where will Reformed Baptists of conscience worship in coming generations if we do not take up the cross now?"[5] That is what we have found in Dr. Malone himself. He is a true Mr. Valiant-For-Truth.

[5] Malone, *The Baptism of Disciples Alone*, xx.

14

Exalting Christ by Contending for the Faith

Earl Blackburn

To the one who believes upon Him and His saving gospel, Christ is precious (1 Peter 2:7). The greatest joy and delight for the true Christian is to love, worship, serve, and honor Christ Jesus the Lord. The believer has tasted and seen that the LORD is good (Psalm 34:8). A follower of Christ has discovered that His gospel is powerful and indisputable (Romans 1:16; 1 Corinthians 15:1–8), His salvation is life-changing (2 Corinthians 5:17), His love is measureless (1 John 3:1), His church is wise (Ephesians 3:10, 21), His precepts and commandments are not burdensome, but light (John 14:15; 1 John 5:3), and His glory and honor are of greater value than eating or drinking (1 Corinthians 10:31). This has been the Christian perspective for over two millennia.

However, something has changed in Christianity, especially in Western culture. Paul wrote of perilous and difficult times in the "last days" (2 Timothy 3:1–9). He knew there would be periods when the professed church "would not endure sound doctrine" but would "turn away their ears from the truth and will turn aside to myths" (2 Timothy 4:3–4). We are living in such days. These are similar to what C.H. Spurgeon called the "downgrade" in the late 1800s. Biblical Christianity is on the decline in our Western civilization, specifically in the United States. These are days our fathers and grandfathers never dreamed would materialize in our nation. In 2009, President Barak Obama emphatically stated that the United States is no longer a Christian country. (There is a question of whether it had ever been one, but that is beyond the scope of this chapter.) In the year 2017, it is popular to be anything but a Christian. What once was the mainstay of Western society is now the brunt of many jokes, the whipping post for the media, the disdain of college professors, and worst of all, the abject complacency of the general population.

Tolerance has become the war cry of the age against a Christianity that has a biblical conscience and conviction. D.A Carson correctly notes this attitude: "Tolerance currently occupies a very high place in Western culture, a bit like motherhood and apple pie in America in the early 1950s: it is considered rather gauche to question it."[1] This present culture wants people to be tolerant of everyone and everything, without being judgmental. Carson further explains that those who cry the loudest for tolerance are the most intolerant of biblical Christianity, and the truth it claims upon the unbelieving world. Herein lies the duplicity of the movement for tolerance.

Christian doctrine is disrespected, the Christian church is deemed unimportant, personal beliefs based on Holy Scripture are belittled, and moral convictions derived from God's Word are challenged. A Christian's faith, though frequently given an outward smile of seeming approval, is inwardly mocked, especially if that person stands for the exclusivity of Christ. If anyone confesses that Jesus is the *only* Way, the *only* Truth, and the *only* Life, and that there is no other way to God and heaven except through Him (see John 14:6), that person will be resisted with bitter vitriol. Such Christians are often called unloving, hate-mongers, and anti-social bigots. All sorts of sarcastic, ridiculing, scornful, and insulting labels are attached to them. If Christians remain faithful to Christ and His inerrant Word, society will view them as arrogant and as self-righteous "holier than thou."

Furthermore, there are those who call themselves "spiritual" and talk about having faith but never mention the object of their faith. Quickly, the discerning Christian begins to understand that "spiritual" means something ambiguously vague, and faith is little more than a positive thinking or faith in faith. The scornful often tolerate this misguided mindset even though they perceive it as naïve.

How are orthodox, evangelical Christians to respond? Should they artificially smile and simply seek to live a good and godly life before an unbelieving world? Should they be passive and quietly accepting of everyone and everything as they exemplify respectful lives and nothing more? Or is there another posture that must be taken? Must they honor Christ by speaking up boldly and graciously, challenging the pervasive skepticism and pluralism of this present age? Are they to be content with the way

[1] D. A. Carson, *The Intolerance of Tolerance* (Grand Rapids, MI: William B. Eerdmans Publishing Company, 2012), 1.

things are or are they to contend for the faith in an adverse environment? These are the questions and issues that will be addressed in this chapter. Before doing so, we must begin by considering the source and definition of the Christian faith.

The Source of the Faith

There is a body of belief taught in the Holy Bible that is called "the faith." There are many who contest this claim saying the Scriptures are little more than human compilations of moralistic stories and pietistic platitudes. The prevailing conventional wisdom conveys that it is okay to be religious and even Christian if that is a person's preference, but to press individual beliefs upon others or to state that someone or something is wrong is considered hateful or ignorant. This notion has permeated much of twenty-first century society. The Bible is a good book, many will affirm, but it is only one among many spiritual books that can be beneficial. One should keep personal faith private and deferentially respectful without saying anything negative about another's beliefs or unbelief, their behaviors or misbehaviors. However, when the Christian reads the Holy Bible another directive is taught.

Before this thought is considered, one must ask what is the apostolic and conservative evangelical understanding of the Holy Bible? Is it another religious book that is of equal value and importance as the *Qur'an* to Islam, the *Vedas* and *Bhagavad Gita* to Hinduism, the *Sutras* to Buddhism, and *The Book of Mormon* to the Latter-day Saints?

The above question forces the Christian to return to *epistemology*. Epistemology is "a theory of knowledge or an inquiry into how we gain knowledge,"[2] or, the foundation of the source of knowledge. King David, the psalmist, understood the necessity of having a proper foundation: "If the foundations are destroyed, what can the righteous do?" (Psalm 11:2). Peter, the apostle, affirms this indispensable truth that was laid by the Old Testament prophets (2 Peter 1:16–21). According to Peter, the Holy Scriptures are "the prophetic word more sure" than if Christ was here upon the earth corporally. For the orthodox, evangelical Christian, the Holy Bible alone is the foundational source of our epistemology, of all spiritual knowledge. There are seven characteristics of the Holy Bible and they are wonderfully rich and underpinning.

The first characteristic of the Holy Bible is that it is ***inspired*** (2 Timothy 3:16–17; 2 Peter 1:20–21). The word "inspired" (theo/pneustoj) means

[2] Millard J. Erickson, *Concise Dictionary of Christian Theology* (Grand Rapids, MI: Baker Book House, 1986), 49.

"God breathed," as in breathed out by God. God moved upon holy men of old, and by His Spirit, breathed out and into them His sacred Word. It is a unique product, a very special revelation of God that is self-authenticating, a divine *self-disclosure* revealing the very mind and heart of God the LORD.

Second, it is ***inerrant.*** Inerrancy means freedom from error of any kind: factual, moral or spiritual. The Holy Scriptures are exempt from the liability of mistakes. They are incapable of error. The word inerrant refers only to the original transmissions and manuscripts, not to the numerous translations. In spite of sleepy scribes, misguided devotees, evil intentions of enemies, and human foibles, the Word of God is without error.

Third, it is ***infallible.*** Inerrant and infallible are not interchangeable terms. The Holy Scriptures are inerrant because they contain *no* errors. They are infallible because they *cannot* err! Due to its infallibility, the Word of God has not, will not, nor cannot lead someone astray in anything it declares or teaches. The Bible is not primarily a book of science, but when it addresses scientific matters, it is infallible. The same is true in all other matters such as medicine, history, economics, jurisprudence, etc. Whatever subject it addresses, it addresses the subject infallibly.

Fourth, it is ***authoritative.*** It is recorded in the Bible that the LORD spoke 3,808 times. Since God entirely inspired and transmitted the Holy Scriptures to mankind via His Holy Spirit, they are vested with *His* holy authority. It is an authority that no other entity or power can bestow or take away. The Bible is permeated with God the Creator and Lord's sovereign authority. His imprimatur is stamped upon it in every page and part. Its disclosures are glorious; its declarations are true; its commandments are decisive; its threatenings are horrible, and its promises are emphatic. This means that whatever God reveals about Himself must be embraced; whatever He declares must be believed; whatever He commands must be obeyed, whatever He forbids must be avoided; whatever He promises shall surely come to pass. No other earthly authority equals or surpasses the Bible.

Fifth, it is ***perspicuous.*** The word comes from *perspicuity*, derived from the Latin and it means transparency or the *"see-through-able-ness"* of an object. In other words, the Bible is clear and possesses the quality of clarity. While some passages are difficult to understand, if all four-syllable names and places are removed from the Bible, it is written on a fourth-grade reading level. There are those who are untaught and unstable who "twist them to their own destruction, as they do also the rest of the Scriptures" (2 Peter 3:16), but with a little effort and careful study the passages will become clear and understandable. One need not be a Hebrew or Greek scholar to read and comprehend the Bible. A humbly educated farmer, a moderately learned housewife, or a little child can read and understand it.

Sixth, it is ***preserved***. The psalmist declared in Psalm 12:6–7: "The words of the LORD *are* pure words; *as* silver tried in a furnace on the earth, refined seven times. You, O LORD, shall preserve them from this generation forever." When textual critics argue over the variants in the various manuscripts and the proliferation of translations, they can be reminded that 99.9% of all the manuscripts agree. The one tenth of one percent that does not agree is minuscule in comparison to the whole. While men may have failed, God has not. He has preserved His Word and we have it today! Jesus said in Matthew 24:35, "Heaven and earth shall pass away, but My words shall not pass away."

Seven, it is ***sufficient***. This is the crux of the situation presently faced. Many believe the Bible is a holy book, a good book, maybe even the best of books, but it is an ancient book and does not fully meet us where we are. It is outdated and not sufficient to address and meet every problem or need faced in the twenty-first century. It is not a sufficient guide for those who desire to live under the authority of God and worship and serve Him in this present day. Other things are needed, such as prophecy, dreams, words of knowledge, and other assorted charismata (spiritual gifts). Contrarily, Jesus said in Matthew 4:4: "It is written, man shall not live by bread alone, but by every word that proceeds out of the mouth of God." Jesus was speaking of the inscripturated written Word of God of the Old and New Testaments. Granted, the Word will not sufficiently instruct a person on how to repair a computer, but it is unquestionably sufficient to meet every spiritual, moral, and ethical situation encountered. Never before has the battle cry of the Reformation — "Sola Scriptura" — been needed as in this incredulous, self-destructing, and post-modern generation!

What is the Faith?

In addition to knowledge of what God's Word is, there must be an understanding of the difference between faith and the faith. Faith is the subjective personal belief of someone in Christ as Savior and Lord. The faith is that objective body or system of belief revealed in the Holy Bible. Many scholars agree that the New Testament contains statements that form a creedal and confessional basis of the Christian faith (e.g., Philippians 2:5–10; 1 Timothy 1:15; 2 Timothy 3:16; and Revelation 5:9–10). If one is a Christian, or is to remain a Christian, these statements must be believed *ex animo* (to use the old Princetonian Latin expression—*from the soul*). Below are six biblical passages that pertain to *the* faith.[3] Each is cited

[3] The passages used in this chapter are from the NASB, which is Dr. Fred Malone's version of choice.

and given a brief exposition. Notice carefully in the passages that it is not the personal (subjective) faith that a Christian exercises in Christ for salvation the writers have in mind, but the objective faith, which God revealed from heaven and is contained in the Holy Scriptures.

The first passage is 2 Thessalonians 2:13–15:

> But we should always give thanks to God for you, brethren beloved by the Lord, because God has chosen you from the beginning for salvation, through sanctification by the Spirit and belief in the truth. [14] It was for this He called you through our gospel, that you may gain the glory of our Lord Jesus Christ. [15] So then, brethren, stand firm and hold to the traditions which you were taught, whether by word of mouth or by our letter from us.

The books of Thessalonians are the first inspired epistles written by Paul. As the apostle mentally rehearses his entrance into that ancient city of pagan Greece, he is filled with thanksgiving. Already, he had taught them their election by God (1 Thessalonians 1:4), and once again, reminds them of their particular position and privilege as beloved and chosen (v. 13a). Their salvation was affected by the effectual, setting-apart work of the Holy Spirit and their belief in *the truth* (v. 13b). *The truth* refers to the whole counsel or purpose of God (Acts 20:27), not merely the nondescript preaching of a vague and nebulous Jesus. Paul did not skimp in his evangelistic work by simply sharing the "ABCs of Salvation," but was thorough in declaring a full-orbed body of *the truth.* The focal point of the truth was the all-powerful gospel of the death, burial, and resurrection of Christ Jesus the Lord. He is purposefully recapping the doctrinal foundation of their salvation, which will eventuate in their gaining glory (v. 13–14). Why did the apostle reiterate this foundation?

Paul's reason was clear. He wanted to exhort the Thessalonian church (i.e., believers) to obey a direct imperative (v. 15): hold fast to the traditions they were taught by his own mouth and in the epistles! He knew the danger of drifting in a Christian's life, which can break unity and fellowship with the true Body of Christ. Trueman's explanation captures the thought:

> Again the verbal emphasis is clear: these traditions were taught by words spoken or written; and they are to be the norm of life and teaching in the church in Thessalonica. Similar statements can be found in 1 Corinthians 11:2 and 2 Thessalonians 3:6, where Paul makes conformity to the tradition of his teaching a condition for fellowship.[4]

[4] Carl R. Trueman, *The Creedal Imperative* (Wheaton: Crossway, 2012), 77

To head off that danger of drifting, Paul exhorted them to remember *the truth* and hold fast to the apostolic *traditions* they received. There is a body of truth, a system of apostolic traditions that is to be steadfastly cherished and tenaciously embraced.

The second passage is Ephesians 6:16:

> in addition to all, taking up the shield of [the] faith with which you will be able to extinguish all the flaming arrows of the evil one.

Paul concludes the practical applications of the book of Ephesians by exhorting the believing church to put on the "full armor of God" (Ephesians 6:10–20). There are many commentaries that give excellent exegetical expositions on the whole armor of God. The most noteworthy importance to this chapter is in verse 16. All the major English translations are remiss in translating the Greek as "the shield of faith." This translation causes the casual reader to believe that when the devil assaults and spiritual warfare rages, the Christian is to be strong in personal faith and trust the Lord to assist in the battle. According to this understanding, the outcome depends upon the exercising or strength of faith. However, the original language of the New Testament states something more emphatic-the shield of *the* faith![5]

The definite article before the word "faith" demonstrates that it is not a personal, subjective faith or a trust in the Lord of battles, which can be weak or strong and even change. The faith that is referenced is the objective, unchanging faith that was once delivered unto the saints. It is taking the body of divinely revealed truth, that entire corpus of sufficient revelation, as a shield against the fiery arrows of Satan's lies. This does not mean that personal faith should not be exercised, which it must, but it is the absolute truth of God that will beat back and ultimately defeat the wicked one's lies.

The third passage is Titus 1:1–3:

> Paul, a bond-servant of God and an apostle of Jesus Christ, for the faith of those chosen of God and the knowledge of the truth, which is according to godliness, [2] in hope of eternal life, which God, who cannot lie, promised long ages ago [3] but at the proper time manifested, even His word, in the proclamation [preaching] with which I was entrusted according to the commandment of God our Savior;

[5] Greek: τὸν θυρεὸν τῆς πιστεως.

Paul quickly turns to "the faith of those chosen of God" (i.e. "the faith of God's elect" — AV). His entire reason for being a bond-servant and an apostle was for "the faith of God's elect and the knowledge of the truth." There are several details about this body of belief known as the faith: it leads to godliness, which is contrary to sin; it produces hope and the assurance of eternal life; it was given by God, who cannot lie; it was promised long ages ago, denoting before the ages or time began; and it is manifested or made distinctively known through preaching.

Notably, a fixed body of truth and faith was incorporated into the mindset of the apostles. "The Christian Church from the very first accepted and taught specific truths as the very foundation of Christianity (Acts 2:42, 6:7; Romans 6:17; Galatians 1:23, 3:23)."[6] Paul expressly testifies that he did not receive the faith and the gospel from man, nor was he taught it by man, but through the personal revelation of Jesus Christ. This took place in Arabia where he studied under the tutelage of the Lord Himself for three years (see Galatians 1:11–17). Thus, Paul could speak of the faith with authority.

The fourth passage is Jude 1–4:

> Jude, a bond-servant of Jesus Christ and brother of James, to those who are called, beloved in God the Father and kept for Jesus Christ: 2 May mercy, peace, and love be multiplied to you. 3 Beloved, while I was making every effort to write you about our common salvation, I felt the necessity to write to you appealing that you contend earnestly for the faith that was once for all handed down to the saints. 4 For certain persons have crept in unnoticed, those who long ago were long beforehand marked out for this condemnation, ungodly persons, who turn the grace of our God into licentiousness and deny our only Master and Lord, Jesus Christ.

Much could be said about Jude, the brother of James, but that is best left to the commentaries.[7] What is important is the theme of the book. Jude possessed a strong desire to strengthen the believers that had been scattered because of persecution. He indicated his original purpose for writing in verse 3a: he "was making every effort" to write about their "common salvation." (Salvation is common not in the sense of being plain and ordinary, but in the consensus of it being shared by every true believer in

[6] D. Edmond Hiebert, *Second Peter and Jude* (Greenville, SC: Unusual Publications, 1989), 219.

[7] An excellent detailed explanation of the historical author of *Jude* can be found in Hiebert's commentary *Second Peter and Jude*, 185–205.

Christ as Lord and Savior.) Very quickly, Jude indicates, the Holy Spirit made him feel the necessity of altering his original purpose to something more crucial: "contend earnestly for the faith which was once handed down to the saints" (v. 3b). Ungodly persons had "crept" into the churches and were perverting the gospel of God's grace. They were turning God's grace into "licentiousness," which gave a license to sensuality and immorality. This could not be tolerated because, in essence, it denied Christ, the holy and sovereign Lord. Jude declares that these persons were foreordained or "long before marked out for this condemnation."

Jude's inspired remedy was an appeal to "contend earnestly" for the faith. To which specific faith is Jude referring? (Interestingly, Jude does not use the word salvation, or the word gospel but *the faith.*) It is the unique belief system that "was once for all handed down [delivered, AV] to the saints." In essence, "handed down" means being expressly distributed from heaven to earth, from God to His redeemed, believing, and holy people. Unlike all the other fabricated religions of the world, the faith for which the saints are to contend is not a religion that originated with humanity, but is the exclusive deposit of truth from God the Lord of what is to be believed and practiced. At all costs, the saints are to fight for this precious treasure.[8]

The fifth passage is 2 Timothy 1:13–14:

> Retain the standard of sound words which you have heard from me, in the faith and love which are in Christ Jesus. 14 Guard, through the Holy Spirit who dwells in us, the treasure which has been entrusted to you.

Before making this charge to Timothy, Paul asserts his divine calling from Jesus Christ, the head of the church, to be "a preacher and an apostle and a teacher." This means his words come with unquestionable authority. Before addressing the two main verbs, "retain" and "guard," the "standard of sound words" must be understood. What is this pattern or standard? It is "the simplest and most primitive dogmatic formulas of the Christian faith."[9] Stott calls it "the apostolic faith,"[10] and Knight describes it as "the

[8] For a full-orbed, exegetical, pastoral, and rich exposition of this passage by a Puritan, see William Jenkyn, *An Exposition upon the Epistle of Jude* (London: Samuel, Holdsworth, Paternoster Row, 1839).

[9] Donald Guthrie, The Pastoral Epistles (Grand Rapids: Wm. B. Eerdmans Publishing Company, 1979), 132.

[10] John R.W. Stott, *Guard The Gospel: The Message of 2 Timothy* (Downers Grove, Illinois: InterVarsity Press, 1973), 43.

contents of the apostolic teaching,"[11] contained in the Holy Scriptures of the Old and New Testaments. John MacArthur's assertion is correct: "In Scripture we have God's own truth and standards, all we need or should want to have. It is the only divinely inspired, divinely revealed, absolute, unique, perfect, and sufficient truth. In it is found everything necessary for salvation and for living out the saved life."[12]

What did the aged apostle charge the young pastor regarding the faith? Timothy must "retain" (*eche* — to hold) that is keep a firm grip on the faith. He must not dangle it or play loosely with it but steadily clench his hand around it. Furthermore, Timothy must "guard" (*phylassō*) with vigilance and sustain a close watch on the faith so it is not lost or damaged. Heresies and corrupt teachings abound that beguile uninstructed souls, and even some weak believers. Like Nehemiah, the young pastor needs a trowel in one hand and a sword in the other (Nehemiah 4:17, 22). Timothy must constantly be on watch and sacrificially protect the priceless treasure of God's truth and holy gospel entrusted to his stewardship.

The sixth passage is 2 Timothy 4:7:

> I have fought the good fight, I have finished the course, I have kept the faith.

These are the last inspired record of Paul's words. The sentence of death had been pronounced, there was no escape from the Roman prison, and death was a few days away. The apostle had no regrets and nothing to hide or retract. His passionate heart for Christ, His church, the unsaved, and God's truth were burning still within his bosom, which is evident in this chapter of 2 Timothy. Without flinching and in the face of imminent death, he could testify of several things.

In particular, Paul could claim that he had fought a good fight. He understood the Christian life and gospel ministry was a battle: a war for God's glory against the pseudo-gods of this world, for Christ the Truth against the falsehoods of fallen humanity, and the holy reign of the triune God over the depraved empires of the ages. Paul could affirm that he had completely finished his course (i.e. race). He had not given up and quit. Neither had he become distracted and paused, nor compromised and swerved from the path set before him. He had finished! Paramount to

[11] George W. Knight III, NIGTC, *The Pastoral Epistles* (Grand Rapids: Wm. B. Eerdmans Publishing Company, 1992), 381.

[12] *2 Timothy*, The MacArthur New Testament Commentary (Chicago: Moody Press, 1995), 30.

Paul's testimony is that he had "kept the faith," which was in contrast to Hymenaeus and Alexander that made shipwreck of *the* faith (1 Timothy 1:19–20). "The faith," as J.H. Bernard observes, is "the Christian Creed, regarded as a sacred deposit of doctrine."[13] Patrick Fairburn describes it as: "faith objectively, as the great treasure of gospel verities."[14] Coder explains it as "that extensive body of Bible doctrine which makes up the perfect whole of the truth revealed by God…"[15] "The faith" as Michael Green notes, "is here a body of belief, *fides quae creditor*, as opposed to the more usual meaning of *pistis* as 'trust,' *fides qua creditor*."[16] And Homer A. Kent, Jr. confirms the Greek as meaning "the truth of God, which constitutes the Christian faith."[17]

Paul, in keeping the faith, had not held back unpopular themes that offend fallen minds. He had not smoothed off the angularities that prick darkened consciences. He had not softened the hammer of God's Word that pound misguided emotions. He had not sweetened the salty certainties that are often distasteful to human palates. He was not embarrassed by any of God's truths revealed in the biblical text, nor did he feel that he needed to apologize for what God had spoken. He boldly testified to the Ephesian elders that he had not shunned or shrunk back from declaring the whole counsel of God (Acts 20:27). He had not simply maintained personal faith in Christ, but had faithfully kept *the faith* of God's elect, that body of truth deposited to him, to the end.

In conclusion, contrary to postmodern thinking, there is a body of absolute truth that is divinely revealed from heaven to earth, from God to humanity. It is found *only* in the Holy Bible, and it is called the faith. This faith is not up for debate; God requires everyone made in His image to believe it and submit to its government and rule.

How Did the Early Church Encounter their Culture?

While many received Jesus' message and found a deliverance from sin, new life, and joy, others were antagonistic. That is evident from the narra-

[13] *The Pastoral Epistles in the Cambridge Greek Testament for Schools and Colleges* (Cambridge University Press: Cambridge, 1906), 143.

[14] *1&2 Timothy and Titus* (Edinburg, Scotland: The Banner of Truth Trust, 2002), 391.

[15] S. Maxwell Coder, *Jude: The Acts of the Apostates* (Chicago, Illinois: Moody Press, 1958), 17.

[16] *The Second Epistle of Peter and the Epistle of Jude*, TNTC (Grand Rapids, MI: William. B. Eerdmans Publishing Company, 1968, 1979), 159.

[17] *The Pastoral Epistles* (Chicago: Moody Press, 1958, 1982), 288.

tive of the four Gospels. Carried over into the book of Acts, antagonism and persecution began quite early. The first attack on the early church commences in Acts 4:1–22. The event that starts the first concerted, religious violence upon Christianity was the healing of a man lame from birth (Acts 3:1–10) and the subsequent preached explanation that followed (Acts 3:11–26). The religious leaders of Judaism were "greatly annoyed" (Acts 4:2); they confronted and arrested two apostles (Peter and John). It was not a criminal act or some form of roguery that provoked the confrontation, but a kind and gracious work of healing and compassion. Luke chronicles this and subsequent persecutions throughout his book.

At the close of the New Testament canon (ca. AD 95), the assaults against Christianity continued and increased. The malicious aggression came on two fronts: an apostate Judaism and a philosophical paganism. Judaism rejected its God-sent Messiah and paganism gloried in its fallen, humanistic reasoning. Arrests, imprisonments, confiscations, executions, and general harassment could not be ignored by the early believers in Christ. Quickly, men arose in defense of the body of truth revealed in Holy Scripture against these two assaulting fronts. These defenders of the faith are known as the Apologists. The earliest known apologists were Quadratus (c. 117–138), whose writings are lost, and Aristides (c. 138–147), of whom very little is known.[18] These were quickly followed by the best known of the early apologists, Justin Martyr, in his *First Apology*, written in Rome to Emperor Antonius Pius and his son, the future emperor Marcus Aurelius. Many more followed in the first Apologists' footsteps including Irenaeus (c. 130–200), Clement of Alexandria (c. 155–220), Tertullian (c. 160–220), and Origen (c. 185–254). They engaged individuals privately, addressed groups in the forum, and wrote stalwart epistles. Harry Y. Gamble gives excellent insight into the early apologist's attitude and approach:

> The burgeoning number of apologies attests both the need and the effort of the churches to respond. Apologists usually went beyond mere rebuttals of specific charges and pleas for toleration. They vigorously attacked popular religious ideas and practices and appealed to the thoughtful by representing Christianity as consistent with the best of classical philosophical reflection. They were defensive, polemical, and even evangelistic.[19]

The early church modeled a pattern for evangelicals to follow today. Cries for toleration abound, especially from the media. Christians, fearing exclusion by certain segments of society, often retreat into silence and

[18] *Encyclopedia of Early Christianity*, second edition, vol. 2, A-K, ed. Everett Ferguson (New York & London: Garland Publishing, Inc., 1997) 84.

[19] *Encyclopedia of Early Christianity*, 85.

acquiescence. Not so with the first believers. They did not retreat into holy huddles, nor were they quiet, even in the face of death. Their love for the risen Savior and triumphant Lord, their devotion to the faith of God's elect, their pity for the suffering and persecuted brethren, their longing for the extension of Christ's kingdom in a darkened world, and their thirst for the salvation of lost, perishing souls motivated them and their church leaders to speak, and speak loudly!

Contend for the Faith

Frequently in well-established Christian communities, the faith is taken for granted and its preciousness fades into the background of secondary or tertiary subjects. The cross and the central, glorious themes of the law and gospel lose their luster in minds and hearts. Preoccupied with work and the necessities of life, believers easily become ensnared with the cares of this world. Wrapped up in selfish ambitions and personal struggles, they lose the focus on Christ and His great salvation, as it drifts into the mundane. Spiritual fervor and zeal are lost, and coldness encases the heart. Christians unmindful of erroneous ideologies and humanistic worldviews that surround them frequently live in a motionless vacuum. Heretics take advantage of such situations. Spider-like, ungodly false teachers dressed in sheep's clothing, creep into Christ's churches. (Jude vividly exposes these apostates in his epistle: vv. 5–16). Naïve and gullible professors of faith can be drawn into their cleverly spun webs of deceitful error.

There is a tension here. The honor and crown rights of Christ are at stake. The purity of the church can become compromised. Plus, poor sinners who need salvation are in a state of perishing (1 Corinthians 1:18), and shall perish endlessly, if they die without Christ (Revelatians 20:15, 21:8). What actions must churches, her leaders and members, take to stop these insidious intrusions? Furthermore, what must Christians do to expose the damning lies of fabricated religions and amoral cosmologies in a hostile social order that hates Christ? Pluralism — "a theory or system that recognizes more than one ultimate principle"[20] — reigns in Western civilization, and is militant against the claim of an absolute authority, especially biblical Christianity. Belief-systems collide and conflict, and the tension is felt by Christians and non-Christians alike.

Jude gives an exhortational antidote for the poison of all error, whether it arises in the world or emerges within the church. He begins by "appealing" or exhorting these beloved ones, who are called and kept by Jesus

[20] *New Oxford American Dictionary*, Third Edition, Edited by Angus Stevenson & Christine A. Lindberg (Oxford: Oxford University Press, 2010), 1346.

Christ. Hiebert accurately observes: "'Exhorting you' (*parakalōn*) at once indicates the character and tone, as well as the contents, of his letter. His approach is not didactic but hortative, persuading with authority."[21] What follows is not optional!

Jude urges his readers to contend earnestly for the faith! What, then, does this look like? By way of negation, it does not mean to take up swords or explode bombs, like the militaristic technique of jihadists against perceived infidels. Neither does it mean to craft laws and pass legislation to make a state or nation Christian. It does not mean to strike with clubs or fists, yell and scream profanities, and be mean-spirited to those who oppose the faith or with whom you disagree. Jude understood what Paul writes: "For though we walk in the flesh, we do not war according to the flesh, for the weapons of our warfare are not of the flesh [carnal — AV], but divinely powerful for the destruction of fortresses" (2 Corinthians 10:3–4).

Positively, it is twofold. First it is to stand without shame or embarrassment for the faith revealed in Holy Scripture, particularly any truth that is under attack. Second, it means to engage error in such a manner as to change, or at least correct, the false representation set forth by the enemies of Christ.[22] It involves contentious, energy-draining struggle so that the faith be preserved, maintained, cherished, and propagated to the entire world. Hiebert gives an excellent description:

> "To contend earnestly for" (*epagōnizesthai*) translates an expressive compound verbal term which appears only here in the New Testament. The simple form of the verb (*agōnizomai*), which appears as "agonize" in its English dress, was much used in connection with athletic contests to describe a strenuous struggle to overcome an opponent, as in a wrestling match. A more general use was in reference to any conflict, contest, debate, or lawsuit. It involves the thought of the expenditure of all one's energy in order to prevail. Here, as often, the verb is metaphorical, describing the spiritual conflict in which believers engage.[23]

Here again, another tension arises. A number of evangelical pastors possess "an embarrassment before the biblical text,"[24] and are either ashamed or afraid to speak what God has spoken in His Word. They real-

[21] Hiebert, *Second Peter and Jude*, 218.

[22] Who are Christ's enemies? Anyone that is not for Him. Jesus said: "He who is not with Me is against Me; and he who does not gather with Me, scatters" (Luke 11:23). There is no neutrality! One is either with and for Jesus or against Him.

[23] Hiebert, *Second Peter and Jude*, 218.

[24] Albert R. Mohler, *He Is Not Silent: Preaching in a Postmodern World* (Chicago: Moody Press, 2008), 15.

ize that faithful expository preaching of the Word, especially those controversial parts, may cause a loss in membership and attendance. People want to leave church feeling good and do not want to be instructed, convicted, disturbed, or drawn closer to a thrice-holy God. Salaries must be paid (above all, their own), expensive facilities must be maintained, and innovative advertising supported, which cost money; a church cannot get money without people. Serious preaching, usually, will not gather a large crowd. Thus, a faithful exposition of books of the Bible is usurped by topical, motivational talks that deal with felt needs and self-fulfillment. To preach a sermon on contending for the faith is thought to be counter-productive, not to mention unloving.

Likewise, evangelical believers face tensions between faith and fear. There are numerous, sincere believers who love Christ and the gospel, but fear the consequences of faithfully sharing their faith and the gospel. Fear of losing their jobs, exclusion from family and friends, and what others may think have caused a guilty silence. *Why speak up when I can lose out?* is the widespread thought of many. Contending for the faith has not penetrated their minds.

One must leave his or her comfort zone to contend for the faith. The earth is not heaven, but a battleground on the way to heaven. Those who earnestly contend will be misunderstood, maligned, hated, mocked, rejected by the world, possibly excluded by family and friends, and maybe killed. But so was Jesus the Messiah! And so were the prophets, apostles, apologists, and martyrs. Contenders for the faith of God's elect are in a good and noble company; a true band of brothers!

Why Must Christians Contend for the Faith?

Why does God, who gave the truth and established it upon the earth, who is almighty and absolutely sovereign, instruct His church and people to contend for the faith? Is He not capable of arising and pleading His own cause? (Psalm 74:22). Most certainly, He is! Nevertheless, He has called His people to be activists, to be co-involved in His work on earth. While many reasons can be given, only six will be briefly stated.

The *first* is the honor of Christ. Without Christ there would be no Christianity; it would exist as another quasi-moral religion. "He who comes from above," declares John the Baptist, "is above all" (John 3:31). The Father has given Christ "all judgment…so that all will honor the Son even as they honor the Father. He who does not honor the Son does not honor the Father who sent Him" (John 5:22–23). Often, the name of Jesus is nothing more than a swear word. The only Mediator between God and man (1 Timothy 2:5) is the brunt of foul jokes and cartoons. Despite the rabid skepticism of a pluralistic society, God has appointed a day in which He will judge the entire world in righteousness by Jesus Christ (Act 17:31). That Day is inescapable and unavoidable and every unbeliever will then confess Him as Lord (Philippians 2:9–11). It is time for the church to arise, contend for the faith, and honor Christ her Lord!

The *second* is the purity of Christ's body, the church. Never before, unless it was during the Middle Ages, has the visible church of the Redeemer been in such disarray. Its walls are in desperate need of repair. Redactional higher-criticism, Liberalism, and a watered-down evangelicalism has left the church dazed, confused, and without discernment. Transgression of God's holy Law is tolerated; sexual immorality (of all sorts) abounds, and the people of God live in the same manner as people in the world. Some ministers commit adultery or some other sexual perversion, are removed from their pulpits, and within two years are ministering in another church. Church discipline is mostly neglected or mocked while various scandals are excused, even accepted. The result is little gospel holiness! Yet, it is "time for judgment to begin with the household of God;" and as Peter notes, "if it begins with us first, what will be the outcome for those who do not obey the gospel?" (1 Peter 4:17). It is time to seek the purity of the church by contending for the faith!

The *third* is the temptation to compromise. There was a time when people blushed and were ashamed of sin. Some things were unspeakable! Now the world has become loud and boisterous, flaunting unutterable sins, and committing virulent attacks upon biblical Christianity. Believers are easily intimidated and are hushed into silence. Rather than standing up for the faith or speaking against iniquity, some believers compromise by saying nothing or going along with the crowd. They do not want to lose their friends in the world, forgetting that "friendship with the world is hostility toward God" (James 4:4). Paul, rather than yielding to the temptation and compromising the gospel of grace, and in the presence of powerful persons, publicly confronts and rebukes Peter (Galatians 2:11–14). The church today must also contend for the faith and resist the temptation to compromise.

The *fourth* is the case of divine testing. Paul wrote in 1 Corinthians 11:19: "For there must also be factions among you, so that those who are approved may become evident among you." Factions (divisions) arise often in Christ's churches. What most do not realize is that they are unavoidable and necessary! Why? Charles Hodge answers: "By the prevalence of disorders and other evils in the church, God put his people to the test."[25]

[25] Charles Hodge, *Commentary on the First Epistle to the Corinthians* (Grand Rapids: Wm. B. Eerdmans Publishing Company, 1965), 218.

True Christians desire visible unity in Christ's church because they are in spiritual union with Christ. Nonetheless, factions arise. God, who could stop them, instead allows discords so that those who are really His "approved" will become clear to both the church and the world.

The *fifth* is false teachers and the damage and destruction they produce in the church. Jesus warned: "Beware of false prophets, who come to you in sheep's clothing, but inwardly are ravenous wolves" (Matthew 7:18). Paul, also, knew of this reality as he taught the Ephesian elders: "I know that after my departure savage wolves will come in among you, not sparing the flock; and from among your own selves men will arise speaking perverse things, to draw away the disciples after them[selves]" (Acts 20:29–30). For two millennia, Christ's churches have been plagued with false teachers. Today is no different! They fill pulpits and are on the radio, TV, and the internet. With intentional guile, they look good; they sound good, and are usually quite charming. They even use Jesus' name, and thus deceive many, especially the young and uninstructed. They play on people's emotions, cause church splits, damn souls, and damage the Lord's people. The fourth and fifth reasons are reminders of the necessity of contending for the faith in the church!

The *sixth* is abounding apostasy. Professed Christians today are very fickle. They go from one church to another, from one prominent leader to another, looking for the constant spiritual high. Because Christ's gospel and the whole counsel of God do not satisfy their souls, their fickleness soon drains them of spiritual energy. They either turn back to the world for their gratification, or they become complacent and turn from Christ's church. Paul warned that the Day of the Lord would not come until there was first the apostasy or falling away (2 Thessalonians 2:3a). This falling away is not referring to the world because it is already fallen. Rather, it is indicating the professed church. In his last epistle, Paul braces Timothy for the whimsicality of many professed Christians, which looks very much like today: "For the time is coming when people will not endure sound doctrine, but will accumulate for themselves teachers in accordance to their own desires [passions in the ESV], and will turn away their ears from to the truth and will turn aside to myths" (2 Timothy 4:3–4). People want to feel good, and sound doctrine often makes them uncomfortable. Should pastors accommodate and please people, or be faithful to God's Word and please Him? The answer is simple-contend for the faith; seek to stem the tide of apostasy, and please the triune God.

How Should Christians Contend for the Faith?

There is a variety of opinions expressed among Christian leaders on this topic. Some are hesitant to teach Jude's imperative, lest Christians are thought intolerant and contentious. The concept of contending for the faith appears to be contrary to Christ the Prince of Peace. The regenerate person is the only one at peace with God, possesses peace within himself, and desires to live peaceably with all people. But, it must be remembered that our Lord Himself said: "Do not think that I came to bring peace on earth; I did not come to bring peace, but a sword" (Matthew 10:34). Jesus instructed that the cross will bring controversy and division, even among the most intimate of family relationships. Christ was a controversial man of His time, and the most controversial person of this day.[26] The writer of Hebrews gives insight into why Christ was controversial: He "loved righteousness and hated lawlessness" (Hebrews 1:9a).[27] Thus, if someone stands faithfully for Christ, His gospel, and the faith, loves righteousness and hates lawlessness, and earnestly contends for the faith, controversy will ensue.

However, there is a difference between contending for the faith and being contentious. The former is biblical and the latter is not. Some people love to fight and it is a part of their personalities to always engage in some sort of conflict and controversy. They are not happy unless they are fighting something. Not so with Christ's people; they only contend when necessary. However, when it becomes necessary, there are certain things that must accompany contending for the faith. D.A. Carson addresses this issue and gives ten "ways ahead."[28] In addition to his ten, four basic guidelines are given below. These four will help in any given situation where contending for the faith is compulsory and indispensable.

Contend for the faith with knowledge. Ignorance of the Holy Bible is pervasive. Most unbelievers have never read the Bible. What is heart-rending is that many Christians have never read it in its entirety. Know

[26] See John R.W. Stott, *Christ the Controversialist* (Downers Grove: InterVarsity, 1970).

[27] Note the beautifully-anointed balance Jesus exhibited. He loved righteousness and actually hated lawlessness. Often Christians are told they need to more loving like Jesus, which is true, but they also need to learn to hate the things that Christ hates. This is not hypocrisy. Instead, it is part of the moral balance of Christian godliness, which brings the oil of gladness upon Christians just as it did upon Jesus.

[28] "Ways Ahead: Ten Words" in his excellent work *The Intolerance of Tolerance*; 161–176.

the Holy Bible: know its history, its chronology, its books, its characters, it redemptive purposes, its way of salvation and how to be accepted by God, its ethical instructions, its church, its plan for the ages, and especially its main resurfacing theme — the Person and work of Jesus Christ. This theme is not always front and center, but it is never far away (see Luke 24:27b & 44b; John 5:39; Acts 3:24).

Contend for the faith with conviction. If the Holy Bible is false, then it has no value, and there is no obligation to heed it. Conversely, if it is absolutely true and without error, then embrace it, believe it with your whole heart, and order your life by it. When confronted with evil and error, have the conviction that the Bible is not your Word, but God's Word: the self-authenticating revelation of Himself. Contend without wavering from this verity.

Contend for the faith with boldness. Seldom is prayer needed for opportunities to speak of Christ and His gospel. Many are given every day. What is often lacking should be the heart-cry of our prayers: boldness to speak when the opportunities arise. The apostles understood this. When commanded by the authorities not to preach again in Jesus' name, they did not complain or throw a pity-party. Instead, they gathered for prayer. What was their unadorned request? Remove the opposition? Cause the people to love and accept them? No! The modestly asked: "…and grant that Your bondservants may speak Your word with confidence [boldness as in the AV and ESV]" (Acts 4:29). Do not say "in my opinion," but boldly declare "This is what the Lord God says. It is not my Word but His. I am merely telling you what God has spoken." Boldness may cost you, but God will own it and bless you.

Contend for the faith with compassion and humility. The Christian faith is unique, contrary to the thoughts and ways of fallen humanity, and authoritative. Because of this, the one contending is often viewed as hating others and arrogant. This is virtually unavoidable. However what can be avoided is contending with hate and pride. Remember God loved His people when they were hateful and hated others, vile sinners by nature and choice, and filled with self-conceit— "Such were some of you" (1 Corinthians 6:11a). Remember the pit from which you came and understand that the person with whom you are contending could be yourself. Love and show compassion, be meek and humble to those who oppose themselves. Trust the almighty Spirit of the living God to grant them repentance leading to the knowledge of the truth, that they may recover themselves out of the snare of the devil who has taken them captive at his will (2 Timothy 2:24–26). Employ these elements in contending, and error can be averted and many won to the faith.

Conclusion

There is a body of divinely revealed truth, from God to humanity, called *the faith*. It is unparalleled in every way. It is non-negotiable, and must not be tampered with, added to, subtracted from, or changed (Revelation 22:18). Believe and receive it, and be saved. Reject it, and be damned and lost forever. Furthermore, Christians must love the LORD their God with all their hearts, minds, souls, and strength (Mark 12:30), and out of honor to Christ their preeminent Lord, earnestly contend for the faith in *and* against an unbelieving world. May grace be given to Christ's churches and people to do so. Amen.

15

Exalting Christ by Connecting with Church History

The Faith of Ezra Courtney, Pioneer Missionary in the South

Joe Nesom

Courtney's Life

Ezra Courtney (1775–1855),[1] was born, according to the inscription on his gravestone, in the Darlington District of South Carolina. Other sources have the year as 1771 with Pennsylvania as his birthplace.[2] According to the records of Bethel Black River Church in Sumter Country South Carolina, he was "working" for the church in the year 1790. Whatever the word "working" may refer to, it indicates involvement in the affairs of God's kingdom in a notable fashion when Courtney was only a teenager. As a young man Courtney married Elizabeth Dearmond. Their first child, a daughter named Sarah, was born on August 25, 1792.[3]

[1] First Baptist Church, Clinton, Louisiana, where Fred Malone has served for many years, was founded by people who sat under the teaching of men like Ezra Courtney. He lived near Clinton and is buried just a few miles to the southeast.

[2] For example, Jesse Laney Boyd, *A Popular History of the Baptists in Mississippi* (St. Louis, MO: 1888), 37–38.

[3] "Elder Ezra Courtney (1775–1855): Bringing the Baptist Faith to the Wilderness," Journal of Louisiana Baptist History, Vol. 1, 1988, 52–54.

After living for a time in the Darlington District, where Courtney was listed as a licensed preacher at the Ebenezer Church, he and his family moved to Amite County, Mississippi.[4] Just to the south lay West Florida, which was then under the dominion of the Spanish king. Oppression by Roman Catholic authorities in the area had already been felt by newly arriving Baptists, and when Courtney preached for a group of them some nine miles from Baton Rouge, the Catholics threatened him with arrest. However, the Alcalde, a local official of the Spanish government, protected him. As the American population increased, a new day of political change and church growth arrived.[5]

Ezra Courtney was, from the first, active in the establishment of numerous churches in both Mississippi and Louisiana,[6] and helped to organize the Mississippi Baptist Association in 1806. He served eight terms as its moderator. The Mississippi Association was comprised of churches located in southwestern Mississippi and southeastern Louisiana.[7]

Ever a theologian of discernment, he never lost his balance and was quick to oppose the anti-missions sentiment that had a growing appeal for many in the early 1800's. At a time when English Baptists were still often tentative in their support for William Carey's work in India, Ezra Courtney enthusiastically supported the missionary cause in the newly opened territories. And when the heterodox doctrines and practices of the Campbellites seduced some of the most prominent Baptist pastors, Courtney stood his ground. In House Upon a Rock, the official history of the Louisiana Baptist Convention, Glenn Lee Green called Courtney, "a vigorous and faithful Calvinist, unrelenting in his stance." Green also described him a man who knew the difference between "authentic Christianity and all proposed substitutes."[8]

[4] Ibid, 55.

[5] W.E. Paxton, *A History of the Baptists of Louisiana from Earliest Times to the Present* (St. Louis, MO: 1888), 37–38.

[6] Editors Note: First Baptist Church of Jackson, LA was founded by Ezra Courtney in 1835. Joe Nesom has served as the pastor of this church since 1982. Its sister church, First Baptist Church of Clinton, LA (15 miles to the east of FBCJ) was founded in 1836 through efforts of the Mississippi Association in which Ezra Courtney ministered. Fred A. Malone served as senior pastor of FBCC from 1993 to 2016 and continues to serve as one of its pastors to the present.

[7] T. M. Bond, *A Republication of the Minutes of the Mississippi Baptist Association from its Organization in 1806 to the Present Time* (1849) (New Orleans, LA: 1849), 12.

[8] Glenn Lee Green, *House Upon A Rock* (Alexandria, LA: 1973), 72.

Courtney's Faith

Was Ezra Courtney in the mainstream of Baptist doctrine and practice or was his teaching aberrant? What did Ezra Courtney believe to be scriptural doctrine?

Courtney's faith was a God-centered faith. His primary concern was the doctrine of salvation. He taught, (1) the total depravity of all human beings, that all of Adam's children are sinners and therefore unable of even desiring the favor of God unless God should grant them grace, (2) the unconditional choice of God in salvation, that God chose his elect in eternity and that the choice of God does not depend on any human action, (3) that Christ's atonement was definite, that is for the elect alone, (4) effectual calling, that those who have been chosen by the Father and atoned for by the Son, will be called by the Holy Spirit to regeneration and, (5) the perseverance of the saints of God, that God is the author and finisher of our faith; therefore, we may be certain that those who were chosen by the Father, redeemed by the Son, and sealed by the Holy Spirit will continue in faith until death, and will not fail of the grace of God for all eternity.

The Articles of Faith, which Courtney helped draft for the Mississippi Association, are a concise guide to the doctrines he preached. They are as follows:

1. We believe in one true and living God; and that there are a trinity of persons in the Godhead—the Father, the Son, and the Holy Ghost, the same in essence, equal in power and glory.

2. We believe the scriptures of the Old and New Testament were given by inspiration of God, are of Divine authority, and the only rule of faith and practice.

3. We believe in the fall of Adam; in the imputation of his sin to all his posterity; in the total depravity of human nature; and in man's inability to restore himself to the favor of God.

4. We believe in the everlasting love of God to his people; in the eternal unconditional election of a definite number of the human family to grace and glory.

5. We believe all those who were chosen in Christ before the foundation of the world are, in time, effectually called, regenerated, converted, and sanctified; and are kept by the power of God through faith, unto salvation.

6. We believe there is one mediator between God and man, the man Jesus Christ, who by the satisfaction which he made to law and justice, "in becoming an offering for sin," hath, by his most precious blood, redeemed the elect from under the curse of the law, that they might be holy and without blame before him in love.

7. We believe good works are the fruits of faith, and follow after justification, are evidences of a gracious state, and that it is the duty of all believers to perform them from a principle of love.

8. We believe in the resurrection of the dead, and a general judgment, and that the happiness of the righteous and the punishment of the wicked will be eternal.[9]

The Articles of Faith of the Mississippi Baptist Association are obviously a succinct presentation of the theology of the Magisterial Calvinistic Reformers with Baptist ecclesiology. The dominant doctrinal interest is clearly soteriological.

An examination of other associational articles of faith, and of the confessional statements of the numerous Baptist churches organized in the eighteenth and nineteenth centuries, reveals a common commitment to these same principles. The wording may vary a bit but the doctrine of salvation is always the central feature, and the five soteriological concerns of the Synod of Dort are always represented.[10]

But why should there be such a monolithic stand for evangelical Calvinism among the Baptists of the South? Why should they, in common with the Presbyterians, and the pre-Oxford movement Episcopalians, espouse such doctrines? Not only do the confessional statements set forth the "doctrines of grace," the same is true of the Baptist catechisms most often used in the early 1800's.[11]

The Baptists living in the southern colonies were, like most of their brethren in the North, heirs of the English Particular Baptist tradition. In the 1640's an assembly composed of Puritan divines produced the Westminster Confession of Faith. The Particular Baptists of England had already issued their own confession in 1644 but in 1677, wishing to show their similarity to the more numerous Presbyterians and Congregational-

[9] Bond, *Minutes,* 7–8.

[10] Author's private collection (I have not discovered any associational articles of local church confessions in the states of Mississippi and Louisiana that vary from this pattern).

[11] Thomas J. Nettles, *Baptist Catechism,* (Memphis, TN, 1983).

ists, the Baptists drew up a new confession based upon the Westminster and Savoy Declaration. Its ecclesiology was Baptist, yet it retained word for word most of the Westminster Confession. Years later, James P. Boyce, the founder of Southern Baptist Theological Seminary, would still be calling the Westminster Confession, "our confession."[12]

In 1689, the Baptist Confession was re-issued. For 200 years it would remain the confession of faith of the Baptists in England and Wales. In 1742 Baptists in the Philadelphia Association added an article on congregational singing and one on the practice of "laying on of hands," and republished is as the Philadelphia Confession. The printer was Benjamin Franklin.[13]

In the South the Charleston Association would publish the 1689 confession in its pristine form. Along with the Keach's Catechism and a church manual, the 1689 confession would become the only confession of great influence in the life of Baptists in the south. Dr. Richard Furman, pastor of First Baptist Church, Charleston, S.C., gathered all the children, both white and black, before large congregations to examine their progress in Keach's Catechism.[14]

By 1845, the year the Southern Baptist Convention was born, the doctrines set forth in the 1689 confession would reign supreme. W. B. Johnson, John L. Dagg, P.H. Mell, R. B. C. Howell, Richard Fuller, Basil Manly, Sr., Basil Manly, Jr., Jesse Mercer, James P. Boyce, and John Broadus are all representative early SBC statesmen who unequivocally held to the Reformed doctrine of salvation.[15]

Men like Ezra Courtney brought to the frontier a commitment to the same doctrines. They stood shoulder to shoulder with their well-known brethren and they enjoyed a practical ecumenicity unknown in our day, as men from different denominations addressed the meetings of associations and presbyteries. Although the followers of John Wesley were not in agreement, the influence of George Whitefield produced Calvinistic brothers even among the Methodists.

It should be noted that these "frontier" preachers were not uneducated men. The stereotypical circuit rider full of zeal, and owning only a Bible

[12] James Pettigrew Boyce, *Abstract of Systematic Theology* (1887), 339.

[13] William L. Lumpkin, *Baptist Confessions of Faith* (Valley Forge, PA: 1969), 350.

[14] Jesse L. Boyd, *A Popular History of Baptists in America Prior to 1845* (New York: 1947), 100. Keach's catechism is essentially the Westminster Shorter Catechism revised for Baptists.

[15] For example, see John L. Dagg, *A Manual of Theology* (Southern Baptist Publication Society: 1857).

and perhaps a hymnal, is off the mark. Numerous academies for the instruction of young pastors came and went. They were often taught by one man, as was the case with Courtney's teacher, John M. Roberts, of Statesburg, South Carolina. Roberts, a graduate of Brown University, operated a school in the classical tradition.[16] Courtney, and the many other men who received their training in this fashion, would have had a working knowledge of Latin and Greek, and sometimes even of Hebrew. Their libraries included many of the standard commentaries of the day.

The circular letters written by Courtney reveal a refined literary style and testify to his resolute steadfastness in defending the orthodox faith. In 1832 Courtney wrote,

> Dear Brethren, we have often thought that the growth of errors was owing to the ignorance of want of information that prevailed … to our astonishment, the same errors that these dark ages produces are proclaimed and received by more than we could expect. When Alexander Campbell first came before the public as a writer, his religious views and feelings were thought to be identified with the Baptists. Some thought him a champion in Israel; but it was not long before some discovered a want of stability in him. Like clouds that are carried about of the winds, like a wandering star, he has gone from the highest views of Calvin to the lowest grade of Arminianism. Poor man, how desperately he has fallen! When Mr. Campbell announced that historically believing that Jesus Christ was the Son of God was the only requisite to baptism and that baptism was regeneration itself, the Baptists knew too well what these heresies had done and would do again if admitted.[17]

Demise of Historic Baptist Soteriology

Today, many years after Ezra Courtney wrote those words, Arminian doctrine, with the addition of a truncated version of the Reformed doctrine of perseverance, is the dominant soteriology of many Baptists. Furthermore, contemporary evangelism often degenerates into the practice of calling for the acceptance of several propositions followed by the repetition of a ritual prayer. The differences between modern Baptist practice, and old-fashioned Campbellism, may not be as great as some would like to think.

It is impossible to say when this doctrinal declension began, but by 1843 a question was raised concerning the advisability of a change in one

[16] Joe M. King, *A History of South Carolina Baptists* (Columbia, SC: 1964), 45.
[17] Bond, *Minutes*, 138.

of the Mississippi Association's articles of faith. Courtney was made chairman of the committee assigned the task of investigation. The article in question was the fourth, which asserted "the unconditional election of a definite number of the human family to grace and glory." Courtney marshaled many passages of Scripture in order to show that the article should be retained without alteration.[18] The Association voted to reaffirm the doctrine. According to Boyd, the article was still held by the Association when he wrote his history of Mississippi Baptists in 1930.[19]

Still, the necessity of mounting a defense for the old confession suggests that some were moving in a different direction. Why should this have been the case? First, the advent of hyper-Calvinism with its assault on the biblical doctrine of human responsibility and its anti-missions agitation probably caused many people to react in the extreme, so as not to appear to give aid and comfort to heretics. Men like Courtney were able to maintain their evangelical character in both doctrine and practice. They would fight on two fronts at once: against Campbellism and its faulty doctrine of salvation and against the so-called "primitives" and their faulty doctrine of evangelism.

Second, the nineteenth century was preoccupied with ecclesiology not soteriology. The burning question for many was not, "How can I be saved?" it was, "What is the true church?" Campbellites inaugurated a "restorationist" movement, and judged themselves to be the true church. The Oxford movement called Anglicans to look again to apostolic succession. It was in the nineteenth century that Rome officially promulgated the doctrine of papal infallibility. Various sects and cults gave their own answer to the question. Joseph Smith claimed a latter day revelation and established the "true church" himself.

Among Baptists J. R. Graves would teach a high church system that we have come to know as Landmarkism. The old Baptist doctrines would be partially retained, some would be ignored, and others would be rejected entirely, as in the case of the doctrine of the universal church. Because of Landmark influence, it would be 1963 before the Southern Baptist Convention would adopt a statement containing an affirmation of the real existence of the church universal.[20]

A third reason for the eventual rejection of Reformation theology in popular practice was the gradual neglect of catechetical instruction. Failure to teach the doctrines of grace would considerably weaken them in the minds and hearts of Baptists. Still, as late as the 1918 publication of *The*

[18] Bond, *Minutes*, 8-9.

[19] Bond, *Minutes*, 78.

[20] See *The Baptist Faith and Message*, 1963, 13.

New Convention Normal Manual for Sunday School Workers, the confession of faith that F. H. Kerfoot had written for the Eutaw Baptist Church in Baltimore and that had been adopted by many other churches was included. Kerfoot was Boyce's successor at Southern Baptist Seminary and later corresponding secretary for the Home Mission Board. It is entitled, "What We Believe According to the Scriptures," and includes a section identifying doctrines held in common with other denominations. It read as follows:

> And, in common with a large body of evangelical Christians nearly all Baptists believe what are usually termed the "doctrines of grace."
>
> 1. The absolute sovereignty and foreknowledge of God.
> 2. His eternal and unchangeable purposes or decrees.
> 3. That salvation in its beginning, continuance and completion, is God's free gift.
> 4. That in Christ, we are elected or chosen, personally or individually, from eternity, saved and called out from the world, not according to our works, but according to his own purpose and grace, through sanctification of the Spirit and belief of the truth.
> 5. That we are kept, by his power, from falling away, and will be presented faultless before the presence of his glory. Read Romans 8, 9, 10, 11; Acts 13:48; Ephesians 1:4, 5; Ephesians 2:1–10; 1 Peter 1:2–5; Jude 24; 2 Timothy 1:9; Titus 3:5.[21]

And the same allegiance to Reformation theology persists in the "Baptist Faith and Message," a modified version of the New Hampshire Confession of Faith which has been the theological consensus statement of the Southern Baptist Convention since 1925. The priority of regeneration is acknowledged, and repentance and faith are called "inseparable experiences of grace." The statement on election, free agency, and perseverance could have been written by Courtney himself.[22] It is consistent with the historic Reformed, Puritan and Baptist traditions.

Nevertheless, it is clear that most Baptists early in the twenty first century are ignorant of their heritage and of the doctrines that their denomination regards, on paper at least, as the standard for our faith and practice.

[21] *The New Convention Norman Manual for Sunday School Workers*, (Nashville, TN: 1918), 307–308. See *Founders Journal* 9 (Summer 92):27–28.

[22] "The Baptist Faith and Message", 1963, 12.

What factors contributed to the popular demise of the doctrines of grace in the twentieth century?

Thomas J. Nettles has identified two developments that have played a very important part. One, the tendency to overlook doctrinal distinctives for the sake of fiscal unity. Orthodoxy has come to be defined by many as support for the Cooperative Program.[23] Thus, often when a presbytery is called for the purpose of examining a candidate for the ministry, little attention is given to his understanding of doctrine and much attention is given to his commitment to denominational support.

In the second place, there is a great difference between the attention given to doctrine in the Baptist Press after the nineteenth century. Nettles says, "A second factor in the change involves increasing indifference toward doctrine in the literature and Baptist papers. In fact, not only is doctrinal distinctiveness overlooked, it is actually discouraged by many contemporary Southern Baptists.[24]

Another factor is the popular dominance of Dispensational theology. Southern Baptists were not forced to form alliances with Dispensational, and often Arminian teachers, in the fight against Liberalism, as were orthodox men in other denominations, (the Presbyterian Church being one example, which resulted in a weakening of that denomination's adherence to the Westminster standards). Still, among Baptists, the influence of popular, non-Southern Baptist, evangelical literature along with growing acceptance of the Scofield Reference Bible brought doctrines into Southern Baptist Life that were not consonant with the doctrines of grace.

Resurgence

A generation ago it was possible, but difficult, to find seminary professors and denominational leaders who believed and taught the historic Southern Baptist doctrine of grace. Today there are professors, seminary deans, editors, denominational employees, missionaries, agency trustees, a growing number of younger well-educated pastors, and a host of enthusiastic church members who would agree with the theology of Ezra Courtney. The resurgence of reformed theology in the evangelical world has had its manifestation among Baptists generally. Among Baptist churches associated with the Southern Baptist Convention, this resurgence has been fostered and conserved, in large measure, by Founders Ministries, the out-

[23] Thomas J. Nettles, *By His Grace and for His Glory*, (Grand Rapids, MI: 1986), 244.

[24] Ibid, 244–245.

growth of The Southern Baptist Conference on the Faith of the Founders.[25] That movement continues to provide encouragement and help to many through its publishing efforts and online services, as well as through a number of regional conferences and fellowships.

Like Mark Twain, who when informed that his death had been reported in the press, responded that his demise was "highly exaggerated," the faith of Ezra Courtney endures, and by God's grace prospers.

[25] Fred A. Malone has served on the board of Founders Ministries since its inception in 1982.

16

Exalting Christ by Serving the Church as an Elder

Mitch Axsom

The heart of a biblical elder wants no title. He wants no fame. He wants Christ to be exalted and the souls of men to be established in Him. He wants no acclaim, but instead desires that every heart may be rooted and grounded in the Ever Living One seated on high. O, that the Lord of the harvest might raise up an army of such men to stand as watchmen of Christ's church—loving them, overseeing them, feeding them, and praying for them in love to Him who owns His flock (Matthew 9:37, 38; Luke 10:2).

This chapter assumes that the reader knows that the qualifications of 1 Timothy 3:1–7 and Titus 1:6–9 require that one who is being considered as an elder be a holy man of God. These qualifications speak much more to his holiness than to his ability to teach, though he must be apt in this sphere. He is not a sinless man, as there was only One sinless Being in all of time. Rather, he is a blameless man, one that the people can follow as an example in all areas of his life. This man does not have various sinful quirks of temperament—bad baggage—for which others inside or outside of the local church have to make apology. He is apt to teach. That is, he can teach more than one Sunday lesson on a given topic. He is able to feed and establish the saints in Christ from the whole counsel of God. According to Ephesians 4:8–14, these elders are gifts to the flock to help all the members one by one grow together into the image of our Lord Jesus Christ.

There are many aspects to the making of an elder and an eldership. This chapter is a brief survey of five aspects of the role of an elder: (1) a man exalting Christ in fellowship with his Lord, (2) a man exalting Christ with his family, (3) a man exalting Christ with his church, (4) a man exalting Christ with his fellow elders, (5) a man who aids the local church to exalt Christ in helping it maintain association with other churches. The last two aspects will be particularly considered.

A Man Exalting Christ in Fellowship with His Lord

All Christians belong to Christ. All Christians love the lord. Not all Christians are called to be elders. Those that are called to be elders are called internally by the Spirit and externally by the church.[1] They are a gift of Christ to His church (Ephesians 4:11, 12) to watch over them, feed them, and edify them so that as one body they may glorify the Lord, being conformed to His image. This called man is one who loved the Lord long before he was called as elder (overseer, pastor) of His local church. He is a man whose heart pants after the water brooks of the Lord's mercy because he is saved by astounding grace. His heart was and is following hard after God, the living God because He has redeemed him from certain destruction so that he might continually feast upon Him. His heart is now fixed on the Lord and his eyes are ever searching His Word, laying it in his heart that he might not sin against Him (Psalm 119:11). He thirsts not for leadership per se, but he thirsts for following the Lord of Glory. His family experiences the blessing of his relationship with the Lord; his church is edified by his love for the Lord and them. We are to pray that the Lord raises up such a host of men "for … the laborers are few" (Matthew 9:37, 38; Luke 10:2).

An elder's relationship with the Lord is one that will be evident whether he is installed or not. To be an elder is not his goal in life. The eldership is merely an outworking of what God has already worked within him—an insatiable love to His Lord fueled from heaven itself. He makes no show of his religion. His secret time with the Lord is his daily feast. Two of his greatest delights are the Word of God and prayer manifested by a holy life of obedience to His commands. So then, God's elder is a man who exalts the Lord Jesus Christ in his personal life.

A Man Exalting Christ with his Family

He is also a man whose heart is singular toward his wife. He is not flirtatious. His wife can trust him ministering to other women because she

[1] John Gill, *Body of Divinity*, 2 vols. (London: W. Winterbotham, 1796), 245.

knows she is number one and he has no number two. His heart is constantly putting off the sins of the flesh and the mind which would interfere with the self-denying love he is to show to his wife each and every day (Ephesians 5:25).

He trains his children for the glory of God. He first is their example, and then he is their guide. They see him as one who honors the Lord as he resists their sinful natures and chastens them with a loving heart. He trains them in the Word of God and seeks to fulfill the commands of Deuteronomy 6:5, Ephesians 6:4, Colossians 3:21 and a host of commands in Proverbs given to help this father fulfill his God-given trust. He helps them see that only Jesus can cleanse away their sins and that He loves to receive children to Himself. He delights in time with his children not for the purpose of achieving an elder's status, but that they may be readied for heaven. They see him not as perfect, but as one who repents quickly and flees to the throne of forgiveness. He owns his sins before them and seeks reconciliation when needed. They see demonstrably his humble, loving, servant heart and eventually long to be a parent after his pattern. They have been shepherded by his wisdom, nursed by his tenderness, and rescued by his love for the Lord, their mother, and them. He is one who helps them see that Christ is building His church with children eventually to be pillars in that edifice. He leads them in family worship and then leads them at church without hypocrisy. They know that he should be able to take care of the church of God because they know he has cared well for them. In short, he is Christ's representative in the home to both his wife and his children, and they would be the first to vote for his candidacy for the eldership. He is a man exalting Christ in his home.

A Man Exalting Christ within His Church

An elder is not a man who seeks preeminence, but one who lowers himself in following the example of Christ who washed the disciples' feet. He is satisfied with being unnoticed. He does not see his training as a fast track to the ministry, but only a means for God to use if He so desires. His training, whether formal or informal, and his care for his family speak volumes to a church that then says, "May he care for us also." His love for the Lord and His Word are evident to those who have been praying that the Lord would raise up shepherd laborers among them. He is not chosen because he is high and mighty, but because he really has the gifts and virtues requisite for an elder in the Lord's church.

He is a man known for his servant spirit and his willingness to be a member of the flock, whether he a member of an eldership or not (Matthew 20:26, 27; 23:11). He is personable and approachable. He has shirked ministerial airs and looks. He is a saint with all the saints. His heart loves the rich and the poor, the young and the old, the feeble and the strong (James 1:1–7). He loves them for the sake of Christ. He is filled with the Spirit of God to minister to them where they are. He is not looking at the church as a stepping stone to a higher plane of work. He knows that he must be called by a local church to serve them as an elder or he is not an elder at all. He is content with his sphere of labor, trusting the Lord of providence to guide his life and to place him where he is to serve. He exalts the Lord Jesus Christ as head of the church.

We will now turn to the last two aspects of the eldership in which Christ must be exalted as mentioned at the beginning of the chapter. First, an elder is a man exalting Christ with his fellow elders to establish the saints according to Ephesians 4:8–14. Second, an elder is a man who aids the church in exalting Christ by maintaining association with other churches (Acts 15:1–29, Colossians 4:12–16).

A Man Exalting Christ with his Fellow Elders

According to the commandments of Christ

Elders can sometimes see themselves as merely checks and balances in a system that requires accountability. Or they may see themselves as opponents vying for the top position or the place of prominence. We know that these are sinful postures and ones that must be put away in the interest of Christ's commands for all saints and for elders in particular.

What are those general commandments of Christ that will help the elders function together most effectively to the exaltation of Christ? They are to love the Lord and they are to love one another. They are to love the Lord who died for them and washed them from every sin. They are to love Him who has justified them, who is sanctifying them and who will glorify them eternally. Furthermore, they are to love one another. "Love is the divine glue that holds the elders and congregation together through conflict and disagreement."[2] Elders are to be an example to the flock and if they are not an example in love, what do they have to give? "Love never fails" and love among the elders will rise like an aroma that distills over the whole congregation. Without it, the pollution of bitterness and dissention will prevail, as Galatians 5:15 graphically warns, "But if you bite and devour

[2] Alexander Strauch, *Biblical Eldership: An Urgent Call to Restore Biblical Church Eldership* (2nd Edition) (Littleton, Colorado: Lewis and Roth Publishers, 1988), 111.

one another, beware lest you be consumed by one another!"

Not only are they to be examples of love, but they are to be examples of every other fruit of the Spirit: joy, peace, longsuffering, kindness, goodness, faithfulness, gentleness, self-control. Each of these fruits are to abound in the elders' interactions. The peace they have with the Lord through the death of the Lord Jesus must reign in their relations one to another. Patience must abound because He is so patient with them. Faithfulness to the Lord and to His word is essential. Gentleness must mark their actions when they disagree. Quick repentance and full reconciliation must be their hallmarks. The enemy would love to divide an eldership, but the bonds of the Spirit of Christ must be stronger.

God's called elder must be a man given to prayer (Acts 6:4; Matthew 17:21; 21:13; Romans 12:12; Ephesians 6:18; Colossians 4:2; 1 Thessalonians 5:17). Prayer should be his every breath as he seeks to care for the household of God. He has not when he prays not, and the church suffers. He learns to pray by praying, and prays better by praying more. He prays in secret without fanfare, and prays openly before the saints with humility. He prays to be praying more because in prayer he fellowships with His Lord. He moves forward on his knees and rises only to continue in prayer. The Lord is honored by his resolute callings and the saints are blessed (2 Corinthians 1:11).

The elders must serve one another as Christ served us. Consider that the Lord washed the disciples feet (John 13:12–14). This attitude must be in each elder's mind as they serve together. The Lord said that the greatest among us would be our servant (Matthew 23:11). Each elder is then to be the servant of the others even as the Lord Jesus Christ serves us.

He is a man who ministers alongside and well with other elders. He is not striving for the ascendency among them, but the opportunity to support them in their own service to the Lord. He does not think of himself more highly than he ought to think (Romans 12:3). He defers to others when proper, and leads with the encouragement of the other elders who may be able to assess his gifts better than he himself. He is content with the level of service allotted to him by the other elders and the church. He leads like Christ, not like Diotrephes (3 John 9, 10). Love for the Lord Jesus marks all his dealings with his fellow elders, who see in him an example of the Lord to follow (Philippians 4:17). He is careful and prayerful in controversy, thinking and hoping the best. He is, in summary, the Lord's loving servant among servants, remembering that the Lord Jesus Himself is the great Shepherd over all the flock (1 Peter 5:2–4).

What then should elders do when they sin against one another (James 3:1)? They are to exercise the forgiveness that the Lord has extended to them according to Mark 11:25, "And whenever you stand praying, if you have anything against anyone, forgive him, that your Father in heaven may also forgive you your trespasses." This attitude of forgiveness is one that should reside in the heart even before a brother is confronted with a sin. This heart of forgiveness is of paramount importance when elders have sinned against one another.

We must never forget that humility must rest upon the heart of each elder servant. He is to have the humble mind of Christ.

> Let this mind be in you which was also in Christ Jesus, who, being in the form of God, did not consider it robbery to be equal with God, but made Himself of no reputation, taking the form of a bondservant, and coming in the likeness of men. And being found in appearance as a man, He humbled Himself and became obedient to the point of death, even the death of the cross. Therefore God also has highly exalted Him and given Him the name which is above every name, that at the name of Jesus every knee should bow, of those in heaven, and of those on earth, and of those under the earth, and that every tongue should confess that Jesus Christ is Lord, to the glory of God the Father (Philippians 2:5–11).

We often think that assertion and firmness will resolve conflict, and yet it is humility that will win the day in an eldership. Preferring others before oneself is Christ's command, and the humble servant will reflect the character of Christ in his dealings with other elders and among those in the body of Christ (Romans 12:10; Philippians 2:3).

Elders exalt Christ when they obey His specific commands together regarding the ministry. Generally speaking, they are to oversee the flock and feed the flock of God as those who must give an account (Acts 20:28, 1 Peter 5:2, Hebrews 13:17). As overseers, they are like shepherds who protect the flock from harm. In protecting them, they must be able to answer unsound doctrine with pure truth (Titus 1:9). They must be able to lift up the saint who is weak and correct the one who is going astray (Hebrews 12:12,13; Galatians 6:1; 2 Timothy 2:24–26). They may have to rebuke a brother or sister in the spirit of the love of Christ (2 Timothy 4:2, Jude 22, 23). As pastors or feeders of the flock, they must be able to rightly divide the Word of truth (2 Timothy 2:15). They must seek to obey the great commission in that they are to teach the saints, "all things that I have commanded you" (Matthew 28:20). They are to teach the wholesome words of the Lord Jesus Christ (1 Timothy 6:3). They are to teach the "whole counsel of God" (Acts 20:27). They must be fair, patient, and careful in matters of church discipline (Matthew 18:15–20; 1 Corinthians 5; 2 Thessalonians 3:6–15). Regarding specific commands for the ministry, they must consider that there are no less than 67 groups of commands given in the pastoral epistles alone (see Appendix A). Who is sufficient for such responsibility? How are two or more elders to work together in harmony to fulfill these commandments to the glory of God and the blessing of the church? No one can succeed unless the Lord of the Church be their continual Guide and Helper (John 15:5).

According to the gifts fitted by Christ

They must not only keep general and specific commandments by His grace, but they must know well their own gifts and how they fit together in and among the other elders for the service of the body. (Not every elder can exercise his teaching gift before the whole congregation in every given service. On the other hand, elders who are more gifted, who spend more time before the congregation, should consider how other elders may serve as well.) Let us consider how 1 Timothy 5:17 provides an initial direction for an eldership, where each man has varying gifts, but all are "apt to teach." "Let the elders who rule well be counted worthy of double honor, especially those who labor in the word and doctrine." This verse is not teaching that there are three tiers of elders within the body of Christ, for they are all elders. What it does teach is that there are pathways of giftedness. There are elders that rule (who can also teach). There are elders that rule well and there are elders that rule well while they labor in the word of God and doctrine. It is not that the first group do not know how to labor in the word of God and doctrine, it is that there are those among the elders who do this best for the good of the flock. They are particularly fitted by giftedness, or experience, or by simply plain diligence so that they are first among equals.[3]

How is this designation for each elder to be determined? There is an internal call that cannot be denied, but there must be an external call as well within the church. At times, the saints of God know the gifts of those teaching them better than the teachers themselves. They know when one elder's ministry provides a more certain and lasting foundation in their lives. Many times, the congregation has voted that a certain elder should be fully compensated for his service to them. This vote should reflect the depth of blessing they have known in this man's teaching and ministry. Some churches denote this man as a senior pastor (note James place in the Jerusalem church, Acts 12:27; 15:13–21; 21:18). They do receive double honor, or full compensation if the assembly can so afford, so that they do not have to work as bi-vocational elders (1 Corinthians 9:14). Many congregations cannot afford more than one fully supported pastor or elder. In that case, one or more of the elders must be non-supported or only partially supported. Contentment must reign in such situations, particularly for the elders who are not fully supported and serve the pulpit in a lesser capacity.[4]

The relationship between Barnabas and Saul is a good example. In the beginning of their ministry together, Barnabas was the more experienced minister. His name is stated first by the Word of God when they are initially mentioned (Acts 11:30, 12:25, 13:3, 13:7). In Acts 13:9 Saul is also called Paul. From this point in Acts onward, 8 of 11 times they are mentioned together, Paul is mentioned first. Acts 14:12 says "And Barnabas they called Zeus, and Paul, Hermes, because he was the chief speaker." By this time, Paul had become the more prominent speaker. He would later become the chief writer in the New Testament. The same occurs within an eldership. One (or more) brother's gifts are more useful to the saints and they should then have more time in the pulpit.

There is no room for competition. May the Lord ban that from the hearts of men. There is no place for a Diotrephian spirit among those who should be vying for the lowest seat. The glory and honor of Christ requires that each man in an eldership take careful stock of the place that he has among the others and that each be willing to take the lesser spot if this is most beneficial to the growth and well-being of the church.

In addition to the pulpit ministry, there is much ministry to be done outside of the pulpit. Some elders have more administrative gifts for overseeing projects within the church. They may be particularly skilled at assisting other elders in mission trips or the setting up of special weeks within the church. There are too many ministerial decisions for this to be the work of a deacon. These projects must be overseen by an elder with the whole counsel of God on his heart in order to administer them properly. In addition, some elders are specially gifted with the sick, with widows, or with the homeless. There are nursing home ministries and jail ministries that need pastoral preaching and oversight. In short, there is enough ministry to go around for all the elders to work together in concert and in love, supporting one another and helping one another shoulder the burden of ministry together so that no elder (hopefully) is over-taxed. There is no place for division or a party spirit. There is no place for self-pity or self-exaltation. Only Christ Jesus is to be exalted in a church and among the elders.

[3] Alexander Strauch, *Biblical Eldership*, 248–251.

[4] Bi-vocational elders would do well to remember that Paul was bi-vocational during parts of his ministry and that this was his chosen lot so that the gospel would never be hindered (1 Corinthians 9:1–15; 1 Thessalonians 2:9; 2 Thessalonians 3:7–9).

So then, elders are to obey the general commands of our Lord Jesus in loving one another and serving one another in humility. They are to obey the specific commands incumbent upon all elders according to the pastoral epistles and all other Scripture. They are to be very mindful of their individual gifts and serve in those capacities in harmony, to the glory of Christ, their Head and Chief Shepherd.

A Man who Aids the Church in Exalting Christ by Maintaining Association with other Churches

1. According to the testimony of the New Testament

2. By the example set in church history

    a. The Second London Confession of Faith of 1677/1689

    b. A comparison of episcopacy, presbytery, and independency

    c. The founding principles of the Particular Baptists in 1652

Is it Scriptural for a church to work in association with other churches? John Thornberry wisely this question by appealing to churches in the New Testament:

> They had concerns which reached beyond the boundaries of their own communities and touched the whole Christian movement in which they were involved. The churches did have common interests and shared activities. For example, in Acts 15 we find the early churches seeking a resolution of a doctrinal problem by a council at Jerusalem. Representatives of at least two churches, the Jerusalem church and the Antioch church, were present; and since, according to Acts 9:31, there were many churches in Palestine at the time, it is reasonable to assume that there were believers, not only from Jerusalem proper, but also from the whole region, present at the conference. The conclusions were undoubtedly agreed to by all the churches represented, and they were also documented by a letter sent "to the brethren who are of the Gentiles in Antioch, Syria, and Cilicia" (Acts 15:23). There were common projects such as the collection of money from many churches to be taken for the relief of the famine-stricken believers at Jerusalem (2 Corinthians 8:1–11); and the provision for the support of missionaries was shared jointly by all the churches (2 Corinthians 11:9; Philippians 4:15).[5]

5 John Thornbury, "Cooperation and the Autonomy of the Local Church," in *Biblical Shepherding of God's Sheep*, ed. Steve Martin (Leominster: Day One Publications, 2010), 192.

Earl Blackburn points out that the churches of Galatia received but one letter (Galatians 1:2, 22). Furthermore, he mentions that the Colossians were to share their letter with the Laodiceans and vice versa. Finally he comments on the book of Revelation (especially verse 1:11).

> One of the most overlooked facts in modern 20th century evangelical Christianity is the recipients of the book of Revelation. To whom was the book written? The book was *not* written to individual Christians at the end of the 20th century. It was written as *one* circular letter to seven local churches during the latter half of the first century; not to private persons, but to congregations of churches. Chapters 2 and 3 bear this out.[6]

All seven of these churches were true churches of the Lord Jesus Christ and they were all to receive this letter, indicating that there had to be mutual cooperation and association between the churches. So then we see that the churches of the New Testament worked in association with one another.

We know that each individual church must care for itself in terms of teaching and administering discipline, but it is abundantly clear that the churches of the New Testament cared for one another in theological considerations, cared for missionary endeavors and cared for needy saints among them. How then has this been borne out in church history?

The Second London Baptist Confession of Faith 1677/1689, in chapter 26, paragraphs 14 and 15, seeks to apply what is found in the New Testament:

> As each church, and all the members of it, are bound to pray continually for the good and prosperity of all the churches of Christ, in all places, and upon all occasions to further every one within the bounds of their places and callings, in the exercise of their gifts and graces, so the churches, when planted by the providence of God, so as they may enjoy opportunity and advantage for it, ought to hold communion among themselves, for their peace, increase of love, and mutual edification.
>
> In cases of difficulties or differences, either in point of doctrine or administration, wherein either the churches in general are concerned, or any one church, in their peace, union, and edification; or any member or members of any church are injured, in or by any proceedings in censures not agreeable to truth and order: it is according to the mind of Christ, that many churches holding communion together, do, by their messen-

[6] Earl Blackburn, "The Biblical Basis for Associations of Churches," in *Biblical Shepherding of God's Sheep*, ed. Steve Martin (Leominster: Day One Publications, 2010), 192.

> gers, meet to consider, and give their advice in or about that matter in difference, to be reported to all the churches concerned; howbeit these messengers assembled, are not intrusted with any church-power properly so called; or with any jurisdiction over the churches themselves, to exercise any censures either over any churches or persons; or to impose their determination on the churches or officers.

James Renihan asserts that the phrase, "holding communion among themselves" used in both paragraphs means that churches ought to form associations with one another for their "peace, increase of love, and mutual edification."[7] Good elders will assist their flocks to see like-minded churches in such light and make opportunity for them to be in association with one another.

We know that some groups of churches have chosen to work together in denominations such as Presbyterians, Methodists, and Episcopalians. Baptists, on the other hand, have rejected any hierarchy above their local congregations. They have rejected an episcopacy, "a system of *descending* church power that is centered on *bishops*"[8] and the presbytery, a system of *ascending* church power" that begins in the congregation rises to elders. The elders of such congregations form the session which is over the local church. This power then may ascend to synod and a general assembly, all of which have power over the local church.[9]

Baptists, on the other hand, have chosen independency. James Renihan comments on this system of government.

> Rather than independency being a system of descending or ascending power, it is a system of *reciprocating*, or perhaps *cooperating*, power, because this system views all participating churches in an equal light, with equal status, and equal rights. The church in this system can only be the local congregation. So you have episcopacy and presbytery, which ultimately form on large church, but you have independency which recognizes various churches and equates them in status and in rights.[10]

That is, each local church, though an independent creation of God, is working together in association with other churches of like mind and confession.

However, some Baptist churches have actually become what could be called TIBC churches — Too Independent Baptist Churches. These are

[7] James M. Renihan, *Associational Churchanship* (Palmdale, CA: RBAP, 2016), 53–55.

[8] Renihan, *Associational Churchanship*, 9.

[9] Ibid., 10–11.

[10] Ibid., 13–14.

churches (led by elders) who think it unscriptural or unwise to associate with other churches in any way. This was not the case in the history of Particular Baptists in England who did form associations. This practice and their doctrinal convictions have been duplicated by associations of churches in America from the founding of the SBC (the Southern Baptist Convention) and other Baptist associations such as ARBCA (Association of Reformed Baptist Churches of America).

The elder who serves his flock well will seek Scriptural ways to work in association with other churches of like doctrine as we have seen in the New Testament and as we note further in church history. For example, the Particular Baptist churches in England formed the Abingdon Association in 1652. Their founding principles are stated as follows:

1. That Particular churches of Christ ought to hold a firm communion each with [the] other in point of advice, in doubtful matters and controversies (Acts 15:1f, 6, 38, 38; 16:4f). Which scriptures compared together show that the church at Jerusalem held communion with the church at Antioch, offering help to them as they could.

2. In giving and receiving in the case of want and poverty (2 Cor. 16:3).

3. In Consulting and consenting to the carrying on of the work of God as choosing messengers, etc. (2 Cor. 8:19) and in all things else wherein particular members of one and the same particular church stand bound to hold communion each with [the] other for which conclusion we render these Scriptures readings.

   (a) Because there is the same relation betwixt the particular churches each towards other as there is betwixt particular members of one church. For the churches of Christ do all make up one body or church in general under Christ their head as Ephesians 1:22, Colossians 1:24, Ephesians 5:23, 2 Corinthians 12:13. As particular members make up one particular church under the same head–Christ, and all particular assemblies are one Mount Zion (Is. 4:5; S of S 6:9) ... Wherefore we conclude that every church ought to manifest its care over the other churches, as fellow members of the same body of Christ in general do rejoice and mourn with them according to the law of their near relation in Christ..

   (b) From that which is a main ground for particular church communion, v12 to keep each other pure and to clear the profession of the gospel from scandal which cannot be done (1 Cor 5:5) unless orderly walking churches be owned orderly, and disorderly churches be orderly disowned. Even as [just as] disorderly walking members of a Particular church [would be disowned], yea the reason is more full in respect of the greater scandal by not witnessing against the defection (1 Cor 7:11) of a church or churches.

(c) For the proof of their love to all saints, particular church communion being never appointed as a restraint of our love which should manifest itself to all the churches.

(d) The work of God wherein all the churches are concerned together, may be the more easily and prosperously carried on by a combination of prayers and endeavors.

(e) From the need they have or may have one of another to quicken them when lukewarm, to help when in want, assist in counsel in doubtful matters and prevent prejudices in each against other.

(f) To convince the world, for by this shall men know by one mark that we are true churches of Christ. In order thereunto we unanimously agree at our next meeting to declare the principles of the constitutions of the respective churches to which we belong. These things to be offered to the churches to be approved.[11]

One notices how these churches asserted that they collectively were one in Christ as His body. They were to declare Him to the world by their love to one another (John 13:35). They did not see associationalism merely as a means to get certain goals accomplished that they could not do so alone, but that associationalism itself glorified the Lord who had formed them to love one another as churches just as we are to love one another as brethren within the same church. The elder who is leading his church in this God ordained direction must be prepared to spend some of his time with associational matters. David Kingdon states,

> Between meetings of the Association contact was maintained by correspondence. Arrangements were also made with the approval of the associated churches for gifted brethren to visit the churches between each general meeting. For example, at an association meeting at Tatsworth, several churches agreed to delegate two gifted men to visit the various churches. It was also resolved that churches able to release men to help elsewhere should do so. In this way the life of the association was

[11] B. R. White, ed. *Association records of the Particular Baptist of Engliand, Wales and Ireland to 1660. Part 3. The Abingdon Association* (London: Baptist Historical Society, 1974), 126–27 in David Kingdon, "Independency and Interdependency" in James M. Renihan, *Denominations or Associations?* (Amytyville, NY: Calvary Press Publishing, 2001), 11–13.

> strengthened and the weaker churches especially were encouraged and helped.[12]

One notes that through this association's work, weaker churches were strengthened who lacked gifted brethren. Not every church has the gifted brethren needed to fill the pulpit. This association was mindful of this and used their cooperative efforts to solve the problem. Kingdon continues,

> Each associated church was required to send an account of its spiritual state to each general meeting of the association. This was with a view to promoting prayer, and to enable the associated messengers to discern where help was needed. As early as the fifth general meeting of the Abingdon Association in April, 1653, it was agreed that "such churches as want [lacked] gifted brethren to hold forth the Word among them should make the same known to the rest of the churches or, at least to [such] church or churches as in probability may be most able to help them, that help might be afforded them accordingly.[13]

So in this way churches with greater needs were cared for through the strength of other churches so that the Word could go forth to all. What can be learned in this historical account is that an elder working in an association can find means to assist other churches, that they may be blessed as well with the Lord's Word, until such time as they are provided with a gifted brother to serve continually among them.

These churches were not only concerned about pulpit supply, but the substance of the theology that was being preached. The Particular Baptists of England adopted the 1689 Confession of Faith. Their confession became the basis for the confession of the Philadelphia Association in the United States some eighty years later. These churches were very active in assisting one another "in ministerial training, church planting, ministerial relief, benevolence, and a variety of other causes."[14] Elders were used of God in promoting and maintaining such associations as the Charleston Association (1845), the Sandy Creek Association (1755) and numerous other associations. Though this function of an elder is not one of his primary functions, it is one that is seen in the Scriptures, and should be one of the aspects of a good elder's ministry—the care of the churches, not with invasive ecclesiastical oversight, but with love for the Lord's own in those churches and their need for sound doctrine and practice.

[12] David Kingdon, cited in James M. Renihan, *Denominations or Associations?*, 19.

[13] Ibid, 20, 21.

[14] Renihan, *Denominiations or Associations*, 61.

Conclusion

Christ is exalted. He is exalted at the right hand of God, waiting until His enemies be made his footstool (Psalm 110:1; Hebrews 1:13). Christ is exalted in that He is the head of the body, the church (Colossians 1:18a). The Lord Jesus should and must be exalted in His under-shepherds. They should be men who exalt Christ in their private walk with Him. They exalt Him in their families. They are to exalt Christ in their churches and among their fellow elders. They assist their churches to walk in association with other churches.

Elders are called to oversee the body and feed it so that it may be conformed to the image of Jesus Christ (1 Peter 5:2, Colossians 1:28). The eldership of a church is called to exalt the Lord Jesus Christ in every message and counseling session as Paul stated, "I determined not to know anything among you except Jesus Christ and Him crucified" (1 Corinthians 2:2). He is to be exalted by every decision and direction the church may take. The eldership is not a self-exalting agency. They are a group of men called to exalt Christ.

Each elder is personally fitted by the Lord Jesus Christ for the oversight and edification of His local church. They are men internally called by the Lord for this work, and called externally by the church which they serve. They do not serve according to their own egos, but at the direction of Christ through His Word. They do not serve above the people to hold them down, but they serve at the feet of Christ and for the washing of the feet of the saints to whom they minister for the purpose of building them up. They serve for the strengthening of their own congregations to the glory of God, and they lead their church into fellowship and service with other churches in association. They are sinners saved by the grace of their loving God and walk in humility before Him and their fellow saints.

May the Lord raise up many more such laborers that the name of Jesus Christ our Lord might be exalted in all the earth.[15]

[15] The author of this contribution, by the grace of God, has served as a co-elder with Fred Malone since the end of 2005. Fred is a true example to all elders of what it means to exalt Christ in the five areas discussed within this chapter. If he had written this chapter it would have been much more encouraging and gracious, much more Christ-centered, and much more complete.

Appendix A

Commands in the Pastoral Epistles (NKJV)

1. [We are to] teach no other doctrine, nor give heed to fables and endless genealogies, which cause disputes rather than godly edification which is in faith (1 Timothy 1:3,4).
2. I exhort first of all that supplications, prayers, intercessions, and giving of thanks be made for all men, for kings and all who are in authority, that we may lead a quiet and peaceable life in all godliness and reverence (2:1,2).
3. I desire therefore that the men pray everywhere, lifting up holy hands, without wrath and doubting (2:8).
4. In like manner also, that the women adorn themselves in modest apparel, with propriety and moderation, not with braided hair or gold or pearls or costly clothing, but, which is proper for women professing godliness, with good works (2:9,10).
5. Let a woman learn in silence with all submission. And I do not permit a woman to teach or to have authority over a man, but to be in silence (2:9–12).
6. This is a faithful saying: If a man desires the position of a bishop, he desires a good work. A bishop then must be blameless, the husband of one wife, temperate, sober-minded, of good behavior, hospitable, able to teach; not given to wine, not violent, not greedy for money, but gentle, not quarrelsome, not covetous; one who rules his own house well, having his children in submission with all reverence (for if a man does not know how to rule his own house, how will he take care of the church of God?); not a novice, lest being puffed up with pride he fall into the same condemnation as the devil. Moreover he must have a good testimony among those who are outside, lest he fall into reproach and the snare of the devil (3:1–7).
7. Likewise deacons must be reverent, not double-tongued, not given to much wine, not greedy for money, holding the mystery of the faith with a pure conscience. But let these also first be tested; then let them serve as deacons, being found blameless. Likewise, their wives must be reverent, not slanderers, temperate, faithful in all things. Let deacons be the husbands of one wife, ruling their children and their own houses well. For those who have served well as deacons obtain for themselves a good standing and great boldness in the faith which is in Christ Jesus (3:8–14).

8. If you instruct the brethren in these things, you will be a good minister of Jesus Christ, nourished in the words of faith and of the good doctrine which you have carefully followed (speaking of 4:1–5).
9. But reject profane and old wives' fables, and exercise yourself toward godliness.
10. These things command and teach (4:11 speaking of 4:1–10).
11. Be an example to the believers in word, in conduct, in love, in spirit,[fn] in faith, in purity (4:12b).
12. Do not neglect the gift that is in you, which was given to you by prophecy with the laying on of the hands of the eldership (4:14).
13. Meditate on these things; give yourself entirely to them, that your progress may be evident to all (4:15).
14. Take heed to yourself and to the doctrine. Continue in them, for in doing this you will save both yourself and those who hear you (4:16).
15. Do not rebuke an older man, but exhort him as a father, younger men as brothers, older women as mothers, younger women as sisters, with all purity (5:1,2).
16. Honor widows who are really widows (5:3 see also 4–16).
17. Let the elders who rule well be counted worthy of double honor, especially those who labor in the word and doctrine (5:17 see also 18).
18. Do not receive an accusation against an elder except from two or three witnesses. Those who are sinning rebuke in the presence of all, that the rest also may fear (5:19,20 see also 21).
19. Do not lay hands on anyone hastily, nor share in other people's sins; keep yourself pure (5:22).
20. No longer drink only water, but use a little wine for your stomach's sake and your frequent infirmities (5:23).
21. Let as many bondservants as are under the yoke count their own masters worthy of all honor, so that the name of God and His doctrine may not be blasphemed. And those who have believing masters, let them not despise them because they are brethren, but rather serve them because those who are benefited are believers and beloved. Teach and exhort these things (6:1,2).
22. If anyone teaches otherwise and does not consent to wholesome words, even the words of our Lord Jesus Christ, and to the doctrine which accords with godliness, he is proud, knowing nothing, but is

obsessed with disputes and arguments over words, from which come envy, strife, reviling, evil suspicions, useless wranglings of men of corrupt minds and destitute of the truth, who suppose that godliness is a means of gain. From such withdraw yourself (6:3–5).

23. But those who desire to be rich fall into temptation and a snare, and into many foolish and harmful lusts which drown men in destruction and perdition. 10 For the love of money is a root of all kinds of evil, for which some have strayed from the faith in their greediness, and pierced themselves through with many sorrows. But you, O man of God, flee these things and pursue righteousness, godliness, faith, love, patience, gentleness (6:9–11).
24. Fight the good fight of faith, lay hold on eternal life, to which you were also called and have confessed the good confession in the presence of many witnesses (6:12).
25. I urge you in the sight of God who gives life to all things, and before Christ Jesus who witnessed the good confession before Pontius Pilate, 14 that you keep this commandment without spot, blameless until our Lord Jesus Christ's appearing (6:13,14).
26. Command those who are rich in this present age not to be haughty, nor to trust in uncertain riches but in the living God, who gives us richly all things to enjoy. 18 Let them do good, that they be rich in good works, ready to give, willing to share, 19 storing up for themselves a good foundation for the time to come, that they may lay hold on eternal life (6:17–19).
27. Command those who are rich in this present age not to be haughty, nor to trust in uncertain riches but in the living God, who gives us richly all things to enjoy. 18 Let them do good, that they be rich in good works, ready to give, willing to share, 19 storing up for themselves a good foundation for the time to come, that they may lay hold on eternal life (6:20).
28. Therefore do not be ashamed of the testimony of our Lord, nor of me His prisoner, but share with me in the sufferings for the gospel according to the power of God (2 Timothy 1:9 see also 10–12 for explanation).
29. Hold fast the pattern of sound words which you have heard from me, in faith and love which are in Christ Jesus (2 Timothy 1:13).
30. That good thing which was committed to you, keep by the Holy Spirit who dwells in us (1:14).

31. You therefore, my son, be strong in the grace that is in Christ Jesus (2:1).
32. And the things that you have heard from me among many witnesses, commit these to faithful men who will be able to teach others also (2:2).
33. You therefore must endure hardship as a good soldier of Jesus Christ (2:3).
34. No one engaged in warfare entangles himself with the affairs of this life, that he may please him who enlisted him as a soldier. And also if anyone competes in athletics, he is not crowned unless he competes according to the rules. 6 The hardworking farmer must be first to partake of the crops. Consider what I say, and may the Lord give you understanding in all things (2:4–7).
35. Remember that Jesus Christ, of the seed of David, was raised from the dead according to my gospel (2:8).
36. This is a faithful saying: For if we died with Him, we shall also live with Him. If we endure, we shall also reign with Him. If we deny Him, He also will deny us. If we are faithless, He remains faithful; He cannot deny Himself (2:11–13).
37. Remind them of these things, charging them before the Lord not to strive about words to no profit, to the ruin of the hearers (2:14).
38. Be diligent to present yourself approved to God, a worker who does not need to be ashamed, rightly dividing the word of truth (2:15).
39. But shun profane and idle babblings, for they will increase to more ungodliness (2:16 see also 17–19 for commentary).
40. Let everyone who names the name of Christ depart from iniquity." But in a great house there are not only vessels of gold and silver, but also of wood and clay, some for honor and some for dishonor. Therefore if anyone cleanses himself from the latter, he will be a vessel for honor, sanctified and useful for the Master, prepared for every good work. Flee also youthful lusts; but pursue righteousness, faith, love, peace with those who call on the Lord out of a pure heart ((2:19b–22).
41. But avoid foolish and ignorant disputes, knowing that they generate strife (2:23).
42. And a servant of the Lord must not quarrel but be gentle to all, able to teach, patient, in humility correcting those who are in opposition,

if God perhaps will grant them repentance, so that they may know the truth, and that they may come to their senses and escape the snare of the devil, having been taken captive by him to do his will (2:24–26).

43. But know this, that in the last days perilous times will come: 2 For men will be lovers of themselves, lovers of money, boasters, proud, blasphemers, disobedient to parents, unthankful, unholy, 3 unloving, unforgiving, slanderers, without self-control, brutal, despisers of good, 4 traitors, headstrong, haughty, lovers of pleasure rather than lovers of God, 5 having a form of godliness but denying its power. And from such people turn away! (3:1–5 see also 6–9 for commentary).
44. Yes, and all who desire to live godly in Christ Jesus will suffer persecution. But evil men and impostors will grow worse and worse, deceiving and being deceived. But you must continue in the things which you have learned and been assured of, knowing from whom you have learned them (3:12–14).
45. 1 I charge you therefore before God and the Lord Jesus Christ, who will judge the living and the dead at His appearing and His kingdom: Preach the word! Be ready in season and out of season. Convince, rebuke, exhort, with all longsuffering and teaching (4:1–2 see 3,4 as commentary).
46. But you be watchful in all things, (4:5a)
47. endure afflictions, (4:5b)
48. do the work of an evangelist, (4:5c)
49. fulfill your ministry (4:5d).
50. Be diligent to come to me quickly (4:9). [Since all Scripture is profitable, one may see in this and the next command the need to assist one another in ministry.]
51. Get Mark and bring him with you, for he is useful to me for ministry (4:11).
52. Bring the cloak that I left with Carpus at Troas when you come—and the books, especially the parchments (4:13) [Be ready to assist with the mundane details of life].
53. Alexander the coppersmith did me much harm. May the Lord repay him according to his works. You also must beware of him, for he has greatly resisted our words (4:14,15).
54. Greet Prisca and Aquila, and the household of Onesiphorus (4:19)

55. For this reason I left you in Crete, that you should set in order the things that are lacking, and appoint elders in every city as I commanded you— if a man is blameless, the husband of one wife, having faithful children not accused of dissipation or insubordination. For a bishop must be blameless, as a steward of God, not self-willed, not quick-tempered, not given to wine, not violent, not greedy for money, but hospitable, a lover of what is good, sober-minded, just, holy, self-controlled, holding fast the faithful word as he has been taught, that he may be able, by sound doctrine, both to exhort and convict those who contradict (Titus 1:5–9).
56. For there are many insubordinate, both idle talkers and deceivers, especially those of the circumcision, whose mouths must be stopped, who subvert whole households, teaching things which they ought not, for the sake of dishonest gain. One of them, a prophet of their own, said, "Cretans are always liars, evil beasts, lazy gluttons." This testimony is true. Therefore rebuke them sharply, that they may be sound in the faith, not giving heed to Jewish fables and commandments of men who turn from the truth (Titus 1:10–14).
57. But as for you, speak the things which are proper for sound doctrine: that the older men be sober, reverent, temperate, sound in faith, in love, in patience; the older women likewise, that they be reverent in behavior, not slanderers, not given to much wine, teachers of good things— that they admonish the young women to love their husbands, to love their children, to be discreet, chaste, homemakers, good, obedient to their own husbands, that the word of God may not be blasphemed (2:1–5).
58. Likewise, exhort the young men to be sober-minded, in all things showing yourself to be a pattern of good works; in doctrine showing integrity, reverence, incorruptibility, sound speech that cannot be condemned, that one who is an opponent may be ashamed, having nothing evil to say of you (2:6–8).
59. Exhort bondservants to be obedient to their own masters, to be well pleasing in all things, not answering back, not pilfering, but showing all good fidelity, that they may adorn the doctrine of God our Savior in all things (2:9–10).
60. For the grace of God that brings salvation has appeared to all men, teaching us that, denying ungodliness and worldly lusts, we should live soberly, righteously, and godly in the present age, looking for the blessed hope and glorious appearing of our great God and Savior Jesus Christ, who gave Himself for us, that He might redeem us from

every lawless deed and purify for Himself His own special people, zealous for good works. Speak these things, exhort, and rebuke with all authority. Let no one despise you (2:11–15).

61. Remind them to be subject to rulers and authorities, to obey, to be ready for every good work, to speak evil of no one, to be peaceable, gentle, showing all humility to all men. For we ourselves were also once foolish, disobedient, deceived, serving various lusts and pleasures, living in malice and envy, hateful and hating one another (3:1–3).
62. This is a faithful saying, and these things I want you to affirm constantly, that those who have believed in God should be careful to maintain good works. These things are good and profitable to men (3:8 coming after the commentary of 4–7).
63. But avoid foolish disputes, genealogies, contentions, and strivings about the law; for they are unprofitable and useless (4:9).
64. Reject a divisive man after the first and second admonition (4:10).
65. When I send Artemas to you, or Tychicus, be diligent to come to me at Nicopolis, for I have decided to spend the winter there. Send Zenas the lawyer and Apollos on their journey with haste, that they may lack nothing (3:12–13).
66. And let our people also learn to maintain good works, to meet urgent needs, that they may not be unfruitful (3:14).
67. Greet those who love us in the faith (3:15b).

17

Exalting Christ by Remembering that He is Risen from the Dead

Steve Martin

> "Remember Jesus Christ, risen from the dead, the offspring of David, as preached in my gospel, for which I am suffering, bound with chains as a criminal. But the Word of God is not bound. Therefore I endure everything for the sake of the elect, that they also may obtain the salvation that is in Christ Jesus with eternal glory" (2 Timothy 2:8–10).

Dr. Fred Malone's life text is a potent one and so appropriate for a minister of the gospel. Christ's chosen Apostle, Paul, writes to encourage his young assistant Timothy, even though Paul himself is in one of the most discouraging situations possible. Let's begin by looking closely at Paul's predicament and then how Paul encourages Timothy to "play the man" and persevere.

Paul's Discouraging Situation

First, Paul was in prison, in a Roman dungeon, awaiting execution under the Emperor Nero. This is probably Paul's second time in Rome's prison. The first imprisonment is recorded for us by Luke in Acts 28:16–31. That was more like being under house arrest where the prisoner had some latitude within his quarters and some measure of freedom to teach and receive visitors. Many Bible scholars believe that Paul was released from the first imprisonment only to be arrested later. This second imprisonment has Paul in the infamous Mamartine prison, Rome's maximum-security facility. Paul was awaiting execution for crimes against Imperial Rome. There would be no reprieve. This time it would be death by beheading and it would be sooner rather than later. That is discouraging.

Second, Paul had gone through so much suffering, loss and privation for the gospel to this point—and now his life and ministry were about to be over. In defending his claim to be a true Apostle of Christ, Paul had explained to the Corinthians church a "grocery list" of hardships he had faced in order to faithfully fulfill his calling by Christ. 2nd Corinthians 11:24–29 is Paul's list (to that point) of what he had gone through to be a faithful minister of the gospel. There was a ferocious list of exterior, physical trials followed by a list of his greatest struggles—his interior, psychological and spiritual heartache over the churches and the Christians in them.

Narrator David McCoullough gives an anecdote in the American Experience video, "The Battle of the Bulge," that is instructive here. He said that Napoleon Bonaparte, no stranger to soldiering and battles, once remarked that "the first prerequisite of a good soldier is not bravery; a soldier is only in battle about 10% of his service time. Rather, the first prerequisite of a good soldier is the ability to endure fatigue, hardship and privation and to keep on going and do his duty." Paul was in the infamous Mamartine prison in Rome, under guard and in chains and looking over his life and ministry. There had to be emotional and spiritual struggles as he faced not only the end of his life, but the end of his personal ministry. Others would have to pick up the slack left by Paul's death; others would have to combat the false teachers, the false teaching, and the spiritual attacks of the prince of this world. Paul had run his race; his time was just about over.

Third, Paul's final weeks were made more miserable as close friends and co-workers deserted him. First century Christians knew of physical persecution and its offspring, cowardice. In 2 Timothy 1:5 Paul had already told Timothy that "you are aware that all who are in Asia turned away from me, among whom are Phygelus and Hermogenes". Close co-workers turned away in fear. This was no house-arrest where Paul was free to entertain visitors and have warm times of teaching and fellowship. It got so bad that the saints in Rome had lost track of Paul and stayed away under fear of reprisal against themselves. 2 Timothy 1:16–17 records "Onesiphorus … often refreshed me and was not ashamed of my chains but when he arrived at Rome he searched for me earnestly and found me…." James Montgomery Boice notes in his exposition of Philippians that Paul's imprisonment frightened the believers in Rome and they stayed away from Paul. Believers were too intimidated and self-protective to keep up with Paul's judicial standing and whereabouts. They had heard about his second imprisonment somewhere in Rome but they were not going to stick their heads out of their comfort zones to find out where Paul was. Remember, Onesiphorus had to go searching diligently until he finally found Paul. At the end of this most personal epistle to his beloved assistant, Paul warned Timothy about one further discouragement. 2 Timothy 4:10–17 lists Paul's final discouragement from friends and co-workers, the fact that Demas loved this present world and left to go to Thessalonica and one man went here, another man went there. Luke alone stayed with Paul. He concludes this passage by noting sadly but not bitterly: "At my first defense no one came to stand by me, but all deserted me. May it not be charged against them." How one might be tempted to self-pity and bitterness. Paul apparently did not succumb to it but he must have been tempted to give in to it.

Fourth, Paul, in the darkness of his prison cell, could imagine the encircling eyes in the darkened Roman Empire of the false teachers who would threaten to undo his life work and tear down Christ's Kingdom. All of Paul's letters deal with false teachers and false teaching to some degree. Paul is right to have this focus because false teachers produce false teaching which produces false living. False teachers did not preach the saving gospel of Christ. They had distorted notions of Christ and His person and work. Paul finishes this epistle to Timothy by warning against them. He directs Timothy to the God-breathed Scriptures as the basis of his ministry. The Scriptures had been the basis of Paul's ministry (which Timothy had savingly heard preached by Paul). Scriptures had been the core of the belief in Timothy's own home, his mother and grandmother before him being believers (2 Timothy 3:14–15). Paul then directs Timothy to the sufficiency of the Scriptures in dealing with all things pertaining to Christian faith and practice (2 Timothy 3:16–17). Paul then soberly calls God as his witness and charges Timothy (2 Timothy 4:1–2) to preach the Scriptures faithfully and with authority, when it seems to be the right time and when it seems a bit out of season.

We can learn a lesson here from Dr. Martyn Lloyd-Jones, preaching in downtown London just after the end of World War II. There was a large gathering to hear the Chancellor of the Exchequer (equivalent to our Secretary of the Treasury), the Anglican Bishop of London, and the pastor of the venue they were using, Martyn Lloyd-Jones of Westminster Chapel. The Chancellor of the Exchequer spoke about Britain being bankrupt by the war and the way to get the nation up and running and the economy spurred was through a resurgence of the church and the vital role it played in national morale. The Bishop of London spoke about how many churches had been destroyed and the congregations displaced, the general upheaval caused by the war and the need for the Church of England to be revitalized so that it could take the lead in rebuilding the nation. One layman in the audience noted how different Dr. Lloyd-Jones appeal was. The nation was in ruins because of its sin and turning away from God. God had used the war to chasten Germany and England (and the combatant nations). The only hope for Britain was a turning back to God in repentance and faith and submission to His Word and His will. The layman in attendance said that he could not look over at the first two speakers because Dr. Lloyd-Jones had destroyed their arguments and put the gospel of Christ in its proper role as supreme. In the same way, Paul keeps on showing Timothy how the gospel and the Scriptures are the most important thing and to be read and taught and preached unflinchingly.

Fifth and finally, Paul was saying "Good-bye" to his beloved spiritual son. Much of Paul's ministry was to fall on the shoulders of the young man who had been converted under Paul's preaching. Paul calls Timothy to look to Christ in order to fulfill his ministry; he cannot do it on his own, no one can. Christ must be our sustenance and strength. Paul calls Timothy to boldness, endurance and faithfulness in the face of the realities of persecution and false teachers. Paul was handing the baton of truth over to Timothy and the ministry of the Word. Timothy must run his own race faithfully as Paul had and not lose the truth. Paul was fulfilling his own directive to Timothy that he wrote in 2:2—"And the things that you have heard from me in the presence of many witnesses entrust to faithful men who will be able to teach others also."

Paul had all these things and more swirling around in his mind as he writes his final farewell to his closest associate. Imprisonment, discouragement, desertion, false teachers and false teaching, the end of opportunities and open doors, the end of life itself stared at Paul in that prison cell. It is so instructive to see how the old man in prison encourages the young man free on the outside. How does Paul encourage Timothy? Paul encourages Timothy in three ways: he looks back, he looks forward, and he spiritually reasons his way to a fitting conclusion. Consider each of these.

Paul's Backward Looking Encouragements to Timothy

First, Paul begins his encouragement by looking back to Jesus Christ—"Remember Jesus Christ" (2 Timothy 2:8). Surely that's odd. Is forgetting Jesus even possible? Especially for a minister of the gospel? But the Apostles were passing from the scene; some were dead and others like Paul would soon be. Who was going to continue with the truth? Who was going to take the gospel to the lost Roman world and beyond? What's more, as the authoritative teachers passed from the scene, who was going to stand for truth against the cults and false teachers which were multiplying and spreading around the Mediterranean basin? For a case in point (2 Timothy 2:15–19), Paul directs Timothy to the case of Hymenaeus and Philetus who were upsetting believers with false teaching about the resurrection. The way to deal with false teachers is to be good at teaching orthodox or straight truth. Timothy must work hard to be a good and faithful teacher to have God's favor now and at Judgment Day.

Jesus Christ is the center core of Christianity. If a teacher is wrong about who Jesus is and what He did, then his message is no gospel, no good news, no hope, no salvation and no Christianity! There is no Christianity and no salvation without the Jesus revealed in the gospels and the epistles. The various founders of world religions and cults are not needed for that religion or cult to continue. Moses is not necessary for Judaism to continue; the Buddha is not needed for Buddhism to continue; Mohammed is not needed for Islam to continue. These men laid down their teaching and died and their movement continued on. But biblical Christianity is different. Christianity without Christ is impossible—He is Christianity. He is God come to earth in the flesh. He was born of the Virgin Mary by the Holy Spirit and inherited none of fallen Adam's sin. He lived a perfect life, from the heart obeying His Father's commandments 24/7–365 days/year. He earned the right to be God's sacrificial lamb, to be the perfect substitute for guilty sinners. Christ suffered and died at the hands of the Roman Empire with the instigation of the Jewish leaders. He was crucified between two thieves and buried in a rich man's grave to fulfill Jewish prophecy. God raised His Son from the dead on the 3rd day in the grave. God the Father now exchanges the perfect righteousness of His Son for the unrighteousness of the believing sinner. Christ is counted the Ultimate Sinner in our place! Believing sinners are counted by God as righteous as Christ. The Good News we can preach to men and nations is that Christ invites all guilty sinners to come to Him for pardon and cleansing and new righteousness and eternal life. All sinners who trust in Christ to be their Substitute, their "Great Exchange," find themselves accepted in Christ.

But why did Paul begin the sentence with "Remember?" Because Christians can forget and not focus their mental powers, their thinking, on Christ. Believers are to preach Christ and His finished work to themselves daily and sometimes hourly. It is not that Christians are tempted to forget Christ altogether but we are tempted again and again not to put Christ at the forefront of our thinking. Most Christians think about themselves and their performance when thinking about their Christian life. They do not think about Christ and His performance in living a perfect life and perfect atoning death. We do not think about how Jesus perfectly satisfied the demands of God's violated laws, or that God is pleased with us for Jesus' sake, not for our performance's sake. Jesus is our Christianity so we must focus our minds on Him, remember Him! One pastor and Bible commentator writes that "Paul was not worried that Timothy would entirely forget who Jesus was. Rather he was concerned that under pressure Timothy might not allow Christ (His Person and His Work) the place of pre-eminence and supremacy in his thinking that Jesus rightly deserves." We don't begin with Jesus and then move on to something higher or better. We begin with Jesus, we middle with Jesus, and we finish with Jesus. Jesus is our Christianity.

But Paul has more to say about this in verse 8—"risen from the dead". How critical the resurrection of Christ is for Christianity and for each believer! Scripture makes plain that Jesus had to die on that Roman cross and be raised from the dead. It fulfills the Bible's prophesies that the Messiah would not stay dead. Romans 1 says that Christ had to be raised from the dead to show His claims to be God were true. He claimed to be God but if His claims were proven to be bogus and false, if He predicted that He would be raised from the dead but was not, then He is a fraud and a deceiver. Scripture shows that the resurrection of Christ is the culmination of the whole death, burial, resurrection package that gained the salvation of His people. Without the resurrection, Christians could have no confidence that God the Father was pleased with the Son or accepted His payment on the cross. By being raised from the dead, Christ is shown to have defeated the devil, removing his ability to falsely accuse the brethren by using the Law of God improperly to condemn them. Paul told the Colossians in 2:12–15 that Christ had "disarmed, put to open shame and triumphed" over the devil and his minions. In being raised from the dead, Christ has once and for all shown to have conquered death and the devil and proven His claims to be God in the flesh. Death has no power over believers because Christ paid the penalty of the broken laws himself on the cross and in the grave. The Law of God has nothing to say by way of condemnation now to believers. Its righteous demands have been met. The King of God's Kingdom was raised from the dead, victorious over death and the devil and ever lives to give His death-conquering power to His people.

And Paul reminds Timothy (and believers today) that this risen Christ is "the offspring of David" (translated as "the seed of David" in the NASB). Three times New Testament authors refer to Jesus as this "offspring" or "seed" of David. This is a way for the authors to speak of Christ's humanity and His covenant faithfulness. Paul's encouragement for Timothy is not only that Christ was risen from the dead but that Christ is a human being! Jesus was a physical descendant of ancient Israel's King David. This is a great encouragement because frail Timothy and frail us need encouragement to persevere in hard times and face suffering and persecution. Jesus Christ was fully a human being (but without sin) and as He faced fearsome suffering and persecution, He certainly can encourage us. Timothy (and we) can persevere by looking to Jesus who knew human pain and suffering and yet kept entrusting Himself to His Father to endure the suffering and fulfill His calling (1 Peter 2:20–25). But there is another encouragement in this phrase "the offspring of David". God made a promise to King David that one of David's heirs would sit upon his kingly throne forever. Though we humans are so weak and fickle, God is not and in the New Covenant, all God's people are made strong to persevere and endure and to make it to the end. Why? Because all God's people are united to Christ as their King and He was made faithful in the flesh by the power of God as God fulfilled His covenant promises. Human flesh in the person of Jesus Christ now sits at the right hand of the Father's eternal majesty. Human flesh, but without sin, inhabits eternity with the Father's blessing. God made promises to David and to Jesus and He is still fulfilling them, including, "I will never leave you nor forsake you."

Paul's final backward glance leading to encouragement for Timothy is the last phrase in verse 8—"as preached in my gospel." Paul wants Timothy to remember that the gospel that changed his grandmother, that changed his mother, and that changed him was the one Paul preached. Paul called it "my gospel" not because it belonged to him personally or that he invented it but because it was a sacred deposit personally entrusted to him by Christ at Paul's conversion. Paul said that this gospel is to be "preached." It is not merely to be taught or spoken politely in everyday conversation but actually heralded to all who will listen. A herald was a employee of the King whose job it was to proclaim with a loud voice or "herald" the soon arrival of the King. "Hear Ye, Hear Ye!" meant to drop whatever else you were doing and give me your full attention. Paul saw himself as this kind of herald, a preacher, a bold and forthright speaker of this truth that God has invaded this planet in the person of His Son, Jesus Christ. God had proven that Jesus was God the Son by raising Him from the dead. Rebel sinners were to lay down their arms of rebellion and swear allegiance to King Jesus. All who do so will be fully pardoned and forgiven and taken into the King's family. This is not a fairy tale; this is the gospel.

Paul's Forward-looking Encouragements to Timothy

But Paul not only looked backward to encourage Timothy he also looked forward in 2 Timothy 2:9—"for which I am suffering, bound with chains as a criminal. But the word of God is not bound!"

First Paul reminds Timothy that he, Paul, the encourager, is a prisoner, suffering in a Roman dungeon. Paul was suffering for "his gospel," even to the point of chains in prison. Paul knew that false teachers and glory stealers were using his imprisonment against him. They would say: "How could Paul's gospel be so special when its chief spokesman was in prison for preaching it?" Paul could not escape the reality of his circumstances—he could see and smell that he was in a Roman dungeon, the infamous Mamartine prison. He was being treated as a major criminal. Like his Master, Jesus, Paul seemed weak and powerless and no threat to the *status quo.* But Paul knew what he told the Corinthian church was true. What the world viewed as weak, poor and foolish ("stupid" would be the modern version) by the fallen powers of this world was actually the power of God in disguise. It is no shame to be persecuted for following and serving and preaching Christ. And he was chained to Roman guards with little room to move or change positions or get comfortable. He was at the mercy of the guards. This was truly suffering, it was no "church camp."

Second, though Paul seemed so limited and confined, shackled and in prison, appearances were deceiving. "But the word of God is not bound." Yes, he was bound in chains *but* the power of the Word of God marched onward. When God sends His Word through His appointed servants, it always accomplishes what God had in mind for it to do, though men may not understand what is happening at that moment. God in His seeming weakness, seeming impotence, and seeming foolishness was actually infinitely more powerful than this world and its supposed "never fail" strategies and powers and power-brokers. Our human suffering does not slow down or impede the supernatural working of God. Martin Luther gave this report of the powerful advance of the Reformation and the recovered preaching of the gospel: "I simply taught, preached, and wrote God's Word; otherwise I did nothing. And then, while I slept, or drank Wittenberg beer with my Philip [Melanchthon] and my Amsdorf [Nicholaus von], the Word so greatly weakened the papacy that never a prince or emperor did such damage to it. I did nothing. The Word did it all" (Rupp, *Luther's Progress to the Diet of Worms*; p. 99). This is Luther's quaint way of expressing Isaiah 55:10–11—"As the rain and the snow come down from heaven and do not return to it without watering the earth and making it bud and flourish, so that it yields its seed for the sower and bread for the eater, so is My Word that goes out from My mouth. It will not return to Me empty, but will accomplish what I desire and achieve the purpose for which I sent it." If we carefully comb through the New Testament we read that there were Christians in the Imperial Guard and in Caesar's own household. Even Paul's witness to the guards in prison was not in vain. The guards were changed every 4–6 hours and Paul had a fresh set of pagans to preach to. And they could not get away because as Paul was chained to them, they were chained to him. Dr. Howard Hendricks called that reality a "chain reaction!"

Paul's Reasoned Conclusion after Looking Backward and Forward

I say that Paul reached a reasoned conclusion based upon what he says beginning verse 10—"Therefore." What should Timothy then (and Christians ever since) do when facing persecution and suffering, when false teachers are rampant and the ignorance of the masses is everywhere? What should a believer do when he is tempted to embarrassment for just being a Christian let alone speaking the gospel? Paul wants Timothy (and us) to think these things through starting from the Bible's wisdom and counsel and then bring it to bear on one's present situation.

Paul says "I endure everything for the sake of the elect." All Paul's imprisonments, stonings, starvings, whippings, ship wrecks and inner psychological pain were endured in order that Paul might get the life saving gospel to the elect. God has a people and they must hear the gospel of Christ to believe in Christ. According to Romans 10, that is the sovereign God's sovereignly appointed method. Don't miss what Paul is saying here. He is not saying that you and I are so wonderful that we are worth the greatest sacrifice possible. Paul is saying that redeemed human life, God's elect people whom Christ purchased with His perfect life and sin atoning death are worth the greatest sacrifice. These elect people are infinitely valuable because of the price paid to save them. They are not valuable for *who* they are but for *whose* they are. Nothing less than God the Son, Jesus Christ, was necessary to save guilty sinners. Because God's Word is not bound, Paul will go to any length to preach it in the power of God the Holy Spirit. It is the power of God unto salvation.

Paul's final bit of inspired logic is the end of verse 10—"that they also may obtain the salvation that is in Christ Jesus with eternal glory." Paul is not selfish or nationalistic or racially motivated. Paul works and prays and preaches for the sake of the elect "that they may obtain". There is nothing more important in this world than for a sinner to come to Jesus Christ and find salvation, new life, new righteousness, a new family, and a new eternity! Paul was an intellectual giant, a scholar of Judaism, a sophisticated Roman citizen, and a cultured man. But he was first and foremost a herald of the gospel and an evangelist of the lost. Like George Whitefield or Charles Spurgeon or Martyn Lloyd-Jones, his calling was to lift up his voice and preach the gospel of God. This salvation message, this gospel, changed Paul's life forever and he never forgot that or "got over it." Come what may, Paul had to preach the gospel; he simply had to. It was his inner compulsion! People's eternal destinies hung in the balance. Christ glory in this world depended on faithful preachers getting the Word out to those without Christ. And in the world to come, (i.e. "eternal glory"), Paul can imagine the unending praise and honor coming to the Father, Son and Holy Spirit. As Paul told the Thessalonian believers in 1st Thessalonians 2:19–20—"For what is our hope, our joy, or the crown in which we will glory in the presence of our Lord Jesus when He comes? It is not even you! Indeed, you are our glory and our joy!"

So like Paul today's preachers of the gospel can "remember Jesus Christ, risen from the dead the offspring of David, as preached in my gospel, for which I am suffering, bound with chains as a criminal. But the Word of God is not bound. Therefore I endure everything for the sake of the elect, that they also may obtain the salvation that is in Christ Jesus with eternal glory."

I thank God for the influence of Fred Malone on my life. His love for Jesus Christ and Christ's church, along with his love for his beloved wife, Debbie, and his three children is an example to me. His efforts to pursue holiness urge me on in my walk with God. His painstaking attention to the Word of God and its message has been an inspiration to me.

Bibliography for 2 Timothy

"The Battle of the Bulge." *American Experience*. PBS Video (Narrated by David McCoullough), 1994.

Beale, G. K. and D. A. Carson, eds. *Commentary on the New Testament Use of the Old Testament*. Grand Rapids, MI: Baker Books, 2007.

Bodner, John Peter. *The House of God* (A Book of Meditations on the First Epistle of Paul to Timothy for Students of the Gospel Ministry). Resource Publications/Wipf & Stock, n.d.

Boice, James Montgomery. *An Exposition of Philippians*. Grand Rapids, MI: Zondervan, 1971.

Calvin, John. *The Epistles to Timothy*. Grand Rapids, MI: Eerdmans (translated by Thomas Smail), 1964.

Ellicott, C. J. *The Pastoral Epistle of Paul* (3rd ed.). Longmans, 1864.

Fairbairn, Patrick. *The Pastoral Epistles*. T & T Clark, reprint: Edinburgh, Banner of Truth reprint 1989.

George, Timothy. *The Theology of the Reformers*. Nashville, TN: Broadman & Holman, 1998.

Guthrie, Donald. *The Pastoral Epistles*. Grand Rapids, MI: Eerdmans, 1969.

Guthrie, Donald. *The Pastoral Epistles and the Mind of Paul*. Tyndale Press; 1956.

Kitchen, John. *The Pastoral Epistles for Pastors*. Kress Christian Publications, 2009.

Knight III, George W. *The Pastoral Epistles*. New International Greek Testament Commentary. Grand Rapids, MI: Eerdmans, 1992.

Mounce, William. *The Pastoral Epistles*. Word Biblical Commentary. Thomas Nelson, 2001.

Murray, Iain H. *David Martyn Lloyd-Jones*. Vol. 2—*The Fight of Faith (1939–1981)*. Edinburgh, Banner of Truth, 1990.

Rupp, E. Gordon. *Luther's Progress to the Diet of Worms*. Harper, 1964.

Wilson, Geoffrey. *New Testament Commentaries*, Vol. Two, *Philippians to Hebrews and Revelation*. Edinburgh, Banner of Truth, 2005.

Index of Scripture References

Proverbs

Ecclesiastes

Song of Solomon

Isaiah

Jeremiah

Ezekiel

Daniel

Hosea

Joel

Habakkuk

Zechariah

Matthew

Mark

Luke

John

Acts

Romans

1 Corinthians

Philippians

Colossians

1 Thessalonians

2 Thessalonians

1 Timothy

James

1 Peter

2 Peter

1 John

3 John

Jude

Revelation